T0330195

Managing Intensity and Play at Work

Managing Intensity and Play at Work

Transient Relationships

Niels Åkerstrøm Andersen

Copenhagen Business School, Denmark

Edward Elgar

Cheltenham, UK • Northampton, MA, USA

Published by
Edward Elgar Publishing Limited
The Lypiatts
15 Lansdown Road
Cheltenham
Glos GL50 2JA
UK

Edward Elgar Publishing, Inc.
William Pratt House
9 Dewey Court
Northampton
Massachusetts 01060
USA

A catalogue record for this book
is available from the British Library

Library of Congress Control Number: 2013933497

This book is available electronically in the ElgarOnline.com
Business Subject Collection, E-ISBN 978 1 78254 596 5

ISBN 978 1 78254 595 8

Typeset by Servis Filmsetting Ltd, Stockport, Cheshire
Printed and bound in Great Britain by T.J. International Ltd, Padstow

Contents

Contents

Introduction

This book is about conditions created by organizations for the relationship between the organization and its employees as a way to answer how the organization can continually be in the process of becoming something it is not. The book does not simply argue that the world has become more transient and turbulent. It explores what the possible implications are when the organization sees the world in this way. What does "to organize" mean when the only established premise is that everything is transient?

At the center of my investigation is the relationship between organization and employee. I look at the way in which organizations develop language, concepts and demands concerning interactions with employees. I observe how organizations create expectations of their employees based on the single premise of change, of the constant movement towards becoming something else. How is it possible for an organization to establish expectations for its employees according to which employees can self-manage when the organization expects to be continually moving in the direction of a new and unknown place? I believe that we are seeing the emergence of a problem, which may be boiled down to this: How to create expectations based on the expectation of the unexpected?

The following statements are selections from the book's archive. These quotes reappear inside the book and become the object of a more sustained analysis. Here, I merely introduce them as a way to demonstrate the level of heterogeneity and complexity that they entail but also in order to suggest a pattern in the regiments of expectations placed on employees that I try to describe in the book:

- "Employees need to take responsibility for their own development. Each employee needs to actively relate to his or her possibilities and needs for development in order to acquire the necessary tools for embracing new challenges and requirements."

Here, employees are expected to see themselves as projects of change and to develop based on the new challenges and demands which the employee believes to be at stake in the organization. The self-pedagogization of the employee represents the answer to a changing organization.

- "Offer love and encouragement. The more you give the more you get. Make it your priority to be supportive; seek out those who need support."
- "By listening to employees' hopes and dreams, by encouraging them to express their fears and doubts and by providing them with the possibility to present their vision for the future of the organization, employees are made to feel that the management acknowledges their concerns and remains respectful of their feelings."

Here, employees are expected to be invested in the organization and give to the organization without the organization having to ask for it. By showing love and respect for employees and by not only incorporating their enthusiasm but also their doubts and fears, and by providing them with the opportunity to give to the organization what they believe it needs, the organization seeks to create the loving employee, who anticipates the needs of the organization. The employee relation is made more intimate as the answer to an organization which is no longer capable of expressing its needs and authoritatively representing its totality.

- "To refer to oneself as 'playing' rather than 'working' immediately implies an expansion of the experience of who one is and what one is capable of. It means dedicating oneself to the realization of one's total human potential."
- "We play around with who we are, with what we might or might not be, and through our playful engagement it becomes clear to us what we choose to do and what we need not do. Sometimes we become so consumed by playing that it results in changes in who we are. We refer to this as transformation."

Here, employees are expected to relate to their work and themselves in a playful manner. When work is observed from the perspective of play, it becomes more important to potentialize than to realize. It becomes more important to create possibilities than to realize possibilities. And when observing oneself from the perspective of play, the focus becomes what to create oneself as. It is less a question of self-development within an existing horizon and more a question of a transformation of the horizon in order to allow for entirely new possibilities of development. Transforming oneself means to constantly shift and expand one's potential. The playful employee represents the answer for an organization that is concerned about running out of potential and considers notions of potentiality as a scarce resource.

This book could have been about how organizations increasingly colonize employees' freedom, identity and subjectivity. As Hughes ironically states, "In short, the discourse of emotional intelligence seems to mark a continuation and intensification of well-documented processes that are said to involve the increasing corporate 'colonization' of employee affects and subjectivities" (Hughes 2010, p. 33). It could also have emphasized the perfection of power in contemporary management efforts. One could stress the internalization of power and the appropriation by the organization of identity and emotions. Indeed, the book does touch upon these questions, albeit with a less unambiguously normative and moral judgment. The book shows the production of entirely ambiguous and impossible expectations of employees, who as a result find themselves in various precarious positions. The expectation that the employee is to anticipate the needs of the organization even though the organization never expresses these needs creates a system in which the employee can never know whether or not she has anticipated enough needs. The employee runs the risk of finding herself in a spiral of expectation formation in which she has a feeling of never having done enough. One could always have taken on more responsibilities. The call for the employee to show independent initiative and to self-manage creates an ambiguous expectation that says, "Do as I say – be independent." Thus, the employee never feels certain about when to act independently and when to be subordinate. The expectation that the employee relates to work in a playful way and does not abide by the boundaries of reality puts the employee in a situation in which she is at once expected to disregard reality while still being judged on her results.

However, there is another question which interests me just as much, namely, what happens to the organization as it becomes increasingly more dependent on psychic processes to which it has no access, which it cannot observe, regulate and control. I am interested in the way that modern organizations seem to be in the process of deconstructing themselves as organizations through their production of new employee relations. When organizations require of their employees that they be authentic in their organizational engagement, the organization makes itself reliant on employee self-relations in a way that both increases the organization's irritability in relation to psychic operations while also increasing its uncontrollability. It is easy enough to glorify authenticity and realness in abstract and general terms, but it remains a fundamental impossibility to assess whether or not the statements of a specific employee are authentic. And the articulation of authenticity as something that is generated in an exchange between organization and employee multiplies the challenge. I am interested in the way that the many new employee management models create a backlash in the organization in the form of uncontrollability and organizational self-deconstruction.

These notions run together in the subtitle "Transient relationships". How is it possible to ground an organization in which every relationship is expected to be in a process of becoming? What social forms are able to contain transience as precisely transient? The book focuses on two phenomena and their historical development: *membership* and *contract*. Their function in the book is to serve as a kind of point zero, an "outside", which makes it possible to diagnose the conditions of possibility and impossibility of transience.

- I have chosen *membership* because its form is basically a constituent for any organization. Thus transience, if in play, must emerge in the transformations and tensions of the evolution of the form of membership. The book shows how formal membership is doubled and displaced and becomes the membership of self-enrollment. Self-enrollment as a form of membership allows for transience precisely by defining the concept of member as something one is becoming but can never become. Thus, self-enrollment becomes a fixed form capable of comprising transience. This form of self-enrollment is actualized when the manager interested asks the employee about her time in some exciting projects, about the larger perspectives she sees in these projects and how the manager might be helpful for her. Here self-enrollment as the preferred form is a fixed expectation, but how self-enrollment is loaded with concrete and specific meaning by the single employee in single situations is simultaneous open and volatile.

- I have chosen *contract* as another point zero because it is through contracts that an organization formalizes its dependency on its external environment. Contracts should not be understood in the narrow sense of the employment contract, written with the company, but wider, as the formal and informal agreements to be concluded between the undertaking and the employee. Here the book shows how employee contracts are displaced to employee partnerships. Partnerships enable transience by promising future promises. Thus, partnerships represent another form that incorporates transience. When the employee, for example, at the end of an employee development conversation promises their leader to develop their leadership potential and find a suitable project manager training course, and when the leader, on the other hand, promises to investigate the possibility that the employee can be project leader, they have mainly promised each other that they will create the possibility that it can later be incorporated into a concrete agreement on the employee's future. They have both promised and not promised anything. The agreement is both fixed and transient.

What has been called the "post-bureaucratic" organization has not in fact abandoned bureaucracy. The post-bureaucratic organization is a fold within bureaucracy; a bureaucracy that does not wish to be recognized as such but which cannot escape its bureaucratic form. By diagnosing the organization as a "transient relation" I am not aiming to reawaken old virtues and remind the reader of the strengths of the formal bureaucracy. My objective is to show the way that the organization is unable to ever escape itself. There is never a clean break between the formally bureaucratic and the post-bureaucratic (or whatever we want to name it) organization. The formal structure sticks. Formal membership does not disappear but is folded into partnerships. I wish to diagnose "the transient organization" in all its inherent ambiguity. I want to show that the relationship between organization and employee is both radically transformed and the same. I want to describe the current organizational regime with all its combinations of totality of power and powerlessness, leadership ambitions and uncontrollability, expansion and self-deconstruction.

I hardly have to mention that this book does not provide simple advice and a promise of a brighter future. However, I have striven to take "praxis" seriously. I am not one to give advice. I aim instead at proposing a few impractical questions for "praxis" to consider, questions such as "Is it possible that what you do could be done differently?", "Is what you do fundamentally impossible and paradoxical?", "Doing what you do, you risk undermining these fundamental values and categories. Do you take responsibility for that?"

CHAPTER OVERVIEW

Chapter 1, "Diagnostics of the present and second order observation", develops the book's conceptual focus and analytical apparatus.

Precisely because this book is looking for single traits in different phenomena, including previous analyses, and thus tries to draw a more comprehensive diagnosis of the present, it needs to develop criteria for this. How can we identify the "continuous movements"? How can we engage a diagnosis of the present?

Diagnosis of the present is defined as the effort to capture the creation of contemporary conditions and what is at stake in them. However, a diagnosis of the present has to have an outside, a point zero, from which a diagnosis of how something is put at stake can be established. The chapter asks how to establish an outside without subscribing to a fixed ontology. How to observe from within society where society is headed? How to define an outside from within? The chapter also explains the book's model of second-order observation – that is, how we can observe how organizations observe employees, their feelings, their relationships, and so on. So how do we make observations into the single object of research? I outline and differentiate four different analytical strategies, including the semantic analysis and form analysis.

Chapter 2, "Adapting to adaptability: the machine of transience", explores transience as a unique logic which produces radical effects within organizations. I argue that this logic emerged in the 1980s with a new ideal about adapting to adaptability. I explore the logic of transience by means of the concept of decision. Decisions are perceived as communicative operations that seek to fix expectations and thus contain uncertainty. With the logic of transience, organizations begin to concern themselves with the question of whether the decision's fixation of expectations and containment of uncertainty reduce the organization's possibilities. The chapter addresses how the emergence of the logic of transience results in undecidability as a virtue. The result is decisions that do not want to limit possibilities, decisions that really do not want to be decisions.

Chapter 3, "From membership to self-enrollment: the production of the employee who creates herself in the organizational image", looks at the way that membership as form changes with the emergence of the logic of transience. What form can membership take when the membership decision simultaneously desires a certain level of undecidability? How can organizations take responsibility for their members taking responsibility for their inclusion in the organization? The membership criterion becomes the self-enrolled employee. I show how self-enrollment takes place pedagogically, passionately and playfully, and describe the regime of expectations that they establish. In the discourse of pedagogy, one self-enrolls through continual self-development. One is recognized as a member because one strives to make oneself competently relevant for the emerging organization. In the discourse of passion, one self-enrolls by continually anticipating the needs of the organization. One is recognized as a member because one makes oneself lovable and has defined the organization as one's significant other. In the discourse of play, one self-enrolls by playing with the notion of membership and one is recognized as a member because one dedicates oneself fully to playing.

Chapter 4, "Management of authentic feelings: the trembling organization", discusses the way that organizations make themselves dependent upon the emotions of the individual employee and how this dependency affects the organization as a system. I distinguish between a semantic of emotions as concepts available to communication in the articulation of emotional content and emotions as operations in the psychic system. As psychic operations, emotions are thought operations, which are granted a high degree of diffuseness. In the psychic system, emotions serve as a kind of immune system, which allows the psychic system to continue its operations when its continued existence is threatened by the development of internal problems. As diffuse psychic operations, emotions are incommunicable. One may speak of one's emotions, but the very act of doing so changes the state of the psychic system, which is why the communication of emotion is always burdened by problems of authenticity. When self-enrollment becomes coded through pedagogy, passion and play, personal emotions are deemed relevant for communication, although they cannot be communicated. Chapter 4 inquires into organizations' experiences with incommunicable emotions and development of a language for the management of that which necessarily escapes all management. I study organizational rhetoric of emotions from 1950 until today. I trace the development of one emotional language after the other, all of which do not solve the organizational problem of authentic self-enrollment. The result of this is the trembling organization, which has not simply increased its capacity to irritate individual psychic systems but which increasingly has become more sensitive to psychic irritability.

Chapter 5, "Managing interpenetration and intensity", includes the body and biological systems as system references. I will argue that not only the employee's feelings become constructed as an object for management, but also the interpenetrations between bodies, psychic and social systems emerge as management subjects. It becomes a target for the organization to create intensity between the body, psychic and social systems, because this intensity represents a potentiality resource for the organization. Management of potentiality is about creating a zone of intense interpenetration between the organization and psychic systems, inter-human interpenetration and the interpenetration between psyche and body.

Chapter 6, "Loving layoffs: the intimate strategies of the break-up", explores how passionately coded self-enrollment also affects the way that a membership can be terminated by the organization. At the same time, the chapter looks at the way in which the organization's concern with appearing sensitive to employee emotions radically affects certain types of decisions. The chapter shows that with the doubling of membership into formal membership and self-enrollment, the layoff as form is also doubled into formal layoff and loving layoff. The chapter explores the way in which love as a system has developed certain semantics concerning intimate break-ups, or divorces. The literature on divorce is analyzed for semantic strategies for the handling of break-ups. Then, I look at the semantic of layoffs over the past decade. Contemporary semantics of layoffs have inherited certain figures and questions from divorce literature. The notion of the possibility of a loving dismantling of love emerges in the semantics of layoffs where layoffs are explicitly compared with divorces and explore loving ways to carry out layoffs.

Chapter 7, "Unbound binding: from employee contracts to partnerships", shifts the point of observation from membership to contract. I discuss how the book's questions change if we decide to trace employee contracts as form. The chapter explores the way that employee contracts are challenged in the regime of transience in a similar way to the challenge to membership. The challenge of employee contracts becomes how to create mutually binding expectations between independent units with the expectation that expectations are constantly changing. It becomes a question of creating a form of contractual binding that remains unbound. The chapter shows that this is handled by turning the contracts "meta". Instead of making an agreement, one makes an agreement about making an agreement. This is what partnerships are about. Hence, what I claim is that employee contracts become folded and displaced into employee partnership and I look at the communicative effects of this shift. Moreover, Chapter 7 explores different examples of employee partnerships; the competency agreement, the self-contract, the employee development interview and the personal development plan. The chapter ends by suggesting that employee partnerships are contracts that aim towards a management-employee relationship that they can never achieve.

Chapter 8, "The organization as a nexus of partnerships", discusses the notion that employees enter into partnerships not only with the organization but also with the organization's environment in the form of citizens, patients, students, parents, and so on. I pursue two questions here. The first is how partnership agreements offer the organization's audience a peculiar form of monstrous membership. When a client agrees to a citizen's contract with the social services department, she is recognized as a partner and is granted a certain amount of influence on her diagnosis and treatment. When a student signs a contract relating to a student plan, the student is recognized as someone who is capable of taking responsibility for her own learning and is given a level of influence on teaching goals and teaching. The public becomes individualized and is given the opportunity to assume a limited performative role in the organization. The other question I pursue is about the organizational effects of such partnerships. To the extent that employees partake in multiple partnerships with the organization's environment, the organization becomes represented by a multiplicity of general impressions produced on the interface between the organization and its environment. The chapter proposes a parallel thesis to Williamson's (1983) notion of seeing an organization as a nexus of contracts. My thesis is that organizational unity is recreated as a nexus of partnerships and, as an effect, organizational management becomes the supervision of the creation of partnerships.

In the book's conclusion, "Transient relationships – towards the intensity machine", I discuss the book's contribution as a diagnosis of the present compared with Richard Sennett's *The Corrosion of Character* (1998) and Peter Fleming's *Authenticity and the Cultural Politics of Work* (2009). I try to clarify my contribution and how I pursue a different quality of criticism than Sennett and Fleming. In conclusion, I sum up the current status of the organization/employee relation as an intensity machine, which intensifies and accelerates the interpenetration between the organization and psychic systems and provides the psychic systems with new opportunities to pursue affect in organizations.

1. Diagnostics of the present and second-order observation

My approach in this book can be described as a systems theoretically based diagnosis of the present. I define diagnosis of the present as the effort to capture the creation of contemporary conditions and what is put at stake by them. Rather than assuming a fixed relationship between organization and employee, I explore the different historical forms that the relation has taken. At the same time, I look at the inner tensions and logics inherent in these forms. Given a particular form of relation between organization and employee, what specific inner contradictions are management forced to unfold within? Observing organizing and employee management as a social form means addressing them in their ambiguity and complexity. All social and communicative forms contain insurmountable tensions or even paradoxes, which, depending on the specific form, have to be continually managed and unfolded. In other words: a specific form results in specific and inherent questions to which the social has to respond without ever being able to arrive at a final solution. Thus, diagnostics is a question of identifying prevailing forms and framing the basic questions that they raise. It is a question of describing what is at stake given a particular ordering of the social realm. Unfortunately, employee relations as form do not represent an isolated island. Different forms develop alongside each other, condition each other, sustain each other or contradict each other. And the study of this collaboration of forms thus becomes part of the diagnosis.

Why work with Luhmann's systems theory as part of one's critical ambition? Luhmann has been associated with an anti-normative functionalism and accused of taking a position that is anything but critical. Jürgen Habermas has accused him of making critique impossible: "Reason as specified in relation to being, thought, or proposition is replaced by the self-maintenance of the system. By taking this approach, Luhmann also goes beyond a critique of reason that aims at revealing the power of self-maintenance to be the latent essence of subject-centered reason" (Habermas 1987, p.372). And Luhmann would be the first to admit that "there is no place to represent the good society within society" (Interview with Niklas Luhmann: Sciulli 1994, p.47). Or as Luhmann states elsewhere: "There is no privileged point of view, and critique of ideology is no better off than ideology" (Luhmann 1994a, p. 28). To me, Luhmann represents a way to continue the genealogical line of Michel Foucault and the deconstructive line of Jacques Derrida in a sociological ambition that radicalizes both of them and cuts them off from any remainder of moralism. It is a form of critique that takes its point of departure as the impossibility of critique. As Hans-George Moeller writes: "Social systems theory does not deal with fabricating new hopes, new promises, or new utopias, but it is also not afraid of letting go of hopes that cannot be fulfilled, promises that have never been kept, and fairytale visions of a golden future. It dares to introduce a nonhumanist paradigm shift in social theory – one that may 'perturb' society in a profound and (obviously) entirely contingent way" (Moeller 2012, p. 31).

Conducting a diagnosis of the present is a form of critical social studies practice. However, it is not a normative critique based on a specific ideal which judges society from a particular position. I agree with Luhmann when he says: "Sociologist are not supposed to play the role of the lay-priests of modernity" (Luhmann 1997a, p. 77). Normative critique always leads to discontentment about social developments and to the discrediting of different groups of people, organizations or parties who one believes should have acted differently. Observed from the perspective of a given normative framework, deviations from the norm come into view. For example, a Habermasian perspective that observes the world through an ideal of communications free from any kind of domination sees precisely hegemonic relations and distorted communication. Observing the world from the perspective of a communitarian ideal, one sees the decline of communities. As Luhmann once remarked: "Critical sociology would continue to perceive itself as a success, but society as a failure" (Luhmann 1994b, 126). Normative critique fantasizes about a non-oppositional sociality and finds it difficult to accept the world as it is. In the end, normative critics typically express more about the ideal through which they observe than the society they are looking at. Systems theoretical diagnostics of the present subscribes to a much more humble concept of criticism, which does not seek to place itself outside society in order to judge it but which also does not mindlessly accept the most recent trends. It is very simply a question of asking: "given that we are beginning to think in these different ways, to search in these different ways, to act in these different ways, what is at stake"? One identifies a problem, one finds a solution, but only too rarely does one ask about the implications of these types of solutions for new questions, contradictions and power displays.

So diagnostics of the present in systems theory is about increasing the self-observation within society, not by judging, not by preaching in favor of particular alternatives, but by pointing at blind spots, tensions, possibilities and impossibilities: "Systems theory has a certain capacity to improve the instruments of self-observation, i.e. of communicating within society about society" (Luhmann 1982b, p. 137). So systems theory is not so much about intervening in society with the help of knowledge, as it is about providing the systems themselves with better capacity for self-intervention via alternative self-descriptions: "Sociology could create a surplus of structural variations that could induce the observed function systems to consider alternatives to their own modes of operation" (Luhmann 1994b, p. 136). This includes producing descriptions that might increase the discomfort of systems. Rather than looking for better solutions to problems, we should ask, "what is the problem?" in order to produce unpractical problems so that practice might develop an eye for problems as problems of complexity.

Systems theory presents a multiplicity of contra-intuitive insights that open up towards this kind of unsettling diagnostics of the present. A few preliminary examples:

- Studies about the emotionalizing of work based on a theoretical perspective that perceives the authenticity of feeling as incommunicable and socially uncontrollable. Such studies open up a range of questions which otherwise might have been shut down by simple formulations about the colonization of feelings.
- Today managers talk a lot about "the whole human being" and "the integrated self". What is a whole human being? In order to answer this question in a meaningful way, it seems exceedingly helpful to take one's point of departure in a theory that argues that a human being is not a unity but a combination of systems. This perspective puts into question many unquestioned assumptions and calls for more careful analyses.
- And finally, today the organization and its employees are expected to share meaning, perform dialogues and constitute mutual partnerships. By following the approach laid out by systems theory, according to which humans cannot share meaning, cannot reach mutual understanding and cannot communicate but only take part in communication, the field of study opens up quite a bit.

Together, these approaches increase the possibilities of a contra-intuitive diagnostics of the present.

SECOND-ORDER OBSERVATION

At the heart of this book are a particular epistemology and a specific concept of observation concerned with a program of *observing observations as observations*.

Niklas Luhmann defines observation as an indication within the framework of a difference. All observations operate by means of a difference. When an observation is drawn to something in the world, a distinction is made between this "something" and everything else. What the observer sees is only marked and only becomes visible in the observation in relation to that which is disregarded. This means that the difference decides how observation can take place. A game, for example, is always a game for an observer. A game becomes visible to an observation in different ways. There is a difference between observing a game through the lens of the difference fun/not fun, better/worse learning potential, or to pay/not pay. The first offers the game as play, the second suggests a pedagogical form and the third concerns a consumer product. Another example might be a diploma. How a diploma will appear to an observer depends on the difference framing the observation; that is, the differences between, better/worse learning, legally right/wrong or pay/no pay. In the first frame of observation, a diploma is perceived as a pedagogical premise for access to specific training and as a way of ensuring the visibility of a level of achievement in relation to a training program's learning objectives. In the legal frame of observation the diploma is perceived as a formal document that can be interfered with. Thus it may be either valid or invalid in a legal sense. In the economic frame of observation the diploma indicates a utility value of the workforce for which you can either choose to pay or not.

The point is that every observation represents an operation by drawing up a difference, which is not visible to the observation itself. We see a diploma and decide to recruit its owner, but do not see that we only observed the diploma economically. The observation always indicates one side of the difference and leaves the other side unmarked even though it remains constitutive for the observation. One sees what one sees, but one does not see the perspective and the difference that constitutes one's seeing. Thus, the difference defines the blind spot of the observation.

Borrowing the term from Spencer-Brown, Luhmann refers to the inside of the difference as the marked side (m) and the outside of the difference as the unmarked side (Spencer-Brown 1969, see also Robertson 1999). The blind spot represents the very unity of the difference, that which both separates the two sides and also holds them together in a difference. The unity of the difference between paying and not paying is, for example, a transaction. The unity of the difference between "to commit" and "to

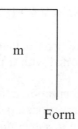

Form

Figure 1.1   The form calculus

be free" is a contract. The contract is a form, constituted by a voluntary binding (obligation) of the freedom of its partners – not just duty and not only freedom, but the unity of the difference between them. This is called the form of difference and is formalized as shown in Figure 1.1.

An observation that indicates that something in the world cannot simultaneously indicate itself. However, a second observation can observe the observation. This kind of observation can both observe the indication that takes place and also observe the difference within which the indication takes place. This allows it to observe the blind spot of the first observation. This is Luhmann's systems theoretical epistemological program: to observe the blind spots of other observations. This is called second-order observation (Luhmann 1993a).

To perform second-order observation is to observe observations as observations. This means that our statements about "observations" as our object of study also pertain to the statement itself. Second-order observation is simultaneously first-order observation, which means that it, too, takes place within the framework of a difference. Thus, there is no privileged position of observation, situated above other observations. The conditions, which apply to the first order also apply to the second. The theory of observation encompasses itself so to speak. The difference through which second-order observations observe is the difference indication/difference. Thus, an observation can be formalized as the unity of this difference (see Figure 1.2).

This means that second-order observations are heavily reductionist. Second-order observations can only see indications and differences, nothing else. Second-order observation is not the pursuit of some master of observations. Observations are to be observed as such in their immediate scarcity and not as something else, and it is precisely this point which gives systems theory its power to deactivate existing assumptions. It is a form of neo-concretism. It represents an insistence on the observations themselves and on the effort not to instantly move away from them towards their context of causes or meanings. Observations need no

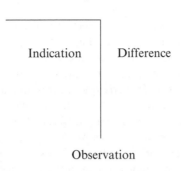

| Indication | Difference |

Observation

Figure 1.2   The form of an observation

interpretation. Their meaning need not be unfolded. Observations also need no explanation. They merely need to be described and diagnosed: What difference is employed in the observation? How is the blind spot defined? How can new observations be added? This is also how I use the gibbet itself (¬). It compels me to stay with the individual distinction, to maintain and observe it. So, I am consistently looking for the drawing and making of distinctions that control how systems observe. Through which differences are organizational systems observing their employees, and how does this govern the organizational horizon of action and decision-making?

COMMUNICATION

Not all forms of observational operations interest me. My focus is organizational communication. I do not observe how individuals observe play, power and organization. I am interested in the communicative observations of organizations.

I do not take communication to mean a special kind of action in which a sender sends a message to a receiver and where communication is considered successful once the receiver understands the message in the way that the sender intended it. In systems theory, communication is defined as a network of retrospective connections. How? Any communicated statement forms a horizon of connectivity. An example: One makes a sarcastic comment to a colleague about something. From the perspective of the colleague, this statement potentially opens up towards many possible future connections, which can take communication in many different directions. Perhaps the colleague does not respond, that is, makes no connection to the possibility of connecting, and hence no communication is established. Perhaps the colleague connects with the communication from the premise that she is included in the sarcasm; perhaps she connects with a literal interpretation of the sarcasm or perhaps she responds with a joke. The point is that it is impossible to determine whether or not communication will take place until the connection to subsequent communication takes place, and just as importantly: subsequent communication also determines the communication's character as, for example, serious, literal or witty.

Thus, communication is essentially different from speech acts. In this perspective, communication consists not of speech acts but of selection, where connecting with connectivity produces new possibilities for connecting, and so on. Communication cannot be reduced to the speech acts of the communication participants; it has its own life, which no individual participant is able to control. Consider a meeting: A manager may have made meticulous plans for the proceedings of a meeting, and yet the agenda slips. Themes are opened up which were not meant to be touched upon and themes, which the manager planned to only discuss briefly, turn out to open up more possibilities for connectivity than desired. Seemingly, however, the planned decisions were made, but at the next meeting in which the minutes are approved it turns out that what seemed a clear decision is later agreed on merely as a discussion.

In this way, communication is created retrospectively or recursively. It is always subsequent communication that determines whether there is communication and how. Each connection opens up towards a new horizon of connectivity and does not become communication until a new connection makes a selection within this horizon. This also means that no one can control communication. None of the communication participants can decide how the communication will move forward. In this sense, communication has a life of its own. Luhmann defines social systems as autopoietical systems, which create themselves on the basis of communication as a network of recursive operations (Luhmann 2000c; for a critique of Luhmann's concept of autopoiesis: Münch 1992).

Another implication of this is that autopoietical social systems are operatively closed. Their closedness lies in the very dividing mechanism of their operations; the fact that they are differences with two sides, which means that subsequent operations have to connect to either one or the other side or change forms and install a new distinction, which then simply means the formation of a new system. The economic communication system cannot be continued through the articulation of love. That would not be a recursive connection but a displacement of the form of communication and therefore the potential formation of a different communication system.

When I stress the fact that communication has its own life beyond the control of any individual communication participant, I also point to the analytical productiveness of a sharp distinction between systems of communication and systems of consciousness. Systems of consciousness can participate in communication but they cannot communicate with each other. Systems of consciousness cannot recursively connect with each other's operations. That would constitute mind reading. By contrast, communication is only possible, one might say, precisely because systems of consciousness cannot connect with each other's operations. In terms of analytical strategy, this touches upon something we have already mentioned, namely the effort to insist on seeing observational operations precisely as observations. It is a question of remaining concrete in relation to communication as operations and not being tempted to shift one's attention to the communication participants; to observe communication as communication without reducing it to individual motives and intentions, which are invisible in the communication and which an observer can only conjecture about. Hence the importance of the sharp distinction. I do not assume that an organization represents the sum of the people who are employed by it. No humans or psychical systems are contained within an organization; only organizational communication. Organizations and their employees remain each other's environment. I consider this a productive approach because it challenges a lot of truisms and dogmas and forces us to analyze them and to seek out alternative explanations; for example, the dogma that one can be in an organization, the dogma that dialogue is possible between employees and between employees and the organization, the dogma of a work community, or that managers and employees can understand each other. It compels an analytical effort that questions such preconceived notions.

ANALYTICAL STRATEGIES OF THE SECOND ORDER

The possibilities for second-order observation are vast (Andersen 2003c, 2011). I primarily employ three guiding differences in this book and thus a combination of three different analytical strategies: semantic analysis, form analysis and coupling analysis. Briefly and somewhat reductively, these strategies can be described as given in Table 1.1.

The Semantic Analysis

The guiding difference of the *semantic analysis* is concept/meaning (Luhmann 1993c, Andersen 2011). The semantic analysis can be used to describe the way in which meaning and expectations become condensed

Table 1.1   The three analytical strategies

Analytical strategy	Guiding difference	Insight
Semantic analysis	Concept/meaning	The semantic analysis provides insight into conceptual structures of expectation
Form analysis	Unity/difference	The form analysis provides insight into the basic "machine" of the individual communication form and the paradoxes created by specific communication
Coupling analysis	Coupling/ differentiation	The coupling analysis provides insight into communication systems' mutual relations, their way to both close themselves around themselves and to observe and connect with each other

into concepts and form semantic reservoirs available to communication. The semantic analysis asks: How are meaning and expectations formed? How do meaning and expectations become condensed and generalized into concepts? How do different condensations establish certain semantic reservoirs and make them available to certain communication systems? The semantic analysis also asks: How are concepts displaced as they generate new counterconcepts, or how do counterconcepts become counterconcepts for a new concept, or how does a counterconcept lose its specificity and create a rush to fill in its meaning.

A concept is comprised of a condensation and generalization of a multiplicity of meaning and expectations. A concept *condenses* expectation in such a way that many different expectations are condensed into concepts. Knowing that somebody is an accountant immediately generates a horizon of different expectations such as, "she is the bookkeeper type", "she is a control freak", "she is a square", "she is honest", and so on. Thus, a concept represents a structure of expectations. To use a particular concept in communication establishes expectations with regard to expectations about the communication and its continuation.

A multiplicity of meaning becomes fixed in the form of concept through the opposition between concept and counterconcept (see Figure 1.3).

There exists no concept without a counterconcept to keep the concept in its place (Koselleck 2004, Luhmann 1993c, p. 15). The counterconcept sets up restrictions for the concept. The expectations that concern the counterconcept establish restrictions for what can be expected when con-

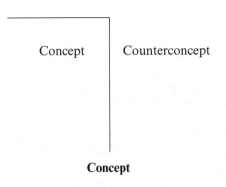

Concept

Figure 1.3   The concept of concept

necting to the concept. In the past, "duty" was an important concept, and someone who was not directed by duties was perceived as "sloppy" or "lazy". Today, employees must be passionate and must be seeking out responsibility. This kind of employee is not driven by "duties" and "given responsibility areas". Thus, "duty" is now a counterconcept to the concept of "seeking out responsibility". A responsibility seeking employee is not waiting to be assigned to a duty.

Form Analysis

The guiding difference of the *form analysis* is unity/difference and is a systems theory equivalent to deconstruction in Derrida's terms (Luhmann 1999). A form analysis observes the unity of how differences are established in an operation. The form analysis directs itself towards the basic forms of communication. Giving a gift is, for example, the device of receiving a gift, on the inner side of the difference, without giving a second gift in return, on the outside of the difference. There are an endless number of differences available to communication. However, a smaller but indefinite number of these differences make up communication forms that other differences connect with. Some of these are forms such as decision, transaction, intimacy and care. These communication forms have their own communicative logic, their own mutually exclusive way of constantly dividing communication into marked and unmarked. Every form creates a paradox. It separates what cannot naturally be separated. The relation between the inside and the outside of the form is always a relation of impossibility, so the aim of the form analysis is to specify the communication form's specific conditions of impossibility out of which communication is forced to create possibilities. It concerns the infinite inner logic of the communication and operational forms.

An example might be forgiveness. Forgiveness introduces into any com-munication a distinction between "the forgivable" and "the unforgivable". Forgiveness represents the unity of this difference. The paradox of forgive-ness is that only the unforgivable can be forgiven. This paradox drives all communication within forgiveness as form and has as one of its effects the fact that forgiveness is never completed. One employee has forgiven the leader his unforgivable betrayals, but as soon as the leader comes close to repeating his or her mistake, perhaps in relation to another employee, it turns out that he has not been completely forgiven.

In other words, a form analysis investigates the fundamental differences through which communication operates and which allow any communica-tion within the form to land either on its inside or outside. The form estab-lishes expectations with respect to continued communication. But precisely because these expectations are linked to a difference, there is always a point at which the expectations break down. So a form analysis tries to specify particular conditions of impossibilities inherent in singular forms of com-munication. The aim of the form analysis is to demonstrate the inner logic of a specific form of communication. It is about the limit of the formation of expectations given a particular dividing operation in the communication.

The Analysis of Structural Couplings

Finally, the guiding difference for the coupling analysis is coupling/dif-ferentiation. It aims to specify the way in which systems allow themselves to be interrupted by one another even though they are operatively closed to one another. Systems theory is incredibly sensitive to systems relations because they are not considered self-evident. Because systems are con-sidered operatively closed, one achieves sensitivity to the "mechanisms" which, despite this closedness, create their own openness and mutual couplings. When communication between systems is not self-evident, one develops an eye for the nature of the systems relations. The coupling analysis thus asks: how are systems coupled while maintaining their differentiation?

Luhmann points out that communication systems are autopoieti-cal systems which create the elements they consist of. A system cannot produce elements for another system. A system can only produce its own internal order. It cannot produce order for others. This also implies that systems cannot communicate with each other. They can, however, observe each other's communication. They can also assign meaning to each other's communication, but only on the basis of their own communication forms. Teubner says that a system can produce productive misunderstandings from another system's communication (Teubner 1991). An example could

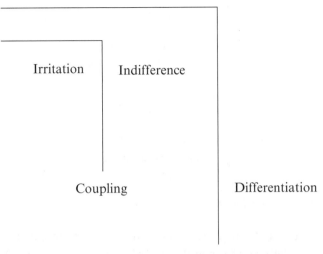

The general form of coupling

Figure 1.4   Structural coupling

be that the legal system communicates a number of new rulings according to which companies' discharge of waste is deemed illegal and fines are issued. Obviously this can be observed in the economic system, but only in economic terms. The legal communication is productively (mis)understood as the price-fixing of waste discharge.

The fact that systems cannot communicate with each other but that they are able to observe each other allows for structural couplings between them. Structural couplings represent forms of simultaneous operations. Couplings can provide the systems with a continual flow of disorder up against which the systems may create and transform themselves. A structural coupling between communication systems can be defined simply as the unity of irritation from other systems and indifference to other systems (Luhmann 1992, p. 1443). I have formalized the general form of the structural coupling as shown in Figure 1.4.

ANALYTICAL STRATEGY AND DIAGNOSTICS OF THE PRESENT

Analytical strategies are not simply methods. They are strategies created to facilitate a diagnostics of the present. Basically, a diagnostics of the present asks questions such as, "When ideas and praxis develop in these

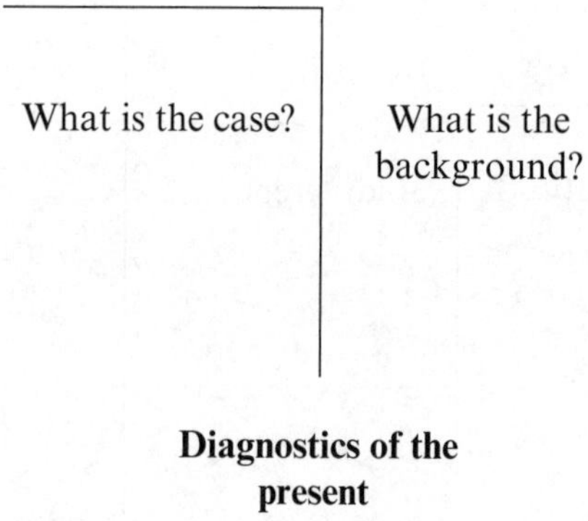

What is the case?   What is the
background?

**Diagnostics of the
present**

Figure 1.5   Diagnostics of the present as form

ways, what is put at stake?" And questions like these need to operate with a distinction between case and background. Diagnostics is, so to say, the unity of this difference (see Figure 1.5).

In order to be able to say anything about the "case", one has to be able to know what the background is. But how is it even possible to make such a distinction? A big problem for any diagnosis of the present has always been that it defines as "background" what later proves to be "the case". One may for example define as point zero the distinction between rationality and emotions by claiming that the modern organization, as we know it from Max Weber's works, created and founded itself on such a distinction. One could then study the way in which this distinction is now dissolving by theorizing the rationality of emotions. One may argue in favor of a new "bodily and emotional rationality" (Townley 2008). The problem with this would be that one would end up confirming the self-perception of the most current discourse and would thus be barred from providing the present moment any insight into its origins. The idea that the distinction rational/ emotional is superseded by emotional rationality has precisely become a robust part of organizations' self-image, so supporting this perspective means to take over the organization's self-perception rather than trying to understand what it involves.

In very general terms, the problem is that an insight generated by a diagnostics of the present is only an insight in relation to a position outside that insight. There has to necessarily be an "outside" up against which any contribution and insight constitutes itself. When diagnosing the present we need an "outside" that allows us to assess whether and to what extent we have delivered a diagnostic contribution. A diagnosis of the present needs an outside in order to define the point zero for determining when something is put at stake.

However, if we take on the epistemology of systems theory, there exists no "outside" that can provide us with a solid diagnostic judgment. An outside is both necessary and impossible. The only way to handle this dilemma is to define the distinction between inside and outside, inside meaning in my case inside systems theory.

Any outside, therefore, is always already an inside. The effort to define an outside takes place on the inside and in a sense never moves outside. Thus, we must define criteria for the internal production within systems theory of what we choose to observe as an "outside" that our analyses contribute to. We cannot begin with a point zero. Where would it come from? We have to create the point zero as our outside as part of the analytical strategy of a diagnosis of the present. Only in this way can we arrive at a self-critical diagnosis of the present because it includes itself, that is, a diagnosis of the present, which also diagnoses the diagnostics of the present. I argue in favor of a cumulative epistemological strategy consisting of three steps, moving from inside to outside, and in which the diagnostic strategy marks the final step in an epistemological accumulation. These three steps represent my blueprint, so to say, for an "inside out" diagnostic of the present.

The first step is connected to the epistemological interest regarding production of contingency; that is, the production of insight into the differently possible. One of the epistemological aims of second-order observation is simply to offer systems new possibilities for self-description through the description of their self-descriptions, and thus through the production of contingency in their possibilities for observation. It is about dissolving what seems self-evident as the differently possible becomes a real possibility. So the first step is insight into the contingency of the system's semantic self-description. When we describe the self-descriptions of systems by analyzing different semantics, we provide the systems with contingency concerning their self-descriptions. In other words, when we, for example, describe how organizations describe their relationship, with their employees, it becomes evident to the organizations that their ways to describe are not self-given, but might be different.

The second step is connected to the epistemological interest in forms. Here, the epistemological objective is to observe the observation of different forms and to use these to describe conditions of impossibility for social phenomena and the paradoxes that function as autopoietic machines within systems of communication. It is about gaining insight into what must necessarily exist given a particular form of communication. So the second step raises subsequent questions about a system's limit of contingency; that is, the form within which a system's contingency must unfold. Systemic production of semantics and self-descriptions always represents the unfolding of the constitutive paradoxes of the communication forms. The formation and condensation of meaning represent the generation of communicative possibilities from formal impossibilities. Formally connected paradoxes function as the internal "machines" of systems, preventing them from "resting" and compelling them towards increasingly de-paradoxifying meaning formation, which never leads to closure but at best generates endless displacement. Hence, formal analyses use semantic analyses as their "outside". A formal analysis does not become a contribution until it provides insight into a system's restless production of new meaning and new forms of meaning. Thus, its contribution to the organization is not that it might do something differently, but rather that the organization in its practice is bound to unfold a particular necessity, which simultaneously is an impossibility. This might be to make decisions. An organization is thrown into decision-making, but any decision entails a cascade of new uncertainties and new decision-making.

The third and final step is connected to the epistemological interest regarding diagnostics of the present. I speak of a diagnostics of the present when second-order observations not only produce contingency for a specific semantic field and not only describe individual communication forms but also observe how semantics and forms in general generate particular social differentiation forms and put different systemic relations at stake in particular ways. It is about how a pattern emerges across semantics, systems and forms. So the third step raises new questions about the communication forms' conditions of formation: How do these forms relate to other forms? What is the unity of differentiation as form, which appears precisely in the formal unfolding of these systems? How are the forms differentiated and coupled? How do different differentiation forms relate to each other over time? This brings us to the diagnostics of the present, where the central focus becomes the condition for the production of forms and how forms are put into play and at stake. In sum, what kind of regime seems to emerge and repeat itself across the different semantics, forms, structural couplings, technologies, and so on? This gradual logic can be illustrated as shown in Figure 1.6.

The implication is that one cannot skip any of the steps and proceed directly with the larger diagnostic questions since that would mean transforming systems theory from sociology into philosophy. A diagnostics of the present has to take as its point of departure the semantic space of possibility and can never be any better than its level of groundedness in the semantic analysis. The semantic analysis is the foundation. Without it, diagnostics becomes a matter of arbitrary speculations.

This provides us with a strategy for how to slowly radicalize our impractical questions as practice. See Figure 1.7.

Diagnostics of the present	Forms at stake in the semantic space of possibility	Diagnosing how societal forms are put at stake in the current space of possibility
Form	Forms of impossibility	Identifying social systems' specific forms of operation and their inherent tensions and paradoxes
Contingency	Semantic space of possibility	Identifying social contingency and the differently possible within contemporary forms through the description of systems' self-description

Figure 1.6   Accumulation of insight based on second-order observation

Diagnostics of the present	You do more than you realize. Take responsibility for your actions	The semantics put the forms of sociality at stake. The forms of membership and contract are put at stake. This changes the meaning of our categories for organization, freedom and responsibility. Do we want these changes?
Form	What you do is impossible	The different semantics introduces different paradoxes into organizations such as the paradox of self-management: "Do as I say – be independent!"
Contingency	What you do is not necessary	There are many alternative semantics for the articulation of the relationship between organization/employee, which establishes different conditions of possibility

Figure 1.7   Accumulation of impractical insight

The semantic analytical strategy explores formations, selections and shifts of semantic reservoirs for communication about the relationship between organization and employee. It provides insight into the semantic contingency of the relation and makes it plausible to argue that a particular management practice is not necessary and given. To the systems we observe our message is "What you do is not necessary."

The form analysis studies the communicative forms that the semantics are attracted to. The analysis explores possible internal tension and paradoxes of these forms, giving credence to the claim that certain management practices are not only contingent but also driven by necessary paradoxes that prevent the management practices from fulfilling their promises. To the systems we observe our message is "What you do is impossible."

Finally, the differentiation and coupling analyses look at the kind of regime established by the joint efforts of different semantics and forms and how they put basic forms at stake. These analyses allow us to point out certain effects of particular management practices and appeal to management practices to assume responsibility for their effects. To the systems we observe our message is "You do more than you realize. Take responsibility for your actions."

2. Adapting to adaptability: the machine of transience

Around 1980, a new ideal emerged in organizations about adaptability. It was not an ideal about adapting to some definite form but rather an ideal about adapting to adaptability. I have primarily studied the emergence of this ideal in the public sector, but today this is no longer specific to a particular sector but applies more generally to modern organizations. I argue that this ideal generates a specific "problem machine", which since 1980 has thematized and recreated a large number of elements in modern organizations, including the relationship between organization and employee. This book explores the effects of this problem machine in the form of changed conditions for the way that organizations produce the organization-employee relationship along with a range of associated phenomena, including membership, role, contract and layoffs. My focus is primarily on the public sector but not exclusively.

The purpose of this chapter is to describe the "naked" problem machine as the engine of the regime of transience.

I do not claim that there is a shift from stability to change or from a small degree to a large degree of change. That would be both an incorrect and imprecise diagnosis. However, what is true is that organizational theory has shifted its focus, which in the 1960s and 1970s was primarily on stability, to being primarily concerned with change. In simple terms, the prevalent notion used to be that an organization existed within a changing environment, which was perceived as a threat to the organization which had to respond with adaptability and stability in a changing world. Today, organizational theories are more concerned with whether organizations are too stable and rigid.

My point of departure is Luhmann's systems theory. As an observational program, systems theory does not assume that changes simply happen on the outside. Rather, each organization finds it inherently difficult to create itself and stabilize its unity.

This also means that my central question does not concern a shift from stability to change. I do not forward a naïve argument about how previously we had more stability and now we have more and more change, or a consultancy narrative about how changes happen with increasing speed. Instead, I ask: *What happens to an unstable system when instability is reintroduced as ideal and program? What happens when a system, which is fragile, in becoming, never stable, always improbable, always continual, begins to develop self-descriptions about its desire to only exist in the present, to capture intensity, to be in becoming and never identical with itself?* This is the problem of transience.

ORGANIZATION AS UNFOLDED INDECISION

Luhmann suggests that an organization can be seen as a system of communication, which communicates through decision operations, creates itself through decisions and consists only of a network of decided decision premises. So decisions are solely observed as a special form of communication that under no circumstances can be reduced to individual choices or something that takes place in the individuals' minds (Luhmann 2000a, p. 141).

Decision is communication that implies taking a stance with regard to social expectations. All communication contains a circulating multiplicity of different expectations. A multiplicity of variant expectations continually circulates in interactions related to the organization, including temporal expectations, factual expectations and social expectations. These interactional expectations do not make up the organization itself but are part of its environment. The organization emerges as a system that takes a stance with regard to these expectations by making decisions.

Decisions do not determine the future. Decisions create and attune existing expectations between organizational members concerning the organization's future, their respective roles and, not least, what to expect of future decisions. Thus, decisions attune social expectations with regard to future decisions.

A decision splits the world into a "before" and an "after". The difference between before and after is a distinction within the operation. When a decision is made, it is an indication that we are now past the decision. "Before", therefore, always appears in the order of the "after" of the decision. From the perspective of the decision, the "before the decision" appears as the space of *open contingency* in the interaction, which will be significant in the future. The decision's "before" is a moment when a specific situation still had many different conceivable outcomes, a moment when much could still be changed. After the decision, this contingency, this openness with respect to the outcome, appears in fixed form, that is, as the notion that the decision could have been made differently. Only one outcome was chosen but other outcomes could have been chosen. What

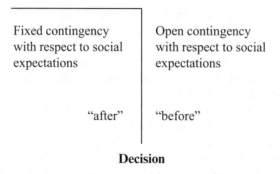

Decision

Figure 2.1   Decision as form

might have been different has now been determined. We could have done something but we did something else. Thus, in every operation, decision communication forms the difference fixed/open contingency with respect to social expectations (Luhmann 1993b). The form of decision can be formalized as shown in Figure 2.1.

Accordingly, a decision represents the unity of the difference fixed/open contingency with respect to social expectations, and as a unity the decision both represents that which divides the world into two sides and that which holds together the two sides within the unity. This means that each time a decision is made, it does not only establish expectations, it also produces uncertainty in the sense that it becomes apparent that the decision could have been made differently. The decision operation simultaneously fixes and opens up social contingency because the fixed and attuned expectations always appear within a horizon of other potential attunements. In this way, new decisions are potentialized at the moment a decision is made. This means that they establish new possible connections for future communication.

The form of decision contains certain paradoxes. The first paradox consists in the fact that decisions establish expectations about the future, *but are made retrospectively*. Not until a decision has been made is it possible to tell if it was actually decided, if expectations were established, if contingency was fixed. A decision does not take on the character of decision except through another decision. It can only be decided retrospectively whether or not a decision really was a decision or just talk, regardless of how the communication was originally perceived. Moreover, this means that decisions constantly decide which previous communications were actually decisions and thus can function as decision premises for future decisions. A decision cannot decide for itself whether it has been decided or not. In order to become a decision it needs subsequent decisions to assign it the character of decision. Almost all meetings begin by deciding what was decided in the previous meeting, for example, with the approval of minutes. Through decisions about the minutes, "previous" decisions are established as *decision premises* for current meetings whose decisions then have to be retrospectively decided on in order to become decisions. Decisions produce decisions. In other words, a decision is not really decided until it has been recognized as a decision premise. Decision communication, therefore, is not only communication *in* the form of a decision but always already communication *about* decisions (Luhmann 2000a, pp. 222–56).

Moreover, decision communication is paradoxical in the sense that *only questions, which are principally undecidable can be decided* (von Foerster 1989, 1992, Luhmann 1993b, Luhmann 2000a, p. 132). It is not possible to calculate the right decision. A decision always potentializes alternative decisions and always contains a shred of undecidedness. Only if it is possible to reach a decision through complete deduction, calculation, conclusion or argument does the decision lead to a final closure or fixation of contingency, which does not simultaneously potentialize alternatives. But if one arrives at a result through factual analysis, it would no longer be a decision but simply calculation and deduction. Decision communication is subject to a freedom, a freedom of choice, which cannot be analyzed away. Referencing Derrida, John Caputo speaks of "the ghost of undecidability":

> Undecidability is taken, or mistaken, to mean a pathetic state of apathy, the inability to act, paralyzed by the play of signifiers that dance before our eyes, like a deer caught in a headlight. But rather than an inability to act, undecidability is the condition of possibility of acting and deciding. For whenever a decision is really a decision, whenever it is more than a programmable, deducible, calculable, computable result of a logarithm, that is because it has passed through "the ordeal of undecidability (. . .) Decision making (. . .) positively depends upon undecidability, which gives us something to decide (. . .) Deciding is a possibility sustained by its impossibility. (Caputo 1997, p. 137)

Finally, a decision can be said to be paradoxical in the sense that *what a decision is, is in itself a decision*. Only the decision can decide when something is a decision, that is, when something can be said to be a fixation of expectations. Organizations do not only make decisions. They continually make decisions about what makes a decision a decision. Who is authorized to make certain decisions? Does a decision need to be confirmed in a meeting in order to function as a decision or is it enough that one's boss says that this is how it is? The distinction between fixed and open contingency, therefore, is itself contingent. Decisions need to decide themselves – and this decision, like any other decision, is obviously

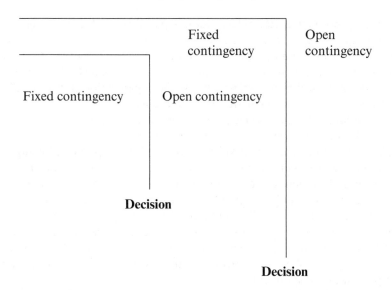

Figure 2.2   The paradox of decision

founded on paradoxy. Hence, there are many different criteria for when a decision has been made. These criteria vary from one organization to the next, from one context to the next, from one organizational level to another, and so on. And the criteria are always only partially fixed. Thus, decision as form is also double and folded onto itself. The decision of the decision is part of the decision. This can be formalized in the following way and constitutes the paradox, which makes up the autopoietical machine in any organization (see Figure 2.2)

DEPARADOXIFICATION AND ORGANIZATIONAL AUTOPOIESIS

The inherent paradox of decision represents the internal machinery of organizations (see also Nassehi 2005). Because a decision cannot be made singularly – once and for all – but instead continues to potentialize alternatives and create uncertainty about the status of already made decisions, a decision has to be constantly followed up by new decisions. This is the driving power of organizational systems, which compels them to engage in ongoing decision communication. When a decision connects with a previous decision it is transformed into a decision premise for further decisions, and that is what creates an organization. Organizations are nothing more than a by-product of unfolded decision paradoxes. Organizations and their elements – staff, structures, strategies, vision, and so on – are created through decision communication when decisions confirm other decisions and turn them into decision premises for new decisions. *What* constitutes an organization is a result of *how* the organization deparadoxifies decisions and converts them into decision premises.

In the study of the formation of organizations, therefore, the focus should be on strategies for the deparadoxification of decisions, which makes it possible to decide despite undecidability. Deparadoxification is a strategy, which handles paradoxes in order to ensure continued communication. Decisions can deparadoxify themselves by basically achieving the freedom to resemble necessity. There are many different ways to study this phenomenon empirically and to localize a multiplicity of strategies by observing the way that organizational semantics and management semantics create conditions for deparadoxification. This might include observing the way that deparadoxification happens differently in the factual, temporal and social dimensions.

Factual deparadoxification can be seen as a way to make decisions look like reactions to facts of the matter and to environmental imperatives. By naturalizing the organization's environment and describing its imperative movement, the decision is transformed into a reaction to the environment. "The market", "globalization" or "the financial crisis" are addressed as a cause for a necessary decision. They become reference points that bring the infinity of undecidability to a stop.

Temporal deparadoxification is about defining decisions as a reaction to the seriousness of the moment. In order for a decision to be made, it has to appear necessary, it has to appear urgent, alarming and immediate (Derrida 1992a, p. 26). A decision is an interruption of that which precedes it; talk interrupted by decision. The moment of decision is always a decisively urgent and abrupt moment regardless of how much time the decision has to allow itself. In the temporal dimension, deparadoxification is about creating this moment of decision, which cannot be postponed for one instant. We know the problem from everyday expressions such as "the time has come", "the time is ripe" or, by contrast, "time is not yet ripe for this decision".

Finally, *social deparadoxification* is about making decisions appear as if they have already been made so that the only thing left to do is to formalize them. Social deparadoxification can take place through "political analysis" or "stakeholder analysis" of the decision circumstances. By pointing to central actors in the environment, assigning them authority, preferences and strategies, the decision eventually takes on the status of social imperative.

The central point here is that the organization is a system of communication whose operations constitute decisions that seek to stabilize expectations but which simultaneously produce uncertainty about expectations. The organization as decided premises for decisions emerges as the fixing and stabilization of expectation but also as its destabilization. What pertains to decision also pertains to the organization. It can only be decided retrospectively and never unambiguously. Undecidability clings to every decision premise. The decision could have been different. And the "structures" of the organization only apply as such once they are assigned value by the continual decision operations. Thus, an organization cannot remain the same. Change and contingency are its fundamental conditions.

More generally and with reference to Heinz von Foerster, Luhmann states that systems are created like order out of noise: "This cannot be emphasized enough. A preference for meaning over world, for order over perturbation, for information over noise, is only a preference. It does not enable one to dispense of the contrary. To this extent the meaning process lives off disturbances, is nourished by disorder, lets itself be carried by noise" (Luhmann 1995d, p. 83). Or as von Foerster expresses it: "'The order from noise' principle (. . .) requires the co-operation of our demons who are created along with the elements of our system, being manifest in some of the intrinsic structural properties of these elements" (von Foerster 2003, p. 13). In his article "Social order from legislative noise?", Gunter Teubner asks: "What do the 'little demons in the box' look like? As stubborn norms, values, rationalities, word-views, ideologies, vested-interest, power patterns material relations of production or all of them together at work?" (Teubner 1996, p. 619). In an organization, the demons are represented by the undecided element of decisions; what John Caputo refers to as the ghosts of undecidability. Undecidability, not as remainder but as a concomitant by-product of any decision and decision premise, is what constitutes the serving demons of the organization. An organization does not need noise and interruption from "outside" in order to change. Decision communication produces its own noise, which it has to then order. An organization only exists if decisions keep connecting with other decisions, and each decision produces uncertainty about itself. Every decision produces both order and noise. That compels change. An organization represents the "sum" of decision premises, but these only exist as premises to the extent that they are being connected to as such. It is simply impossible for an organization to remain itself. It constantly transforms into something else, which at best might describe itself as the same. It constantly produces its own inner demons of expectational uncertainty, which has to be contained in a pursuit that generates ever more demons.

THE ORGANIZATION THAT WANTS THE UNDECIDABLE

What happens if the organization, in its desire for order, not only produces order out of noise, which produces its own noise, but also begins to worry too much about its own stability? What if the organization turns the production of demons into its goal? What if the organization is worried that there might not be enough noise to produce order (Pors 2011c)?

My claim is that this is precisely what we can observe in modern organizations from approximately 1980 until today. If our point of observation is the public sector, we can look to the concept of planning of the 1960s and 1970s to see how change became articulated as reform and adaptation. Public committees and councils identified specific developments in the environment and prescribed reform, which would help the administration and politics adapt to the new conditions. In the administration, a predominant notion was that the world was moving in one particular direction and that was the direction to which one had to adapt. It was typically assumed that a historical analysis would lead to prescription that could then function as the basis of decisions. Change was always seen as change in relation to stability. Stability was the precondition for any kind of learning, for the analysis of own development and the ability to identify elements that needed reform. Stability was valuable as the precondition of change. In the relation between time and case, the case held priority. The precondition of change was factual analyses of history and environment. It was a question of incremental changes. This logic of change can be summed up as shown in Figure 2.3.

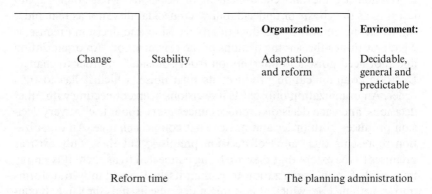

		Organization:	**Environment:**
Change	Stability	Adaptation and reform	Decidable, general and predictable
	Reform time		The planning administration

Figure 2.3   Figures of temporality in the public administration of the 1960s and 1970s

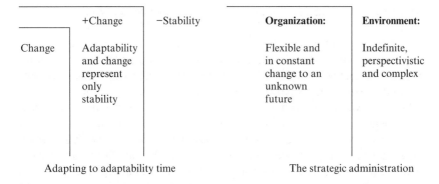

	+Change	−Stability		Organization:	Environment:
Change	Adaptability and change represent only stability			Flexible and in constant change to an unknown future	Indefinite, perspectivistic and complex

Adapting to adaptability time   The strategic administration

Figure 2.4   Figures of temporality in the public sector from the 1980s until today

From the 1980s until today, the concept of temporality has become radically different. The environment and its development are not simply described in definite terms such as "this is the trend". The environment begins to be described in indefinite terms with statements such as "the world is becoming increasingly complex", "changes are here to stay" and "the world is turbulent". How does an administration relate to an environment described in such terms? The answer of the past 25 years has been "adaptability", "flexibility" and, not least, "innovation". The administration is no longer adapting to something specific. It has to adapt to the unknown. We can call it adapting to adaptability. It is a question of constantly being able to be something other than what one already is. It is not a question of reform – to reform is to move in a specific direction. Modern public change management is different. It is about the ability to continue to change direction. Change no longer happens in response to stability, because the only things that are identified as stable are change and turbulence. In other words, the public administration shifts from considering change as a movement towards something specific, a movement based in stability eventually leading to another stable condition, to change as a pulse. It is not change with a specific and final aim. It is not change in relation to something else. It is change or no change. It is change with a view to more change. This also shifts the balance between case and time, so that the temporal dimension is given primacy in the administrative notions. Instead of problem-driven changes we get innovation and adaptable subject knowledge. The logic of adapting to adaptability can be summed up as shown in Figure 2.4 (see also Andersen and Born 2000).

This development has been given many different names in the international literature. John Clarke and Janet Newman speak of the tyranny of transformation and of "the discourse of turbulence" in which "the only continuity is change itself" (Clarke and Newman 1997, pp. 39, 45).

The basic point is that the notion of change based on change removes any concern about stability. In fact, it becomes a concern that the organizational tendency towards stabilization through the fixing of expectations in itself impedes the organization's capacity to constantly be something other than what it is. What interests me in this context is how organizations begin to strive to *increase* their internal undecidability. We might even speak about the emergence of *programs for undecidability* when organizations program decisions to suspend a decision's status as decision premise for future decisions (Andersen 2012b). We end up with decisions that prefer not to be too decided. We end up with decisions that seek to avoid the exclusion of possibilities. One might say that we end up with a kind of transience consisting of decisions that do not want to be decisions but that seek to make undecidability available; decisions that continually suspend themselves as decisions.

My book, *Power at Play* (2009), describes the design of today's organizational games as a way to question and challenge expectational structures (Andersen 2008a, 2009, 2011). The result is a multiplicity of organized games that play organization without being organization. And this increases the total number of possible organizational states and the differences an organization can tolerate. There is a continual production of a surplus of possibilities, oscillating between the virtual and the existing, non-commitment and commitment. The organization's capacity for being something other than what it is, perhaps to be something other than an organization, explodes.

This is the central tenet in the regime of transience; organizations seeking transience in order to get away from themselves, in order to evade the tendency of decisions towards organization and fixation. This organization simultaneously creates itself through streams of decisions but also deconstructs itself through the suspension of its own decisions (Andersen 2009, Andersen and Sand 2012).

Malou Juelskjær et al. (2011) write about potentiality management in an organizational setting that is less concerned with the realization of existing possibilities and more concerned with the constant creation of new possibilities. Generating possibilities becomes a program, which in itself is disconnected from concerns about the realization of these possibilities. The question of realization is transformed into the multiplication of possibilities on the basis of possibilities. Here potentiality indicates a transgression of the possible (Staunæs 2012, p. 245). In relation to municipal management of school management, Justine Grønbæk Pors argues that in order for organizations to be able to focus on the generation of possibilities, they have to suspend their own contexts and reality (Pors 2011a, 2011c). Similarly, Niels Thyge Thygesen and Christian Frankel write about organizations that create strategies for future development in order to immediately suspend these so that they do not block new strategies (Frankel and Thygesen 2012). Moreover, many contemporary organizations wish to enter into committed relationships with other organizations without commitment. Partnerships seem to provide organizations with a way to simultaneously make themselves reliant on another organization while not fully relying. Partnerships represent both a promise and the suspension of that promise (Andersen 2006, 2008b, 2012b).

A similar trend seems to apply to the relationship between organization and employee. Organizations want to simultaneously ensure their employees' commitment while also making sure that the commitment is non-committal; to create employee expectations and also prevent the expectations from stabilizing. In the next chapter I discuss how organizations are concerned with and haunted by how to simultaneously make a decision about membership and include a specific person as an employee while suspending the very same decision by deferring to the employees themselves to self-enroll in the organization in a way that self-enrollment continually becomes obsolete and calls for renewal.

3. From membership to self-enrollment: the production of the employee who creates herself in the organizational image

INTRODUCTION

This chapter provides the basis for the book's evolving diagnoses. It shows how the question of transience challenges formal membership and opens up towards what I have referred to as "the membership of self-enrollment" (the chapter elaborates Andersen and Born 2001, 2007, 2008; Andersen 2007b).

I have chosen membership as my portal to the diagnosis of the present because membership is anything but an arbitrary element in organizations. Our society consists of a multiplicity of social systems constituted in rather different ways. Organizations are social systems, whose social dimension is constituted precisely through membership. Membership, I argue, is the constitutive element for organizational systems. If I can show that membership as a form shifts in accordance with the question of transience, then I will not only have shown that an element of modern organization has changed but also that the constitutive conditions for organization as such have changed. This is a comprehensive question.

Niklas Luhmann wrote his first book about power in 1969. In the final chapter of that book, he observes what was at the time a new development in human resource management. He wonders about observed notions of inclusion, participation, democracy and co-determination. With a good amount of cynical detachment, he writes:

> Nowadays this idea is being sold with help of slogans such as participation or co-determination – hand in hand with the suggestion of false consciousness. Thus "emancipation" becomes management's last trick: denying the difference between superior and subordinate and thus taking away the subordinate's power basis. Under the pretence of equalizing power, this simply reorganizes the power which the subordinates on the whole already posses. (Luhmann 1979, p. 180)

Clearly, Luhmann was not excited about this development – not because of apprehension about a more extensive form of power, which characterizes the governmentality literature today. He simply did not consider it functionally realistic. He writes almost condescendingly that the new management forms would not remain competitive since they resemble "an instance of love rather than power" (Luhmann 1979, p. 180). He concludes: "The error of the 'human relations' movement lay in collapsing different levels of system formation and this error is faithfully repeated in the amalgamation of participation and democracy. If our conjecture that this will not work is correct, it becomes relatively unimportant whether it will be in the interest of domination or in the interest of emancipation that it won't work" (Luhmann 1979, p. 183).

This chapter shows how contemporary forms of membership become embossed on a series of systems perspectives: power, pedagogy, economy, law, play and even love. Perhaps, Luhmann can be said to be right that organizations, in the sense in which he described them in the 1960s, have disappeared. However, notions of co-determination, inclusion and participation are not only widespread, they have also mutated into many different forms. Today, we have concepts such as "the organization as marriage", "management from the heart", "fun programs" and many more. What was once "critical management" bordering on the ridiculous is a reality today. "The good" and "humane" is being realized, remains in force and produces its own challenges.

I am going to discuss the way in which organizational membership shifts from formal membership to the membership of self-enrolment. This represents a shift from a form of membership in which the organization assumes full responsibility for inclusion and exclusion in relation to individual access to and assessment of relevance in the organization to a form of membership in which the organization assigns the individual the responsibility for inclusion and exclusion and thus the responsibility for self-enrollment in the organization. This becomes a transient relationship because self-enrollment does not take place once and for all but becomes an ongoing responsibility. The dominant employee management question becomes how to produce the employee who creates herself in the organizational image.

In addition, I want to show how the membership of self-enrollment becomes coded in the medium of pedagogy, love and play respectively with many radical effects for the relationship between organization and employee. I want to show, in other words, how media, which Luhmann considered dysfunctional and ridiculous in an organizational setting, have now achieved a certain functionality and have made their mark on both new employee semantics and management practices.

Finally, I want to show how self-enrollment as form and its different codifications have comprehensive implications for an employee relationship which is becoming increasingly existential. One implication is the expectation of an employee who splits herself in order to become a learning project and to constantly take shape in response to images of the competencies that the organization finds relevant. Another implication is that it becomes increasingly impossible for employees to know if and when they have lived up to organizational expectations because it has become their own job to create expectations of themselves in an ongoing anticipation of the organization's needs. A third implication is the expectation about an employee's willingness to continue to play around with the possibilities for enrollment in the organization and thus to multiply herself and the membership.

THE FORMAL SHIFT IN THE CONCEPT OF MEMBERSHIP AND THE DESIRE FOR A NEW CODE

In systems theoretical terms, an organization is a communication system whose social dimension is constituted through membership. What constitutes an organization is not its factual dimension, that is, what it talks about. It also is not constituted by its temporal dimension, that is, the question of who is present simultaneously in a communication. Instead, what constitutes an organization is its social dimension, the question of who is socially included as a part of the organization. An organization constitutes itself through membership by only providing access to its communication for people who have been granted the status of members, for example, employees. Membership defines the organizational communicative relevance of individuals. Membership, in turn, defines the scope of validity of the organization's decisions. The organization's limit is defined through its membership and marks the end of the reach of a decision.

An organization is a communication system, which communicates through decisions. In that sense, an organization consists of nothing but decisions.

Membership represents a decided decision premise for access and conditions of access to the organizational system. Membership represents a decision about dependency and connections between communication participant and organization. And that decision is grounded in a principle of exclusion. All communicators are excluded as irrelevant to the organizational communication until the moment when the organization decides to include them through the granting of membership.

Membership is a complex phenomenon. Membership represents the unity of the different between *generalized motive* and *person*. A membership both separates the organization's generalized motives from specific persons but also comprises the unity of this difference. On the one hand a membership decision is about generalized motives and on the other hand about connecting a specific person to this motive. Generalized motives are organizationally motivated motives, which are formulated in general terms and thus elevated above personal issues and specific situations. An example of generalized motives could be description of roles and functions for a particular position in the organization such as, for example, the administration of payment of wages, the description of the information technology (IT) function in a particular department, or the job description for the head nurse in a nursing home. The generalization of motives provides insight into the impersonal character of membership (Luhmann 1982a, pp. 75–8). Generalized motives are not directed at a specific person, whose job it is to realize them, but are beyond the individual. In this way, membership also entails a *zone of indifference* between organization and individual (Luhmann 1996a, p. 341). This zone of indifference implies both the organization's indifference to personal motives for being in the organization, as well as the individual's indifference to the organization's instructions and distribution of responsibilities as long as they fall within the framework of the general motive (Barnard 1968, pp. 167–71). One enters an organization as office clerk with responsibility for paychecks and not as John Smith. A decision about membership links a specific person to the management of the generalized motive. To be granted membership implies that one has been appointed and recognized as a person. But membership also implies that one is assigned generalized motives, which establish one's relevance in relation to the organizational communication. One is employed for a specific purpose. It is only a particular part of the person who has been granted membership, which is included as relevant for the organizational communication. The rest of the person is irrelevant to the communication and is typically given the indefinite label "private" (Kieser 1989, p. 547). Thus, the decision of membership perpetuates the principle of exclusion. One is only relevant to the communication, and therefore included, through reference to the generalized motive. Everything else is excluded until further decisions are made.

A person, however, is not the same as a psychic system. "Person" is a semantic artifact, which is not only employed in organizational systems but in all communication systems for purposes of identifying and addressing a system in the environment as communication participant. Armin Nassehi speaks of "the person as an effect of communication" (Nassehi 2007, pp. 100–20). This trick is entirely necessary in order for communication to be possible:

> A person is a fiction necessary for continuing the process of communication; and it is a function of this fiction to assume the unity of the person and the corresponding individual human being, although the communication itself cannot control what it has to accept as a black box. A person can and will be treated as if it were a human being, and its identity helps to specify the ignorance a social system can afford with respect to bodily and mental processes of the concrete individual. (Luhmann 1996a, p. 343)

My analyses, therefore, are based on the assumption that a person and a specific individual with a biological body and psychic system are not the same thing. The specific individual with biological body and psychic system is radically located outside the social. Social systems can communicate about the individuals but cannot achieve insight into their conscious operations. Communicative operations can connect neither to operations of consciousness nor to different bodily operations. In this sense, they remain the black boxes of the social. Social systems, on the other hand, can form images of individuals. A person represents such an image, which constructs the observing system as an agent, capable of acting and communicating and thus also of being addressed in communication. "Person" is a two-sided image: action and experience. When a system forms a person-image of a different system, it also builds up expectations about this system's ability to act (and communicate) on the basis of an experience of the world. When an event is assigned to a system, the system is transformed into a person and the events into personal events effected by the system. When a system assigns events to another system, it can assume that the system in question, which is now observed as a person, has to experience the world in a particular way. Otherwise the event would simply represent a spasm. And, in turn, when an experience of the world is assigned to a particular system, which then becomes a person, it creates expectations about the specific actions of that person. This unit can be formalized as shown in Figure 3.1.

The form of person is not unambiguously constructed in relation to individuals with bodies and psychic systems. The form can be employed by a social system, when it addresses communication (and hence social expectations) towards a psychic system. But the form of person can also be used by a social system when addressing communication to another social system, which establishes this system as an independent agent. However, this generally requires for the addressed system to be legally recognized as a fictitious legal subject, which can be held accountable for its actions in court. This primarily applies to organizations. Again, organizations are not people. No one has ever seen an organization walking around on two legs. But they can be addressed as such because the law has formulated procedures that determine when an event can be assigned to an organiza-

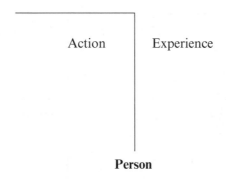

| Action | Experience |

Person

Figure 3.1   The form of person

tion as its action, which means that the organization can be held responsible as if it were a person with its own independent experience of the world and independent motives for action. Finally, a psychic system can reflect on itself through the form of person and connect actions and experiences, for example through reflections on who I am, who can do such and such things. And, similarly, an organization can communicate about itself as an agent, experiencing and acting in a particular way, with a particular history, and a particular appearance, and so on.

Let us return to the form of membership. Membership represents the unity of generalized motive and person. Thus, membership is at once a decision, which specifies a generalized motive beyond "the personal", and also a decision to observe a particular system as a person and link it to the generalized motive. Hence, the form of membership represents a double exclusion of the personal. First, there is the separation of the generalized motive from the fiction of personhood, which is expected to act in accordance with its experience of the world and which is thus assumed to have its own personal motives that are partially irrelevant to the organization. That is, the person as a fiction within communication. Second, there is the separation between the person as fiction on one side and the psychic system on the other side, which operates outside the social and never lets itself be consumed by or summed up in the form of person. The body and the psychic system remains an unknown, unapproachable and obscure environment for the organizational system. The psychic system can partake in organizational communication but remains the communication's environment since communication can never link up with the thought operations of the psychic system. To the organization, psychic systems remain closed boxes located in its environment. This can be formalized as in Figure 3.2.

Membership functions as a flexible decision premise. The generalized motive can be developed over time. New decisions can be made, for

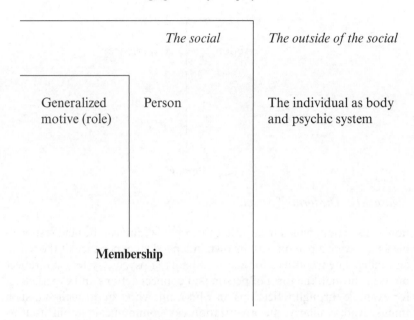

The social	The outside of the social
Generalized Person motive (role)	The individual as body and psychic system

Membership

Figure 3.2   The form of membership

example, decisions about the functions included in a specific job description. On the other hand, membership is simply the equivalent of the existing communicative structural coupling between organization and individual. Communicative operations have their own lives and are not simply determined by decisions. Not everything one does as a member is comprised by the membership. New expectations about one's job are constantly developing as one works. These expectations may follow the premises of the membership, but they may also deviate from it in different ways. As with other kinds of decisions, membership seeks to attune and stabilize expectations in the future but these can only be decided retrospectively by being confirmed as decision premises. In this way, memberships are always preliminary, in the same way that they may disappoint in specific communication. Thus, there is always a tension between the figures of "general motive" and "person", a tension that is reflected in organizational literature, for example, through the distinction between formal and informal (Dalton 1959). So, on the one hand there is ongoing "everyday" communication in the organization, which decides in every operation the question of inclusion and exclusion and continually creates expectations concerning the continuation of the communication and about who is included and how. Luhmann refers to this kind of communication as interaction. On the other hand, there is membership that represents the organi-

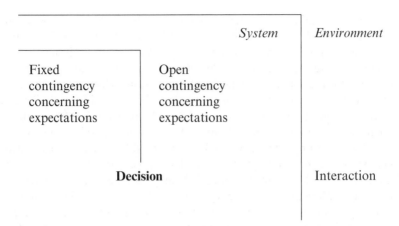

Figure 3.3   Interaction remains the environment of the decision communication

zation's decision about the ongoing formation of expectations concerning inclusion and exclusion. Thus, interaction also remains the organization's environment even though the organization is focused on reflecting on it and attunes expectations concerning the interaction through decisions. This can be formalized as shown in Figure 3.3.

The mutual everyday interaction of employees represents the organization's environment. That which others refer to as "life" is not a part of the organization but of the environment that the organization tries to regulate through decisions. Every decision divides the world into before and after the decision. Before the decision is where a multitude of different expectations came into play without a decision being made. After the decision there is the same contingency of expectation but now a decision has been made about it. This is where we are going but we could have gone in both this and that direction. Thus, an organization comes into play precisely when decisions are made about expectations in the interaction through decision operations. And decision about membership is one such decision.

Even though membership does not equal the operations of inclusion and exclusion concomitant with interaction communication, membership still represents an important part of the organizational premise building: "Members become members by decision. Membership is a way to remember these decisions" (Luhmann 1996a, p. 345). Through membership, the organization remembers its decisions about who is a member and on what premises, and this allows it to reflect on the communication that actually takes place and to align it with these decisions. At the same time, the termination of membership is a way for the organization to forget its

structural connections to certain individuals. Membership can be terminated, for example by firing someone. And when someone is fired, they
are erased from the organizational memory. Bank account, phone number
and email address can all be deleted. Once again, one becomes entirely
irrelevant to the organizational communication. Despite the built-in
flexibility of classic memberships, the form of membership is challenged
with the notion of adapting to adaptation. Membership has always been
challenged by organizational changes. In 1959, a supervisor put it this
way: "The way things change it would be impossible to have a job description that would be accurate. It would have to be revised daily. Things
change too fast. The market changes, your personnel changes, relations
with the union are always changing" (Dalton 1959, p. 220). The notion of
"adapting to adaptation" radicalizes this challenge. When the organization becomes defined by its ability to constantly be something other than
what it is, it causes everything in the organization to be cast in this light.
It is no longer sufficient for the membership to adapt over time. Defined
memberships pose an obstacle to change. Even though memberships can
be changed over time, changing them still requires a decision. Suddenly
what was once the function of the classic membership, that is, to serve
as the memory of who is member and on what premises, is now seen as a
dysfunction. If membership is the memory that reminds the organization
why certain people are members and what their roles are, thus making
it possible for the organization to interject and claim that something
falls outside the framework of membership, when the organization sees
"deviant" tendencies in the interaction communication, then membership
becomes a function of conservation for the organization. Membership
decreases the organization's ability to change. Instead, a need develops
for a membership form, which also has the ability to keep changing. As
I have already mentioned, an organization is basically defined through a
principle of exclusion. No one, except for those who have exclusively been
decided as members, is relevant for the organizational communication,
and through its decisions about granting of membership the organization
assumes responsibility for inclusion. The notion of adapting to adaptation
renders this responsibility highly problematic. It is both too complex and
too time-consuming to place the responsibility of inclusion entirely within
organizational decisions. The question within organizations becomes: *how
to take responsibility as an organization for ensuring that each individual
employee takes responsibility for her own inclusion into the organization,
which is always in the process of becoming something else.* This represents a
small revolution in the functioning of organizations.

My thesis is that this compels a new form of membership, which I refer
to as *the membership of self-enrollment*, and that this membership estab-

lishes a paradox and contains an inherent state of unrest that prompts a process of discovery in organizations. This process of discovery is continual and leaves substantial semantic traces in the form of new concepts and practices for both employees and management. I will address this in more depth below. The membership of self-enrollment represents a fold in the classic membership. Thus, it is not an entirely new phenomenon, which would be rather improbable since that would imply that we no longer would have organizations in the same sense. Nonetheless, it also represents a dislocation of the classic membership and has comprehensive constitutive implications for the conditions of organizational communication (Andersen 2004a, see also Amhøj 2004, 2007 on self-generated membership).

The membership of self-enrollment copies and re-enters into itself the classic membership distinction between "generalized motive" and "person" on the motive side of the difference. That means, on the one hand, that the difference between generalized motive and person is maintained. On the other hand, however, the generalized motive becomes personalized. The generalized motive is now defined as personal self-motivation. In other words, the generalized motive is now defining an expectation that the person who is introduced into the organization will independently define the generalized motive binding the individual as if the motive were motivated by the organization. The general motive is transformed into a demand for a particular articulation by the individual member and fitted to the immediate situation. At the same time, the individual member commits to justifying the particular articulation using the organization's motive as a point of reference. With the distinction between generalized motive/person, the classic membership provides a distinction between the organizationally motivated motive and the personal motive. The discrepancy between the two can be vast. The organization's motive might be to bake bread. The personal motive might be to support one's family. When an individual accepts a membership, she simultaneously accepts that the personal remains outside the organization. The fiction is that the person accepts the organization's generalized motive as the binding of personal freedom. The personal motivation for accepting such binding does not concern the organization. Together, this establishes the notion of a zone of indifference between person and organization. This configuration becomes rather murky in the membership of self-enrollment *because the expectation is that the person's motive simultaneously remains irrelevant to the organization and becomes a central organizational concern.* The organization's motive becomes the employee's personal motivation. The person is expected to be personally motivated to motivate herself as if her motivation were that of the

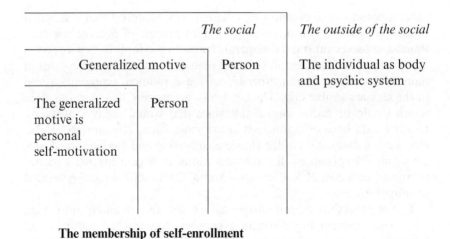

The membership of self-enrollment

Figure 3.4   The displacement of membership

organization. The imagined zone of indifference is transformed into a zone of intensive interest. The organization has to take an interest in the person, her own motives, in order to assign to her the responsibility for self-inclusion into the organization. The question is: How is this possible? This is the question that the organization asks itself. Figure 3.4 is an attempt to formalize the membership of self-enrollment.

FORM SEEKS MEDIUM

When decisions decide, they almost always form a symbolically generalized medium based on one of society's function systems. This can be the medium of economy, money, or the medium of law, existing laws. The choice of medium colors and codes the decision in specific ways. If a decision is made through the medium of money, it becomes an economic decision about whether or not to pay, and the whole world is viewed from this point of view. I have tried to show the relationship between organization and function system, between decision as form and the symbolically generalized medium of the function system in Figure 3.5.

The figure is meant to show that function systems and organizational systems are mutually closed to each other. They represent each other's environment. However, when the organization communicates through decision operations, the form of decision becomes imprinted into the medium of the function system, which causes the two systems to become

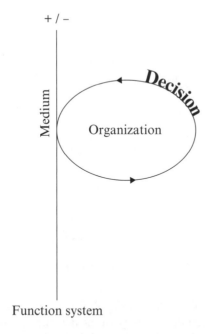

Figure 3.5 The relation between decision and function system

tangentially connected. Within the organization, this finds expression in the particular coding of the decisions.

When the decision is about membership, it has to also link up with a function system by forming its medium. The classic membership typically links up with the legal system and its medium, which is "present law". This results in a decision about membership colored by the code right/wrong, and, in effect, the organization becomes constituted through formal membership, which serves to determine whether or not someone is legally a member of the organization and with what rights and responsibilities. Thus, in the traditional formal organization, membership can be determined legally and is typically supported by a personnel policy, which formulates personnel rules and thus anticipates conflicts, which can subsequently be resolved with reference to the code right/wrong. I have tried to formalize this in Figure 3.6, where the distinction symbol symbolizes the medium into which the distinction and form are imprinted.

The point here is that the difference between "generalized motive" and "person" is drawn in the language and medium of law, which means that the generalized motive becomes recognizable as formalized expectations and the person becomes recognizable as legal subject. Without the

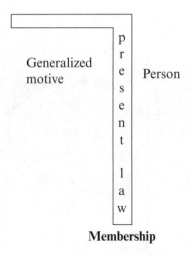

Membership

Figure 3.6   The medium of the formal membership

language of the law, it would be difficult for the organization to decide on membership. Through the language of the law, membership can be formulated through calculable rights, responsibilities and regulations.

The link between membership and law in the formal membership is supported by a semantic of the civil servant emerging in the late eighteenth century and becoming dominant from around 1920 in most of Europe. It is a semantic we all know from boss words like: Fidelity for life, loyalty, diligence, conscientious, discipline, formal qualifications, predictability of decisions, objectivity and legality. This semantic is expressed in a very condensed way in the following quotation from a Danish civil servant in 1928: "With rapidly changing Personnel, with a Staff, which individuals are still considering whether changing job to improve their benefits, the conditions to develop and foster good official traditions cannot be present (. . .) If we imported contracts we would lose the current system benefits towards stability and Solidity" (Kofoed 1928). Stability and solidity were organizational ideals anchored in the formal membership. Stability was observed as the precondition for gathering experience, and experience was again the precondition for organizational development.

The interesting question becomes whether the law can also serve as a medium for the membership of self-enrollment? My claim is that this is only possible with great difficulty. It makes only limited sense to formulate personal self-motivation as responsibility. What would it mean to be obligated to self-motivate? How does one legally determine whether a person is self-motivated? The only thing one can do is to procedural-

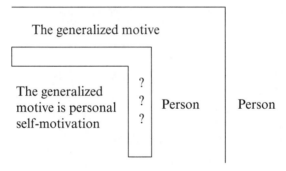

The membership of self-enrollment

Figure 3.7   Form seeks medium

ize the membership, in the sense that the formal membership determines procedures for conversations and similar contexts in which the member's self-motivation is being observed. This could be rules concerning annual performance appraisals. But the law does not provide any language for the conversation, which takes place during the performance appraisal and which is meant to observe self-motivation. At best, the law provides a language for "the difficult conversation" after a negative result from lack of self-motivation results from the use of a different language.

The implication of the fact that the law cannot serve as a satisfactory medium for the membership of self-enrollment is that organizations since 1980 have constantly been looking for alternative media and languages. Organizations are searching for a language for how to take responsibility for ensuring that their employees take responsibility for their own enrollment in the organizations. I have sought to formalize that in Figure 3.7.

What I argue, then, is that since the emergence of the notion of adapting to adaptation, organizations have been looking for a language for how to take responsibility for ensuring that their members take responsibility for their own self-inclusion in the organization, which is in constant flux and in the process of becoming something other than what it is.

There are many function systems in society each with their symbolically generalized medium and communicative code. In addition, there are many other communication forms that organizations may study and try out. Among the function systems are those identified in Figure 3.8.

Since 1980, I argue, three media have been successively tested and embedded in organizational, personnel and management practices. These are (1) The medium of pedagogy: the child, (2) The medium of love: passion, and (3) The medium of play: fantasy. They each provide a

Pay/ not pay	Legal/ non legal	Govern/ governed	Better/ worse	Healthy/ sick	Loved/ not loved	Help/ not help	True/ false
MONEY	LAW	POWER	THE CHILD	MEDICINE	PASSION	CARE	KNOWLEDGE
The economic system	The judicial system	The political system	The educational system	The health system	The system of love	The care system	The scientific system

Figure 3.8   The functionally differentiated society

language for a particular answer to the question discussed above, but none of them is able to provide the final answer. Pedagogy offers its answer but restates the question in a new form, which love is then the answer to. But love also leaves a remainder and the question is displaced and redefined again. The most recent answer is play.

There are also other explorations of the media of function systems. Karen Lisa Salamon, for example, has produced comprehensive studies of what she refers to as the spiritualization of management (Salamon 2002). Described in my own terms, she explores the possibilities for the manifestation of the individualized responsibility for self-enrollment, which exists in the religious system, with faith as its medium. Her focus is particularly on various new religious groups. I have chosen not to follow this path.

THE STRATEGY OF PEDAGOGIZATION

In relation to the membership of self-enrollment, the first medium that public organizations take an interest in is pedagogy. The concomitant communicative code is better/worse educationally. From the mid 1980s, we see the formation of a new semantic with concepts such as "self-development through work", "life-long learning", "responsibility for own development" and "adaptability".

The Semantics and Practices of Pedagogization

Let me begin with a brief description of the pedagogical semantics, which emerges during this period and is still evolving in new concepts such as "talent" and "windows of opportunity".

From the mid 1980s on, employees are beginning to be referred to as self-responsible. Self-responsibility initially refers to a responsibility for the development of one's own competencies. However, if we take a closer look, there is also the question of a much greater responsibility. The concept of "security" becomes redefined. Previously, security meant job security, that is, security that one would not lose one's job without fair warning. Security was a question of rights, which the employee could either have or not have depending on settlements and contracts. However, that is no longer what is meant by security. Security now becomes defined as the degree of one's institutional and labor market relevance. Security presupposes concurrence between employees' qualifications and skills, on the one hand, with the skills and qualifications that the labor market and employers consider currently relevant, on the other. The concept "security" becomes temporalized and personalized. Security becomes causally linked to the effort of the individual employee. The Department of Administration wrote in 1987: "Job descriptions change with increasing speed and the individual's job security is perhaps now more a question of one's ability to 'keep up' both professionally and socially in relation to the growing demands of the job" (Christensen 1987, p. 20, own translation). Security becomes a part of self-responsibility. That means that security becomes individualized and comes to depend on the employee's ability to self-develop in a way that the environment considers relevant. And if one is unable to make oneself relevant to one's current workplace, then there is the possibility of "security through change of jobs". In other words: If one does not "make an effort and latch onto the possibilities for development that the job presents", then one excludes oneself from the labor market (Ministry of Finance 1994, p. 15). The National Association of Municipalities writes: "If employees do not show an interest in lifelong learning, their chances of maintaining their connection to the labor market diminishes rapidly" (The National Association of Municipalities and The Municipal Folk School 1997, p. 17). Elsewhere it says: "The new security can best be described as the possibility to achieve influence, education, and development. At the same time, this security is centered on the individual (. . .) This increases demands on the individual to show initiative and be proactive" (The National Association of Municipalities and KTO 1995, p. 48, own translation). And just one more quote: "The employee that does not evolve is more or less being phased out" (Aalborg Municipality Personnel Administration in The National Association of Municipalities and The Municipal Folk School 1997, p. 16). One cannot say it much more directly than this.

Personal competence development and organizational adaptation to adaptability become linked together:

Competence development and the opportunity to learn create flexibility in the individual employee and institution. Therefore, competence development represents the most important driving force behind adaptability (. . .) Competence development is designed to ensure the institution's adaptability through flexible employees (. . .) To create adaptable, proactive public institutions requires competence planning. The individual employee represents the institution's competence, and the sum of the employees' competences, its development and organization, is of crucial importance to the efficiency of the institution. (Ministry of Finance 1995, pp. 195–6, own translation).

It becomes the individual employee's responsibility, through responsibility for self-development, to ensure the adaptability of the organization. And once the concept "competence" becomes linked to the concept "adaptability" in this way, it loses its referential self-evidence. In the formal organization with traditional membership, competences were simply given formal competences. Now, it is no longer possible to define in any stable way what competence is. As the Ministry of Finance writes, "knowledge no longer has an extended shelf-life" (Ministry of Finance 1998b, p. 25). It even appears as if it is not possible to define current and relevant competences over time on an organizational level. Instead, the question of competency becomes linked to the scope and responsibility of the individual:

Employees need to take responsibility for their own development. Employees should not leave it to the management to ensure their professional and personal development. The individual employee must relate proactively to the possibilities and needs for personal development so that she is equipped to take on new challenges and competence requirements (. . .) But employees must make an effort and be prepared to utilize the possibility for development in their daily work routine. Through continual development and qualification, the individual employee may increase his or her level of security, both in relation to the workplace and also to the labor market as a whole. An independent objective of the State's personnel policy is to ensure security for their employees. In turn, we expect that employees accept job mobility, competence development, and remain open to new challenges. In a shifting world with continually developing demands for qualifications and changing responsibilities, employee security is best ensured through ongoing competence development. (Ministry of Finance 1994, p. 18 own translation)

The organization establishes self-responsibility for own competence development and the balancing of this with the needs of the organization and the labor market. The workplace is responsible for providing a competency assessment in order to take responsibility for the way that the employees take responsibility for themselves and for the organization.

Oddly, what happens is that the concept of competency becomes emptied of all content other than its self-reference: to be competent becomes a question of competence development. Learning to learn becomes detached from learning something specific. The most important employee qualification becomes seeing oneself as unfinished. Thus, the central competency is no longer located within the relationship between the employee and an outside object, which needs to be mastered, but in the employee's self-relation and the mastery of this relation. The employee is expected to be able to relate to herself as potential competency and development. Thus, what is required is the employee's ability to double herself so that one self observes and the other self is observed as competency.

Pedagogization and Its Effects

By moving through this semantic development, organizational systems explore the possibilities for coding the membership of self-enrollment in pedagogical terms. During this period, a language is established for a particular pedagogical articulation of the membership of self-enrollment. A pedagogical articulation of self-enrollment means finding a specific solution to the question of self-enrollment in which the employee can be given responsibility for self-inclusion in the organization in a particular way. What is special about this particular mode is that the employee constantly observes herself through the code of pedagogy, reproduces her own incompletion and makes herself into a project of self-development in order to increase her organizational and workplace relevance. In this context, communicative relevance means to maintain oneself as a strategic potential competency for the organization.

Communicating pedagogically about membership has a number of implications for the expectations that can potentially develop between organization and employee, between employees and in their self-relation. It has implications for the rules that apply to the formulation of and communication about the membership of self-enrollment and it has implications for the possibilities of developing the question of inclusion and exclusion. To shed light on these implications, we have to first address the question of what characterizes pedagogical communication in the first place.

When communication is pedagogical it forms a specific generally symbolic medium of communication, that is, "the child" (Luhmann 1993a). Our modern conception of the relationship between adults and children evolved during the 1700s and superseded the idea that a child's nature is given at birth (Ariès 1973). Instead, the child is now thought of as something moldable. What the child ultimately develops into is now perceived as relating to the environment that molds the child. This idea creates "child" as a symbolically generalized medium across which communication can take place with the aim of effecting a specific set of influences and a specific development so that the child arrives at its proper form as an adult. The possibility of conceiving of the child as moldable creates the condition for pedagogical communication in which no one actually speaks *to* the child but where "child" as a representation comes to symbolize a learning endeavor. The child becomes a symbol thorough which communication takes place. The child is the *medium*, which needs to be *formed* in pedagogical communication.

Which specific form the child is imagined to take on depends upon the pedagogical *program*, that is, what is today referred to as learning objectives. The specific form can be about flexibility, morality, creativity, professionalism, or something entirely different. The fact that the child as medium is a *generally* symbolic communication medium means that there are no restrictions for what types of knowledge can be imprinted in the medium. Theoretically, the child can take any kind of form; a tyrant, artist, environmentalist, and so on. The fact that the medium is *symbolic* means that the child represents the symbolic and recognizable expression of the medium, that about which communication can take place. However, the symbol is variable and can be replaced by student, pupil or course participant (it does not depend on biological age). Regardless of the symbol, the distinction remains: child/adult – moldable/finished.

The binary *code* that the medium "child" comprises is better/worse in terms of learning (Luhmann 1989, pp. 100–106). In pedagogical communication, everything is perceived from that perspective. Everything is perceived with the aim of perfecting the child in relation to learning objectives. Thus, it is a *code of rectification* according to which one can either connect to the code's positive preference value, for example, by considering how the student/pupil/course participant can become better at something, or connect to the code's reflexive side by considering reasons for a lack of success despite the deployment of the most current pedagogical methods. Of course, the code is also used in continual evaluations and tests of the child's abilities: pass/fail, strengths/weaknesses, and so on. In any case, pedagogical communication generally becomes a question of rectifying with a view to perfecting.

Pedagogical communication is aimed at forming a subject, which is treated like a child, that is, as something moldable. Regardless of whether this subject is a child, a student, an apprentice or an employee engaged in "lifelong learning", this molding resides outside the scope of pedagogical communication. Pedagogical communication can observe what a student says and does, but it cannot observe the student's thoughts about a particular class. From the perspective of the communication, the student's consciousness is a "black box". Pedagogical communication can connect to other pedagogical communication but it cannot connect to the thought

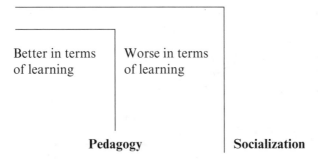

Figure 3.9   The form of pedagogization

operations of systems of consciousness and thus cannot control them. Pedagogical communication can teach and can adjust its teaching on the basis of observation, but ultimately it is unable to teach the pupils, students or employees anything because their learning consists of what they choose to do with their education. Pedagogical communication, therefore, draws yet another line between pedagogy and teaching on one side and socialization on the other. Like the concept of membership, whose outside is constituted by the psychic system and the body, the radical outside of pedagogical communication is socialization. Socialization is perceived by pedagogy as the child's "natural" education and social adaptation. Molding the process of socialization is essentially what pedagogical communication is about. Socialization that does not take shape through pedagogy is perceived as high-risk. Children are either given no form, too little form, or undesirable forms. Thus, it is very important to the pedagogical perspective to ensure that socialization takes a specific direction, but, at the same time, socialization can never become anything but the constitutive outside of pedagogy. Pedagogy desires socialization but has to be content with making the distinction between better/worse in terms of learning. The form of pedagogy is shown in Figure 3.9.

Pedagogized Self-Enrolment

When the membership of self-enrollment is shaped in the medium of pedagogy, it has a number of implications for the pedagogical communication and for the membership. I have tried to illustrate the molding of the medium of pedagogy by self-enrollment in Figure 3.10.

In the membership of self-enrollment, the relationship between form and medium is not a relationship between teacher and student. The relationship between form and medium is expected to be the employee's internal self-relation. It is expected that the individual employee observes herself

+Better/−worst learning

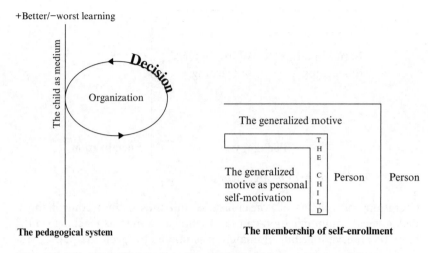

Figure 3.10   The molding by self-enrollment of the medium of pedagogy

through the language of pedagogy. Competency assessments, employee profiles, competency agreements, and so on, are meant to support employees' self-observation and the maintenance of themselves as a medium for pedagogy, that is, as children. Employees are invited to divide themselves into form and medium. In competency assessments, employees are supposed to present themselves as both strategic and competent. The manager does not suggest specific training courses but facilitates and coaches a process through which employees can formulate what they want from their own development. The individual employee becomes the designer of herself as medium: educator and child in one. When ongoing competency development, adaptability and flexibility become the focus, it actually means that one of the most important characteristics of the competence to competency development becomes to maintain oneself as a medium. When the buzzword is lifelong learning, it becomes a question of endlessly deferring adulthood. The problem becomes how to maintain and circulate "child" as a medium so that it becomes endlessly possible for the employee to shape and reshape herself as medium and how to regenerate the pedagogical medium despite constant form formations. In other words, unlearning becomes as important as learning. This problem of the circulation of the medium is operationalized in the competency language, for example, through the division of competencies into general, professional and specialist. Here, general competencies increase moldability and the maintenance of the medium whereas specialist knowledge exhausts the medium and reduces moldability. Circulation is ensured by one's capacity to discard

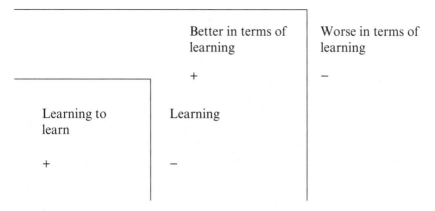

Figure 3.11   The form of pedagogy folded into itself

one's specialist knowledge. One has to be willing and ready to rid oneself of a professional identity defined as a having a great deal of knowledge about a limited area of knowledge in order to be able to maintain oneself as medium. Disloyalty towards one's past concerning knowledge and experience becomes an employee virtue. Obviously, competency assessments also encourage employees to show their willingness to give up something, for example, certain responsibilities and areas where one's competency is well known in order to show that one remains open towards new challenges.

The invitation to employees to pedagogize themselves thus also leads to a particular way for them to see themselves. This perspective is the code of pedagogy, better/worse in terms of learning. Since, however, the most important thing is no longer the ability to learn a specific competence, but to be a learning person, this perspective also means the doubling of the code, that is, not only that one is better/worse at something but that one is better/worse at observing oneself from the perspective of better/worse. That means better/worse at constantly defining new learning objectives, better/worse at constantly developing oneself, challenging oneself, recreating oneself. This requires one to always emphasize what is unfinished about oneself. The central competence, then, no longer resides within the relationship between the individual and an external object, which one needs to master, but in the individual's self-relation and the mastery of this relation. And pedagogical rectification therefore also becomes the rectification of one's self-relation. One needs to perceive oneself and one's personality as something incomplete, which needs further development. In a certain sense, one is expected to see oneself as a child (Andersen 2004b, 2007a). The code of pedagogy is re-entered into itself, which can be illustrated as shown in Figure 3.11.

The pedagogical system (the educational system) observes its own function as cultivation and learning-based development. However, other social systems perceive the pedagogical contribution as classification. Pedagogical communication cannot communicate in its code, better/worse in terms of learning, without also classifying people according to their qualifications. And such classification according to qualifications is precisely a service to the surrounding society when organizations hire people for certain functions, and so on. In the traditional membership, the decision about generalized motives was simultaneously a decision about which formal competencies would be required by applicants. And the pedagogical system functioned as the organization's external environment, which made such decisions possible precisely by developing and classifying qualifications. In the membership of self-enrollment this is radically different when it is coded pedagogically since the organizational perspective is no longer simply focused on the skills already acquired by an individual but the ones that he or she will acquire as a future employee. The classification becomes about having the competence for competency development that benefits the organization, and this competence cannot be conclusively established at the time of hiring but has to be tested throughout the entire period of employment. The organization is not responsible alone for the evaluation of the continued relevance of the employee. From the perspective of pedagogy, it becomes an employee's most important responsibility to evaluate their own relevance for the workplace and subsequently to correct their own self-development. This is basically the condition of membership in the form of self-enrollment when it takes on the form of pedagogy. The result is the expectation about the individual's ongoing self-evaluation with regard to their ability to continually be challenged and to develop in a way that benefits the organization.

This creates the possibility for the individual employee to engage in a distinctively strategic game. Now, competency both means the skills one already possesses and the potential one has for new competence development. The individual employee can use this distinction between real and potential competency strategically by withholding actual competency. By downplaying one's actual level of competency, one increases one's potential, so to speak. One might surprise the organization with quick competency development by having withheld certain competencies from the organization. Thus, the pressure on the individual's ongoing adaptability allows for the individual to "economize his or her talent". There are in fact many different strategic possibilities. One is, as already mentioned, the withholding of competencies. Another possibility is changing jobs. If one is no longer able to demonstrate new talent, one can always be a talent to someone else. That pertains to one's role in the organization, where one might choose new collaborators or a new position, but it obviously also pertains to a shift to an entirely new workplace to whom one is once more "a new talent" who represents new possibilities.

The immanent question in the form of self-enrollment was: *How may we as an organization take responsibility for ensuring that the individual takes responsibility for her inclusion in the organization, which is constantly in the process of becoming something other than what it is?* The pedagogical answer to that question becomes: As an organization, we assume responsibility for hiring people who hold the competency of competency development and ensuring the conditions for continued competence development in the organization, so that the individual may take responsibility for her inclusion in the organization by continually developing and thereby constantly being located in the place where the organization is headed. Employees have to constantly sort through their potential for self-development according to the question of what would be relevant competencies for the organization. It is about potentializing and realizing oneself through the conception of what, in the future, will be relevant conditions for entering the organization.

Thus, within the code of pedagogy, self-enrollment becomes something one has to continually qualify for by molding oneself according to what is relevant for the workplace. This means that one is never fully a member. Membership is always ahead of one, and one always lags behind a little bit. One is always in the process of becoming a member.

Pedagogy provides the membership of self-enrollment with a really good language for how organizations may shift the responsibility for development and inclusion onto the individual member. The question, however, is development towards what? How is it possible for the employee to establish what within the pedagogical language is relevant to the workplace? The problem is that it is not. Typically the educational system employs external reference when programming learning. It generally references well-defined "professions" as external points of reference. However, the very point of the semantic about competency for competency development is precisely that professions can no longer hold this status. At the same time, the organization typically rejects the role of guide for the employee. It is happy to coach employees through their work of finding relevant learning objectives, but the main responsibility remains that of the employees. Therefore, what initially looked like a good answer, that is, pedagogy, runs the risk of causing an introverted self-oscillation in the membership form. The adaptable self becomes both the means and goal of self-development. This is what Karen Lisa Salamon refers to as an own goal when the self is the only goal (Salamon 2007). The problem is that the organization refuses to define what it considers relevant to the workplace, and pedagogical self-molding also does not provide the answer. The peda-gogical code cannot say anything about what it is one needs to become better at except for becoming better at relating to oneself as competence and incompetence, and the self is the medium for this.

The pedagogical coding of self-enrollment leads to employees capable of transforming themselves according to what is considered relevant to the workplace, but the usefulness of this is limited to the extent that the defini-tion of workplace relevance does not become part of the self-enrollment.

THE STRATEGY OF INTIMACY

The strategy of intimacy provides a possible answer to this problem. Through this strategy, organizations explore the possibilities inherent in the medium of the love system, passion. With passion as a medium, the organization becomes the employee's significant other, the other around which everything revolves and whose needs one is constantly trying to anticipate. We might say that love communication is precisely character-ized by providing an answer to the question of responding to the needs of the other without these needs having to be made explicit.

The Semantics of Love

Once more, I will begin by observing the semantic development in order to then focus on the intimate codification in the code of love. Semantically, the semantics of love finds expression in new concepts such as engagement, initiative, responsibility and holistic approach.

In the context of the concept of public servant and thus traditional membership, responsibility was defined as obligation. A public servant was assigned responsibility through the formulation of explicit duties and directions. Duties were not self-assumed. It was the duty of the superior to formulate the duties of the subordinate. Moreover, in the pedagogical semantics about adaptable employees, we see the concept of responsibility for own development where the adaptability of the organization is seen as dependent upon the adaptability of the employee. The concept of the responsible employee adds another dimension to this. Responsibility is no longer seen as a positive reaction in the form of duty to an executive expectation, and it is also not the responsibility for self-development. Responsibility becomes something for the individual to seek out. Responsibility is a self-relation but conceived in such a way that the employee is responsible for finding out what constitutes acting responsibly. Responsibility is not assigned. It becomes something one takes on, something one is responsible for taking on, responsibility for responsibility.

According to this logic, it is seen as a problem, for example, if "employees do not show much initiative with respect to the general situation of the institution but focus on individual cases". It is considered a problem if the management is missing employee "challenge and responsibility toward the collective handling of jobs in the institution" (Administrationsdepartementet 1987, p. 2). As stated in a report by the Ministry of Finance, *Tools for Welfare*, the idea is no longer the employee having responsibility but the person *taking* responsibility (Ministry of Finance 1995, p. 179, own translation).

Responsibility for taking responsibility is about showing initiative and being engaged: "It is by virtue of enterprising employees who are motivated to develop and engage and who are capable of adapting quickly and flexibly that the state can meet new challenges and create the best solutions for the benefit of society as such" (Ministry of Finance 1998b, p. 6). One cannot take responsibility without being engaged. Only engagement makes it possible for the individual to construct an understanding of responsibility in relation to the institution without the interference of a superior. Engagement indicates the employee's attempts to relate to organizational goals and not merely individual cases. In 1987, the Department of Administration wrote: "the individual has to see his or her function as part of a whole and not simply as the sum of individual cases" (Administrationsdepartementet 1987, p. 8). However, the engagement is an internal relationship within the individual employee, which the organization is unable to observe. Therefore, the words "engagement" and "initiative" often appear side by side in various descriptions of employee and personnel policy. *Initiative is the external observable side of engagement.* As opposed to the concept of the public servant, the individual's responsibility within the organization becomes observable not through the following of directions or the carrying out of a duty but precisely in the form of independent initiatives that no one has requested.

This concept of responsibility requires a reconstruction of the relationship between employee and manager. In order to allow the employee to show initiative, her specific tasks are no longer authorized by a superior's definition of those tasks. In this context, we see the emergence of a long list of new buzzwords: involvement, inclusion, delegation of competency and participatory democracy. The Ministry of Finance writes: "In order for the process to be successful through which visions for an institution are created it has to be built on dialogue between management and employee. Without the active and involved participation of employees in the development of visions, they cannot be expected to work with engagement towards their realization" (Ministry of Finance 1995, p. 42, own translation). And: "Managers and employees are expected to take on a shared responsibility" (Ministry of Finance 1998b, p. 5, own translation). But like a marriage, both parties need to develop through the relationship. The Ministry of Finance writes: "Institutions and employees must engage in a mutual development" (Ministry of Finance 1995, p. 179, own translation). And: "Public employees and managers take on a shared responsibility for the development of the institution and employees" (Ministry of Finance 1995, p. 179, own translation).

And obviously it is not only employees who need to be engaged. Managers should too: "Management is also an important focus area because the engagement and ability of the management to ensure a dialogue can support the creation of shared responsibility" (Ministry of Finance 1998b, p. 10, own translation). Engagement spurs engagement.

The asymmetry, which nevertheless is articulated between manager and employee, seems to stem from a difference between *giving* on one side and to *provide the possibility to give* on the other. "The organization" and "management" are responsible for providing the employees with the chance to give. The ministry of Finance writes: "Thus, it is a question of a much broader commitment for both employee and institution, where competency, flexibility, and responsibility are exchanged for possibilities for development and challenges" (Ministry of Finance 1995, p. 179, own translation). Elsewhere it says: "As employer, the state asks of each of their employees that they show responsibility, engagement, and produce results. In turn, the state's personnel policy will provide employees with the possibility for professional and personal development and the security it creates (Ministry of Finance 1994, p. 7, own translation). And again: "Expectations about engagement, flexibility, and joint responsibility for their own development and the development of the workplace is to be countered by attractive working conditions and a flexible workplace setting" (Ministry of Finance 1998b, p. 10, own translation). The general thread here is that management and organization are supposed to provide possibilities: possibilities for being challenged, development, flexibility, independent initiatives and performance. These are possibilities for the employee to give something to the organization, possibilities for the employee to show her engagement in and responsibility towards the organization through independent initiatives in relation to the organization; giving the other the opportunity to give.

If management is about providing the employee with the possibility to give him or herself fully and if employee engagement is a precondition of organizational performance, this implies that the private and the personal have to be defined as a positive element in organizational communication.

It is not enough for the private to be defined as a necessary backdrop and an external obstacle to the completion of work. Private content becomes doubly charged as both the inner emotional life of the employee as well as the employee's private social context. If one wants personal engagement from the employee, there has to be a focus on how to make the job meaningful for the individual:

> Our personnel policy is meant to ensure that individual jobs are defined with the aim to make them as meaningful as possible (. . .) It is not enough that one's workplace and one's job hold a strong image to the outside world if one does not have the sense that one contributes in a positive way to the achievement of the institutional goals and objectives. Thus, it is important for the employee to feel appreciated and respected for his or her contribution (. . .) However, it is also important that the employee does not feel as if he or she is being reduced to a professional individual but also feel welcome and appreciated with his or her particular personality and quirks. Respect and appreciation are not only a question of praise and positive mention but is just as much about criticism – constructive criticism – (. . .) each individual is taken seriously as person and professional. (The Department of Administration 1987, p. 6)

There is no zone of indifference between organization and member but, on the contrary, an intense interest for the personal. We see an organizational interest in "the whole employee": "The whole employee represents a framework around the many relationships that may contribute to employee engagement, responsibility, and motivation" (Ministry of Finance 1998b, p. 31). And the whole employee includes not only all aspects of a person while at work but also that person's life outside the organization: "Those employees who are able to combine in a satisfactory way their work life with their lives outside the workplace are most often the most content, engaged, and productive employees (. . .) [Thus], the relationship between employees' work life and other aspects of their lives should be incorporated into performance appraisals and personnel policy development" (Ministry of Finance 1998b, p. 32, own translation).

The idea seems to be that the organization formulates a positive interest in the emotional and private lives of their employees. Problems at home, difficulties with children become defined as relevant to the organization. If an employee is in the middle of a personal crisis, for example, developing an alcohol addiction, the private becomes articulated as relevant to the organization. How does that make sense? A well-functioning private life is a precondition for the ability to be engaged in one's work. Hence, when engagement becomes defined as a crucial employee qualification, people's family and emotional lives become relevant to the organization as well. Does this abolish the boundary between private and public? No, the boundary has become even more important than before. The boundary is no longer a boundary for what interests the organization. In that sense, it has been abolished. The boundary now constitutes a new speech position within the organization. It becomes possible for employees to speak from the perspective of the private, to advance private reasons in an organizational setting to which employees have privileged access. The private is defined as relevant to the organization, it becomes something that a manager can inquire about, it becomes something that the management needs to consider in their daily planning, but it also becomes a position from which employees can speak without having their statements deemed irrelevant. The relationship between organization and employee becomes intimate.

Love as Form

What this semantic implies is a codification of the membership of self-enrollment in the language of love, and this has a whole range of additional effects on the conditions under which membership develops as well as the love communication. I will first give a brief characterization of love communication and then return to the question of membership. Here, I observe love as a particular form of communication. Thus, contrary to André Spicer and Carl Cederström, I do not observe the relationship between love and organization through psychoanalysis (Spicer and Cederström 2010). I do not inquire about love as a specific structure of desire. I am not primarily interested in the psychological function of love or in the psychological effects of specific organizational forms of inclusion, but in the way in which the medium of love communication is considered relevant in the decision of organizational membership and what the effects are for the organization.

Love communication is characterized by being closed around the function of thematizing the "highly personal". Highly personal love communication communicates about participants in a way that professional content cannot be kept distinct from the mutual recognition and interweaving of identities. In love communication, one either accepts the other with his or her entire life horizon and worldview or one rejects the whole thing. It is not possible in a highly personal relationship to recognize the other without recognizing his or her worldview because this worldview represents their identity (Luhmann 1995b, p. 61). In this context, Luhmann defines intimacy as when "more and more domains of personal experience and bodily behavior become accessible and relevant to another human being and vice versa" (Luhmann 1995c, p. 224). He goes on to say: "Roughly speaking, one loves, not because one wants gifts, but because one wants their meaning. This meaning does not lie in displaced gratification, nor in the indirect satisfaction of needs by diverting through the other. It lies in interpenetration itself, not in performances but in the other's complexity, which is acquired via intimacy as a feature of one's own life" (Luhmann 1995c, p. 224).

Obviously, it is possible to speak of and with the other in other forms of communication, such as for example legal or pedagogical communication. However, communication never becomes highly personal, never intimate. The highly personal communication in the love system is constituted by the binary code of love: love me/love me not, where it is better to be loved than not loved.

This form of coding has a series of implications for the possibility of communication because it affects the way that the individual's environment is created within the communication. Whereas both legal and pedagogical coding refer to the environment as something given, as something universal that exists outside the individual communication, the love coding and its "love me/love me not" turn this relation inside out. The "love me/love me not" coding internalizes the creation of the environment into the communication itself. To say, "I love you", means to define the other as the "significant other" within the worldview of the one who loves. Thus, the other is unable to respond without putting the presupposed worldview at stake. The worldview of the speaker is made immanent in the communication. This means that the other's response does not merely represent a "move" in the communicative game while the rules of the game remain the same, which is what happens in other communicative coding. The response to "I love you" comes to represent both an assessment of the statement and of the worldview of the lover, or more precisely of the identity of the lover and her relation to the world (Luhmann 1995b, p. 62). In short, the response becomes an act in relation to which one either accepts or rejects the speaker (Luhmann 1995b, pp. 61, 65; and Luhmann 1998, p. 22).

Because we are not speaking of something pre-given but something that is created by the speech act itself, the signs of love communication become *expressive symbolism*. Expressive symbolism contains an open space of possible interpretations (in theory, anything can be a sign of love: roses, romantic dinners, but also the dishes that nobody made, the attention not given, and so on), but the expressive symbolism also requires interpretation, which makes the communication itself a high-risk operation. If the other does not want to speak or interpret as expected, it is not only the conversation that breaks down in a way that the next sentence might correct. It threatens the intimate relationship itself. It is love that breaks down in an almost irreversible way because the rejected person experiences a rejection of both her identity and worldview. On the other hand, it is also a communication that may survive for a long time even though what is being expressed has no basis in intimate feelings. As long as the coding and semantics are sustained and the other joins in, communication may go on as hypocrisy and cover up other intentions and worldviews, which remain invisible because the communication so explicitly stages its own relevant surroundings. Clearly, these characteristics of the communicative coding further contribute to the riskiness.

High-risk love communication is only possible because we *take on the other person* in the love communication. Not only in the same way that it takes place in all communication, which has to always base itself on expectations about the other's relevant communicative expectations, but in the sense that we are assumed to consider the life and life situations of the partner, regardless of whether these directly impact the continuation of the immediate communication (Luhmann 1995b, p. 62). Such consideration is of such importance in love communication that it becomes prescriptive: *"The other" is regarded as so significant that the environment of the speaker is created in the image of the environment of the other*, and the communication comes to express not only ideas about the reactions of the other but the very initiative (action) which the other might have taken. The communication comes to express the unspoken wishes of the other.

It is not only a question of initiative but also of taking responsibility for the other by defining the other as a significant environment. Ultimately, love communication ends up being about establishing not only the speaker as agent and therefore giving but also the other as agent and giving; it is about "giving the other the possibility to give" (Luhmann 1995b, p. 67). From this perspective, love communication becomes extremely sensitive to what is done as well as what is not done, sensitive both to anticipation and initiative as well as non-anticipation and non-initiative. Thus, the compulsion to act returns to the speaker in accelerated form. Anticipation becomes the symbolically generalized media, which is at once open to being charged with a specific content as well as pointing to a horizon of possible charges.

With a code that compels action, a code in which statements are no longer statements *about* something but an expression *of* something, a code and a symbolically generalized media which are about anticipation, we see the framework of a communication system with a strict communications economy. Love may intensify communication by largely renouncing communication. It relies on anticipation. It requires no explicit "request" or "pleas" from the beloved in order for the lover to be able to match it. It would be a sign of failure for love to have to ask the other for anything.

However, we also see the framework of communication that threatens to self-destruct. There is a constant risk of total collapse, and there are

Table 3.1   Love communication

The love code	Loved/not loved
The universality of the love relationship	A continual consideration of the partner is expected in all life situations
Love and its environment	Love is the internalization of the other's systematized world relation
Love and anticipation	Love may intensify communication by largely renouncing communication. It relies on anticipation
The symbolism of love	Actions are chosen not for their specific effects but for the actions' expressive symbolic meaning
The contribution of love	To allow the other to give

a constant and endless number of possible interpretations, which nearly makes communication implausible, and yet it continues (Luhmann 1995b, pp. 66, 73). The tension leads the communication system to expound upon its value ascription within the code. It becomes so unambiguously valuable to be loved that communication closes itself around this value. Love can produce love and it requires more love, which, along with the symbolic expressivity machine, results in an ultimate closedness of the code.

Finally, the uncertainty of love communication means that participation requires presence and sensitivity, which in turn expands the repertoire of communicative signals. Few other forms of communication employ non-verbal communication to this extent on a reflexive level. This reliance on the non-verbal is fundamental since intimacy is closely linked to sexuality. Thus, love communication always inherently carries references to a bodily practice, which in turn helps shut down communicative possibilities (Luhmann 1995b, p. 69ff). And without such reference (which will often be the case in organizational communication), one experiences a significant loss of reality for the relationship of communication to practice. The characteristics of love communication can be summed up as shown in Table 3.1.

Loving Self-Enrollment

There are a number of implications for love communication and membership when the membership of self-enrollment is imprinted in the love medium. I have tried to illustrate the way that self-enrollment forms the love medium in Figure 3.12.

When the membership of self-enrollment is codified in the medium of

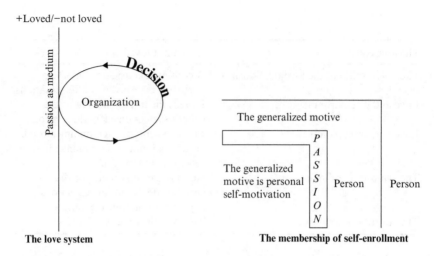

Figure 3.12   Self-enrollment forms the love code

love, it means that the communicative rules of love apply to the determination of membership. I do not argue that employees in fact love their workplace. My claim is simply that we see the emergence of organized games
employing the love code, where one of the rules of the game is that one is
required to express one's love for one's workplace. In the code of passion,
the employee is expected to continually strive to make herself loved by the
organization by anticipating the organization's needs. Today's employees
are expected to take over the organization's worldview. They are expected
to identify the organization's interests and objectives with their own interests and objectives. And in cases when the organization does not have an
explicit worldview, it is expected that employees anticipate such a worldview by actively imagining the organization's perspective on this or that.
In this way, the organization becomes the employee's significant other.

   When the love code is brought to bear on the membership, employees become communicatively concerned with earning the love of their
organization. The love code is not to love/not love but precisely loved/
not loved. Love communication focuses on the experience of oneself in
the loving or unloving eye of the other. When love becomes the code for
self-enrollment, the individual employee becomes concerned with whether
or not she is loved. It is no longer a question of whether one has fulfilled
one's formal obligations, or whether one has produced quality work. It
is a question of achieving constant recognition from the organization for
one's efforts and statements. We might say that whereas pedagogy lacked
language for how employees identify workplace relevance without receiv-

ing this definition from the workplace itself, love is precisely a language for how to direct oneself towards the needs of the other without being told how to do so by the other. Self-enrollment becomes primarily a question of continually making oneself loved by the organization. The language of love fits well with the notion of an employee responsible for constantly inventing herself as part of the organization. Within the love code, one is always doubtful about whether one is loved or not.

Love communication is always difficult, even within its usual relationship setting. However, it is obviously difficult in a very particular way when the significant other is not a person but an organization. Whose recognition is it really that might reveal the organization's feelings of love towards somebody? The organization as a significant other is opaque. It is a many-headed entity, and as employee there is no way to know which head is observing one's action as either loving or unloving. When the organization codes its membership through passion, it simultaneously renounces any form of authoritative center defining requirements and expectations. As an employee, one participates in many specific relations. One has a manager, or perhaps even several managers. One has colleagues. One participates in a number of projects, each with its own set of participants. One has customers and contacts of varying kinds. Who is it ultimately one is supposed to make oneself loved by and when has one achieved enough love from the different faces held by the significant other? This is the fundamental challenge of self-enrollment facing each individual employee. I will elaborate on this challenge in relation to the five variables in Table 3.1.

The universality of the love relationship
In a love relationship, one is expected to consider one's partner in every aspect of life. This is precisely what the semantic about the responsibility-seeking employee articulates through expectations about seeing one's own responsibilities in a holistic perspective. In love communication, employees are expected to constantly take the organization into account in everything they do. Unlike the Weberian bureaucracy, one cannot simply focus on one's specific job and leave the holistic perspective to the management, since the general motive in the form of self-enrollment marked by the love code *is* the whole. Each individual part also always concerns the whole. And this applies even outside of work hours. The concept of the holistic person stresses precisely the fact that there exists no outside of work. When one is defined within a love relationship with one's workplace, one is expected to consider the organization at all times, for example, when planning at home who is dropping off and picking up the children from school next week or when discussing the extent to which

it is acceptable to be checking email and such after the kids are in bed at night. And it remains the responsibility of the employee to find out what the interest of the whole is; whether next week the whole is made up of this or that project, the needs of the manager, the family's needs or something entirely different. From the perspective of the organization, an employee might be considered unfaithful when prioritizing his or her family and not sufficiently prioritizing the organization. However, the employee might also be considered to be unfaithful if she chooses the workplace over her family because she runs the risk of ruining the engagement and the positive energy she is imagined to acquire from her family and which she is supposed to bring with her to work. Engagement represents the organization's most basic requirement of its employees. Within the nuclear family, one has to learn to live with the idea that one is not the only significant other for one's partner. There are always competing love relationships in the form of the workplace of the other. And the employee is placed in an impossible double bind in the workplace where she is expected to be faithful to the job and unfaithful to the job (in order to be able to be faithful later on), and the employee can never know when either one of these contradictory expectations are in play.

With respect to the universality of the love relationship, there is always an inherent tension in the form of self-enrollment. On the one hand, the employee is expected to consider the workplace a partner in every life situation in and outside the workplace. On the other hand, it is also not desirable if the employee becomes too dependent upon the workplace. Anders Bojesen and Sara Louise Muhr remark that employees "might end up experiencing the love that the organization shows transformed into a unifying act of assimilation – wanting to own you; absorb you, direct you to its needs – all in the name of love" (Bojesen and Muhr 2008, pp. 84–5). André Spicer and Carl Cederström formulate it in psychoanalytical terms: "Figures who are completely subsumed and passionately attached to an organizational love object can prove to be a serious risk for the organization. This is because they see no boundaries to the love relationship and will frequently engage in excessive behavior that disturbs the smooth functioning of the organizational machine" (Spicer and Cederström 2010, p. 161). We might say that the power of self-enrollment is so great when passion is the medium that the organization runs the risk of including the employee to excess, with the concomitant responsibility for the life of the individual and the risk that the individual employee can no longer function as a constructive critical force for the many organizational processes of adaptation. In the modern functionally differentiated society, the individual is structurally coupled to a multiplicity of systems through different personifications: as consumer in the economy, patient in the health care system, student in the educational system, and so on. Over-inclusion is when a psychic system permits a particular social system to dominate one's entire reality contact, which prevents inclusion into other systems. Accordingly, a psychic system is over-included in the organizational system when somebody's social identity is made up primarily of his or her work identity. We know the dynamic from the love system more generally when two people have just met and are newly in love. They are not only each other's significant other. The entire world exists merely as a stage for their love. The external environment can only tolerate exposure to this for a relatively short period. In this context, a thesis could be that the preoccupation in the modern organization with the work–life balance is fundamentally a question of handling this risk and tendency towards over-inclusion and over-socialization when the medium of self-enrollment is passion. Anders Raastrup Kristensen writes about the work–life balance without boundaries, in which work "is not just something they [the employees] do during working hours. It takes up their whole life. They do not define their life in opposition to their jobs but see their jobs as a part of their lives. Thus, it is difficult to separate life and work and many people now say: we only have one life" (Kristensen 2011, p. 51, own translation). It is remarkable that it is not so much the unions but the workplaces themselves that show this preoccupation with the work–life balance. The over-inclusion of employees has come to pose a threat to organizations. Employees are becoming too attached to their jobs to also remain a critical innovative force, and many employees cannot sustain in the long term by only having a work life. Jay Roerlich speaks of work-dependency, when an individual cannot do anything but work (Roerlich 1980). Work dependency is seen as an obsession "with precise definitions, goal, policies, facts, list, measurements, methods, procedures and strategies (. . .) The work addict cannot live in the present" (Roerlich 1980, p. 172). Arlie Hochschild analyses the work–life balance technology "Family 360", the central focus of which is the evaluation of a manager's performance in the context of his family through interviews with the manager's parents, spouse, children and close friends in order to coach the manager about improving her family functions (Hochschild 2004). The Family 360 website states: "It's foolish to believe that a person who is unfulfilled in their personal life will be able to turn it off like a toggle switch when they walk through the doors of the company. So, to the degree that you can add fulfillment to their life, you're helping them add value to their employer" (www.family360.com/howitworks.html). Thus, the work–life balance can be seen as an organization's immune system protecting it from over-included employees. Today, it is the manager who tells her employees to "get a life". Concerning the tendency towards limitless work, organizations run the risk of having to assume responsibility for defining their employees' internal boundary in relation to the organization.

Love and environment

Love communication is accompanied by expectations about the internalization of the systematized world relation of the other, that is, the expectation that one sees the world through the eyes of the significant other. This idea is inherent in the very concept of the responsibility-seeking employee. The responsibility-seeking employee is precisely one who seeks out responsibility by perceiving the world through the eyes of the organization. The organization's view of the world becomes installed as a fixed perspective within the employee. And again, this is by no means a simple task since the organization's view is never a given. Modern organizations are multi-centered and polyphonic and do not allow for a reduction of them to a systematic worldview (Andersen 2003c). To seek responsibility, therefore, also means to oscillate between a range of alternative and heterogeneous organizational perspectives on the world, which only occasionally coincide.

Love and anticipation

Love may intensify communication by renouncing communication since it relies on acts of anticipation. Within organizations, anticipation is thought of as "showing initiative", which no one has requested. Taking new initiatives becomes the way in which one shows one's love. Love communication emphasizes the symbolic qualities of communication. Thus, showing initiative is ultimately seen as more important than implementation, which is why some organizations end up with a scenario where many projects are initiated but no one seems particularly concerned with their completion and effects because they have moved on to new projects. Thus, love communication constructs its own hierarchy in which initiatives are at the top and operations and completion at the bottom. Desirable jobs are ones that allow for independent initiatives, which is also reflected in local wage negotiations. Betinna Rennison has shown how the question of pay is framed as reciprocity of love. It pays to show initiative and engagement (Rennison 2007a, 2007b, 2007c, 2011). However, showing initiative is also risky because its central feature is that it symbolizes an understanding of "what we have in common". If you invite a new date to dinner at the hot dog stand and she declines your invitation, it might not be because she is not hungry but because she rejects your proposed view of who she is and what you might have in common. The same logic applies to initiatives in an organization. A rejected initiative simultaneously rejects the employee's comprehensive view of the organization and thus the reality that the employee perceived the relationship to be built on. Therefore, having one's initiative turned down is equal to being told that one is not loved.

The uncertainty about the reciprocation of one's love constitutes the productivity of the relationship. Doubting the love of the organization, the employee has to continually seek to anticipate the needs of the organization, the manager, the projects and colleagues. From the point of view of the organization, this is precisely the point: to have employees who are hypersensitive to the needs of the organization so that the organization no longer needs to express its needs to its employees. This turns into an endless spiral because there is no saying when one has anticipated enough needs. It becomes an inherent contradiction in the membership of self-enrollment when the code is loved/not loved. Bauman writes: "The job is never finished, just as the stipulations of love and recognition are never met completely and unconditionally. There is no time, successes tend to be forgotten a moment after being scored, life in a company is an infinite succession of emergencies . . . This is an exciting and exhausting life; Exciting for the adventurous, exhausting for the weak-hearted" (Bauman 2008, p. 130).

Accordingly, it hardly seems surprising that stress has become a central theme in the past decade. In what we might refer to as "industrial societies", stress was defined as an effect of a disagreement between the organization's expectations on the one hand and the employee's work capacity on the other. Stress was considered an effect of the fact that the employee was unable to live up to existing expectations. Therefore, the imagined solution was to increase employee participation in the workplace. Employee participation was intended to provide a safeguard against the organization's unreasonably high expectations and give employees a sense of control over their work environment. Today, however, stress has transformed into a question of self-stress. Employing the love codification of the membership, we might advance the thesis that stress today is linked to organizational expectations about the ability of their employees to anticipate and create their own self-expectations. Employees expect that the organization expects them to independently develop the needed expectations. Stress, then, becomes a sign of a gap between the expectations an employee has managed to take on and the many expectations the employee has expected to further anticipate. Thus, stress occurs as uncertainty about whether one is loved and whether one is even capable of being loved. Has one gathered up enough expectations? Moreover, stress can become a symbol of the ultimate love of one's workplace. The ultimate proof of love is giving until one has no more to give, no more to offer, once one has sacrificed oneself and risked one's health. My point is not that stress always works this way but that the love codification of membership creates this as a possible communicative dynamic. This also means that stress policies in workplaces become increasingly more complex. A manager who removes certain responsibilities from an employee suffering from stress runs the risk of hurting the employee's feelings by rejecting her love sacrifice. Moreover, when an organization formulates a stress policy about "learning to say no" or "perhaps expectations are not as great as you think", it does not remove the burden of expectation from the shoulders of employees but produces instead a new layer of expectations by not only expecting employees to create their own expectations but also to know their own limits and to say "no" as a way to show their love for the organization. This is yet another example of the double bind that employees find themselves in, where they are expected to simultaneously anticipate the organization's needs and also not. We can all imagine a manager telling an employee: "Your greatest responsibility is to yourself." The employee never knows when to act on either side of the difference, or at least not until she makes a wrong move. Contrary to its objective, stress policies might end up intensifying the spiral of expectations. Michael Pedersen speaks about the combination of a "commitment machine" and a "coping machine", where the individual employee is given responsibility for the management of own stress: "Stress is a lack in one's self-management, something one has to work on (. . .) One is now stressed about coping with one's stress alone" (Pedersen 2008, p. 184). Finally, today's manager is often not capable of relieving employees since most responsibilities are not assigned by the manager but result from projects that employees are involved in with colleagues in teams, which sometimes even work across departments and workplaces. Thus, even if a manager gives a direct order for someone to work less, the employee does not experience this as actually being possible since working less would mean letting down a number of work *partners*. Hence, what results from the manager's effort to protect an employee from herself is further pressure on the employee who is perhaps forced into major hypocrisy, and the manager realizes her lack of actual power. She is not even able to relieve an employee of responsibilities. It is impotence all around.

Communicating stress also takes on specific meaning since, in addition to referring back to a feeling of stress, it also comes to represent a desperate attempt to shed light on responsibilities one has taken on but which one feels are not being recognized and therefore are not visible to others. The responsibilities that employees feel that that they take on may easily seem invisible because they are differentiated across multiple contexts and partnerships, which are not necessarily aware of each other. Thus, when someone expresses stress it can mean: "You might not have noticed everything I do for you but I am approaching my limit and I would like to be seen and recognized for everything I do." Susanne Ekman has analyzed this question in depth. She shows that employees both desire freedom but also require infinite recognition (Ekman 2012). They want the management to be both fully absent and fully present.

The love claim: allowing the other to give. This claim runs through the semantics, which says that it is the responsibility of the organization to allow the manager to provide employees with possibilities, challenges and flexibility in order that they may develop, take initiative and give to the organization. We might say that the claim of love constitutes a way for the organization to invite employees into self-enrollment through passion. The claim of love and thus the entire semantics about possibilities, challenges and flexibility offers employees the chance to show that they want to be members. It is a partnership proposition. But it is also the responsibility of the relationship to ensure the continued possibility for employees to show their love for the organization. Thus perceived, "possibilities, challenges and flexibility" are not just abstract values but something to be concretely produced within the organization. The growing effort in organizations to work on visions and images of the future is also about maintaining the organization as attractive significant other. It is a way to make itself desirable. The formulation of new visions of the future makes new initiatives possible. They allow for new gifts to be given and for the reformulation of one's involvement in the organization.

However, the claim of love is also what allows the organization to address employees' engagement and passion. If repeated possibilities for an employee to develop and take initiative do not yield any result, the organization has to have "the difficult talk", which ultimately may result in divorce. The result of this is organizational communication, which constantly oscillates between considering its workforce as employees (seeking responsibility) and thereby as members of its decision communication or as resource (having responsibility) and thereby as an administrative category to which human resource management (HRM) applies.

The code of love turns self-enrollment into an ongoing question of making oneself loved in the organization. It becomes, in other words, a constituent part of one's role (the generalized motive) to be responsibility-seeking and self-motivated to judge whether one is in or out, relevant or irrelevant. Organizationally, those are made members who are capable of self-enrollment due to their responsibility-seeking attitude, and this happens as a decided and thus as a rational decision premise.

In many ways, love-codified self-enrollment is equivalent to the adaptable organization because the modern highly intimate relationship precisely provides a solution for how to maintain an intimate relationship under problematic and shifting conditions. About typical love relationships, Luhmann writes: "Rather, it also enables both parties to engage in common, or at least cooperative, action in an environment which has become complicated and presents such rapidly changing conditions that the response called for is rarely clear in advance, cannot be defined in morally unequivocal terms and cannot always be agreed between the partners from one case to the next, but rather has to occur in spontaneous harmony" (Luhmann 2010, p. 18). This describes precisely the conditions for modern membership: to maintain membership under continually shifting conditions and expectations. Love communication establishes conditions ensuring "the world in which you and I remain the same" even if external relationship conditions are in a state of continual flux (Luhmann 2010, p. 53).

And yet, this acceptance of shifting conditions is not without tensions. The code of love creates expectations about employee anticipation of organizational needs, but the code of love also entails a conservative danger because the relation risks being marked by security and loyalty and anticipation and becoming routine. The same quality that allows the relationship to endure shifting conditions is also what might prevent the relationship from evolving. Luhmann discusses how history in a relationship can replace its passion: "Passion is transformed imperceptible into history and is simultaneously replaced by history" with the result that "Passionate love turns into established love" (Luhmann 2010, p. 53). Having been in the same workplace for many years, you know your colleagues. You think that you know whom you can work with and not work with. Expectations of the people you work with have stabilized, what they have to offer and what they expect. You think that you know the organization. You begin to be able to tell the story of the relationship, which also stabilizes expectations concerning the future. In other words, you bond closely with your organization, and to bond closely, under the code of love, presents a new risk in relation to the ideal of adaptation. More and more phenomena appear as if they are unchangeable. How to maintain dynamism in a relationship that is taken for granted? How to maintain the openness to the other's needs and the uncertainty of love? How to maintain the ambiguity, which constitutes the energy and dynamic force of passionate self-enrollment?

Love, then, is a solution to the question of self-enrollment, which is the orientation towards the organization's needs without the need for the articulation of these needs. However, as a solution it generates a new problem of how to maintain exploration in a relationship which becomes "established" as it accumulates its own history.

THE STRATEGY OF PLAY

In many ways, the strategy of play provides a possible answer to such questions. Incorporating specific games in organizations is a way to introduce a greater level of imagination into the relationship. Game represents a language precisely for the imagination of the differently possible. With play as communication form and imagination as communication medium, the employee becomes articulated as member because he or she is willing to play.

The Employee Semantic of Play

I return once again to the question of semantic development, which here concerns play, "playability", humor, transformation, flow, "serious play", and so on. From the early 1980s, these concepts became part of a particular articulation of the self-enrolling employee.

I am not suggesting that play has never been used in the workplace prior to the 1980s. Play and work have probably always co-existed in some capacity. Donald F. Roy's famous 1950s study of "banana time" showed how play erupted spontaneously in the context of monotonous work in informal interaction among employees as a response to boredom in jobs involving standing by the same machine for 12 hours a day and doing the same repetitive movements. Roy shows how specific patterns of self-entertainment develop among workers, but also how this entails a range of tensions, which constantly threatens to transform play into mutual accusations and aggression (Roy 1960, p.167). In 1927, Henry de Man pointed to the fact that play served as a way for workers to ensure minimal freedom in monotonous Tayloristic jobs (de Man 1927, pp.80–81). Karl Marx dreamed of dissolving the distinction between work and play, a dream that has since been revived with certain regularity. Herbert Marcuse addressed the question in 1967 in his article "The end of Utopia" in the hopes of an aesthetic convergence between technology and art, work and play (Marcuse 1970, p.68 (orig. in German 1967)). However, Marcuse spotted the danger of repressive exploitation of play as "creative experimentation with the productive forces" (Marcuse 1970, p.66). Productive imaginative power becomes a productive force. Richard Burke is another heir to Marx's utopia. He wrote in 1971: "My formula for utopia is simple: it is a community in which everyone plays at work and work at play" (Burke 1971, p.47). Organized and therefore decided play has existed in certain forms since the 1920s, in the form of competitive games in workplaces, including company sports, for the generation of the desired work attitude and mentality. Moreover, since the 1950s organizations have employed management and business games for the training of managers. However, it was not until the 1990s that we saw the development of an actual semantic for the playful employee and play at work, where play is not an addition to work and membership but the very way in which one becomes an employee and the way in which one works (for a more comprehensive historical analysis, see: Andersen 2008a, Costea et al. 2005, 2006, 2007).

We see the first signs of this development in the early 1980s. Personnel and management training courses, seminars and conferences about organizational development, personnel, strategy and change begin to specifically address social games as a way to support creative and learning processes. The collective heading for these games is "icebreakers". As Ken Jones metaphorically writes, icebreakers are about cutting clear passages in frozen water and opening up channels of communication (Jones 1994, p. 11). Icebreakers are employed specifically in sessions and seminars where the atmosphere is marked by tension because participants do not know each other or to re-energize people after hour-long meetings. But icebreakers are also designed for use in workplaces where there is tension among colleagues, or where tension has developed in relation to new projects, which participants are nervous about starting. One concrete icebreaker example is the game "Barnyard", which is designed for use by a group of people who know each other, but where internal tension and mutual insecurity still exist. The game asks participants to use animal sounds to recognize each other. One of the participants volunteers to be the farmer. The other participants play farm animals. The farmer is blindfolded and spun around. The other participants form a circle around him. The farmer then proceeds to call out the different animals by saying their animal names, for example, "cow". The participant who plays cow responds with a "moo". The farmer then has to recognize the participants by their sounds. If the farmer guesses someone's name, that person takes a turn as farmer. The game ends when everyone has played farmer (Forbes-Greene 1983, p. 9).

In the 1990s, we saw the articulation of a new relation between play and work, which seeks to turn play into a job. The argument being that play needs to be given a purpose and that play and games represent the necessary way to achieve that purpose because play also represents a way to establish social relations and a collective way to learn. Marlene Caroselli, author of the book *Quality Games for Trainers*, writes: "Each game begins with a statement of the objective. Although we call these activities 'games' they are not 'all fun and games'. They are enjoyable work – not mindless busywork" (Caroselli 1996, p. xiii). John Newstrom and Edward Scannell, who share this perspective on fun and games, write: "In short, these games are designed to help team members have *fun* while learning important lessons" (Newstrom and Scannell 1998, p. xxiv). Thus, play must be serious, but seriousness is not defined in opposition to playing. We get the notion of "serious play". Roos et al. define serious play in this way: "We suggest that serious play is a mode of activity that draws on the imagination, integrates cognitive, social and emotional dimensions of experience and intentionally brings the emergent benefits of play to bear on organizational challenges" (Roos et al. 2004, p. 563). In a previous article Statler and Roos wrote:

> On a cognitive level, serious play stimulates people to imagine new possibilities and learn from new challenges. On the social level, serious play engages people in storytelling processes that allow them to make sense collectively of changing their environment. On the emotional level, serious play encourages people not to fear change but rather to embrace it and maintain an open attitude of acceptance and responsiveness. (Statler and Roos 2002, p. 2)

Play becomes a job that maintains central organizational functions. In their conceptual-historical analysis of work and play, Costea et al. conclude that the combination of play technologies and playful architecture sends a specific message: "The message is that work is not in opposition to life, that one's working identity should not be constructed against work (as subjugation or sacrificial) but through it, as an opportunity to enhance life without limitations" (Costea et al. 2007, p. 252).

Play is often associated with change management, organizational change as well as employee self-development. However, the concept of change through play is not about any specific change. It is not a question of planned changes or adapting to the environment. The buzzword is "emergence". Emergence refers to the origin of the moment as pure presence, a present free from any distinction between past and future. Emergence is a present without the repetition of the past. Pat Kane speaks of play as an ethics, which produces a particular attitude that allow us to face emergence directly: "We need to be energetic, imaginative and confident in the face of an unpredictable, contestive, emergent world" (Kane 2004, p. 63). From the perspective of the semantic of play, adaptation is perceived as a primitive mechanical form of change. Play is considered a deeper form of change. As Lloyd Sandelands writes in "The Play of Change": "Play calls upon the deepest vitality of human community and thereby upon its greatest possibilities for adaption and development. Thus, while play is certainly not the only way that change can occur there can be change that is not played – play is the way to deepest and most lasting change" (Sandelands 2010, p. 82). It is a question of generating an appropriate response to a world in which everything does not yet exist but is seen as emergent, as is the self. In a short article from 2002, Matt Statler and Johan Roos write: "Playing seriously helps organizations prepare for the unexpected" (Statler and Roos 2002, p. 1). They expand upon this point in a subsequent book from 2007 entitled *Everyday Strategic Preparedness*. They distinguish between threats to the organization, its necessary preparedness to these threats, and its resources. If the level of threats is raised, the necessity of preparedness grows accordingly and therefore also the need for resources. The limit of preparedness is first of all *the unthinkable*, that is, threats that we cannot even imagine as potential threats, and second, the *impossible*, which is when the organization has allotted all its resources to preparedness. In a world of constant flux, the limit of the unthinkable is pushed beyond itself. And in seeking to strategically prepare for the unthinkable, the number of "thinkable" scenarios becomes almost infinite, as does the need for resources. A central challenge becomes to strategically prepare for unforeseen events and changes (Statler and Roos 2007, pp. 21–38). The solution to this challenge is play:

> Play provides a concrete method of simulating the transgression of the limits of both the thinkable and the possible (. . .) Play appears as a zone for action and reflection in which an increase in the need for preparedness is simulated. By simulating this increased need, organizations can explore the limits of what is thinkable and possible and still remain safe from the immediate risk of overwhelming, real-world consequences. (Statler and Roos 2007, p. 125)

This play zone can be described as shown in Figure 3.13.

In the play zone, the limits of the unthinkable and the impossible can be transcended. The impossible becomes possible and the unthinkable thinkable, which means that the organization can address and prepare for the unforeseen. Statler and Roos conclude: "We can now say that serious play involves: (i) a mode of intentionality attuned to the emergent possible, (ii) a fluid engagement with the milieu, involving holistic operations within an ambiguous frame, and (iii) an opportunity to integrate multi- and mixed-media into a strategic sense making process" (Statler and Roos 2007, p. 125).

Whereas Statler and Roos assume a strategic view of change, Michael Schrage's focus is innovation. He formulates the relationship between innovation and management like this: "You can't be a serious innovator unless you are willing and able to play (. . .) The essence of serious play is the challenge and thrill of confronting uncertainties" (Schrage 2000, p. 2). Likewise, Mark Dodgson, David Gann and Ammon Salter consider play a central aspect of innovation: "The concept of 'play' enables the link between ideas and action. 'Play' is the medium between 'thinking' and 'doing' (. . .) 'Play' gives shape to ideas, enabling selection, manipulation,

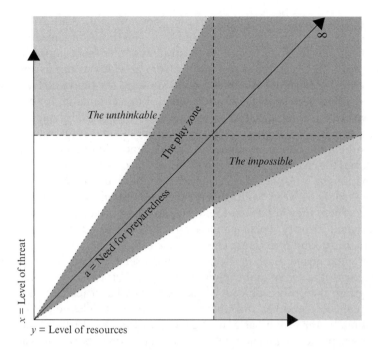

Source: Statler and Roos (2007, p. 125).

Figure 3.13 Statler and Roos' play zone

and learning about possibilities and focusing the mind of doers on action"
(Dodgson et al. 2005, p. 138). The focus of Charalampos Mainemelis and
Sarah Ronson is organizational creativity. According to them, play is the
cradle of creativity. They write: "the role of play is not to abolish purpose,
consistency, and rationality from organizational life; rather the role of
play is to help organizations maintain more flexible and more sophisticated forms of consistency by encouraging their members to occasionally
experiment with possible realities, behaviors, or identities (Mainemelis
and Ronson 2006, p. 117). Pat Kane, in his book *The Play Ethic*, embraces
a similar argument: "Like spirituality, play is about a means of transcendence in the everyday – another 'breath of life' (pheuma) that animates,
fixed situations, accepted boundaries, puts things 'in play'. Like spirituality, play is embracing possibility and change rather than fearing it" (Kane
2004, p. 319). As Costea et al. note, the goal is to overcome the finite and
every finitude (Costea et al. 2007, p. 258).

There are a large number of change games directed at organizations
or teams within organizations. Certain games are about organizational

innovation. Others are about product development. And still others concern the creation of new visions and strategies for the organization. The notion of playing one's way to a new strategy rather than simply deciding on one is to become free of restrictions from previous strategies and from established ideas of what makes a good strategy. As I have already mentioned, there is no shortage of such games. Luke Hohmann, for example, has written a book specifically on innovation games (Hohmann 2007). Some games are designed to generate an innovative employee perspective, others to counter resistance to change, and still others to play forth strategies for change. One of these games is called "Change the picture and the paradigm". The game is designed to encourage participants to move more flexibly between paradigms. Participants begin by each choosing an image. Then, they are asked to cut the image into pieces so that it loses its original identity. Participants are then asked to put the image back together in a kind of collage. The only rule is that it cannot turn back into the original image. Each participant is then asked to share his or her new image with the group and explain what it was before its transformation. The group then proceeds with a discussion of what it felt like to change one image into another and whether it was difficult to let go of the original. Finally, the group has a more general discussion of what it means to reject one paradigm and adapt to or create a new one. Participants are also invited to provide examples of organizational or personal paradigm shifts (Scannell et al. 1998).

My focus in this chapter is membership, so I limit myself here to games which address organizational membership in some way. It seems clear that the discourse, which assigns a specific contingency producing function to play, also applies in relation to the individual employee. Play is not only the answer to shifting and fluctuating conditions. It is also the employee's answer to the same concerns. Statler and Roos write: "We find that serious play encourages people to prepare themselves for the unexpected by constructing new knowledge, sharing meaning with each other, and maintaining an open, poised, and curious attitude towards change" (Statler and Roos 2002, p. 2). Through play, employees can learn to manage the unforeseen, but they can also use play to transform themselves: "We play the way we are, the way we could, or could not be, and through our engagement on play it shows us what we choose to do, not what we have to do. Sometimes, however we get so caught up in our play that it leads us to change who we are: we call this transformation" (Linder et al. 2001, p. 13). Lloyd Sandelands even speaks about the ability of play to effect "self-transcendence", where individual identities are transformed into collective life (Sandelands 2010, p. 76). Pat Kanes formulates the relationship between play and self-development like this: "The player at work is a fully 'potentialized' worker" (Kane 2004, p. 84). Herminia Ibarra and Jenifer L. Petriglieri distinguish between identity play and identity work: "Identity play aims to explore possible selves rather than to claim and be granted, desired or ought selves" (Ibarra and Petriglieri 2010, p. 11). In identity games, employees flirt with alternative "selves". The goal of self-development is not a specific definition of self: "The target identity is multiple, unspecified or unknown" (Ibarra and Petriglieri 2010, p. 16). Identity play is exploratory: "When engaging in identity play (. . .) people may rehearse a variety of possible selves, without necessarily seeking to adopt any of them on a permanent basis (. . .) this play enables them to evaluate possible selves and separate fantasy from reality" (Ibarra and Petriglieri 2010, p. 17). The shift from play identity to work identity is marked by the shift from flirtation to commitment: "The switch from flirtation with many possibilities to commitment, we suggest, may mark the transition from identity play to identity work" (Ibarra and Petirglieri 2010, p. 19). Thus, what we have is a semantics built on expectations about employees who relate to themselves as a multiplicity through a playful exploration of their own alternative selves. It is not simply an expectation about self-development, that is, the further development of a self, but about viewing one's central worldview as contingent and as the object of alternative configuration, redefining the possibilities of thinking the very concept of development.

The question is do employees have the ability to enhance their ability to imagine themselves through play. One critic who has taken great interest in this idea is Alanna Jones, who has written several books and articles on therapeutic games. For Jones, play is a positive form of existence and a resource for self-development. Playing games has an inherent positive therapeutic effect:

> Games have therapeutic value in themselves – the reason people who are depressed are encouraged to engage in activities and why people at a fair or a carnival are smiling and having a good time. Families are encouraged to build better relationships with each other by playing together and by participating in games that are enjoyable and fun for all. Think about your own life and the things that you do that are fun and enjoyable. How do these activities make you feel and how do they help you in your daily life (. . .) Games get you involved with other people, build relationships among individuals, make everyone equal and most of all promote laughter to help people have a good time. (Jones 1998, pp. 11–12)

Accordingly, Jones perceives childhood as a significant source of inspiration for further game development. Because games and play are seen to hold inherent therapeutic value, professional therapists can bring out and develop this aspect: "Think of what you played as a child or even games you like now, and often times these games can be adapted to create a new therapeutic game by changing the game slightly or adding a discussion, and before you know it you will have a new game that focuses on specific goals, objectives, and issues" (Jones 1998, p. 14). In conclusion, Jones reminds her readers: "Don't forget to have fun, laugh, and enjoy yourself while in the process of helping others learn more about themselves and the world around them" (Jones 1998, p. 17). The point is to help individuals who find it challenging to create change in their lives to grow emotionally and become better people (Jones 1998, p. 11).

There are an incredible number of games designed to promote employee development in one way or another. Many of these concern how to improve individuals' images of themselves through play. Without self-esteem, there are no conditions for self-development. One example of such a game is "I like me because". It was designed and implemented by Edward Scannell, John Newstrom and Carolin Nilson. Participants are asked to find a partner, preferably someone they do not know very well. Partners are then asked to sit on chairs facing each other with no table in between them. They are encouraged to relax, to not cross their arms, but sit with an "open body position". One of the partners then has to speak to the other for two minutes about the theme "what do I like about myself". The other partner listens and expresses interest through body language. When the two minutes are up, the partners switch roles. Once both partners in all the groups have talked about themselves, participants engage in a group discussion of these questions: "1. What kinds of things do people like about themselves? 2. What kinds of things were noticeably not very frequently mentioned? 3. Why are we reluctant to express a positive self-image to others? 4. What are some relatively safe ways in which we can express our self-esteem at work? 5. What suggestions do you have for helping to build someone's self-esteem?" (Scannell et al. 1998, p. 207).

Another game designed by Alanna Jones to build self-esteem is about exchanging self-images and compliments. The game is called "How I see you, how you see me". Participants are divided into groups. Within the group, everyone has a partner. Everyone is then asked to think of two things, one symbolizing themselves and one symbolizing their partner. It might be a flower, a stone, a branch, or something entirely different. Subsequently, everyone shares their symbols with the group. When presenting the chosen symbol for one's partner to the partner, one explains the symbol and gives the partner a chance to ask about the symbol and agree or disagree. The group discusses whether one actually arrived at a good representative symbol for oneself, whether it was easier to find a symbol for the partner than for oneself, if one was surprised by the symbol

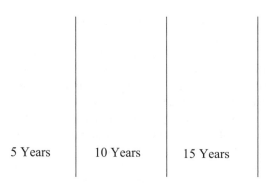

| 5 Years | 10 Years | 15 Years |

Figure 3.14   Possible predictions

chosen by the partner, and so on (Jones 1996, pp. 106–107). For Jones, all people carry good and bad memories and experiences. Negative experiences and negative feedback from others often stay with someone longer and go more deeply than good experiences and this might produce low self-esteem. Society discourages self-praise, particularly in adults, which means that adults depend on other adults for praise and recognition. Therefore, her games incorporate the giving of compliments so that participants hear positive statements about themselves (Jones 1998, pp. 75–6).

However, even with strong self-esteem, someone might choose not to invest themselves in self-discovery. Perhaps, one cannot imagine oneself any differently, or perhaps one is content with where one is. Therefore, another cluster of employee games are about employees' projections of themselves in time. Some games are about telling oneself as a sequence of events and opening up a discussion of what such narratives mean for someone's experience of future determination. Other games are simply about playing with personal futures. One of these games is called "Possible predictions". The introduction to the game states:

> Knowing what you want in your life and striving to get there keeps you motivated, as the more you work towards your goals the more likely you are to reach them. People who don't have goals or who can't picture themselves doing anything positive with their lives often end up right where they expected and they feel unhappy and unfulfilled. Getting people to think about their future is an important step towards creating a good one. (Jones 1998, p. 164)

Participants are given a piece of paper divided as shown in Figure 3.14 into the categories 5, 10 and 15 years. One participant writes his or her name on the paper and passes it on to the next person, who writes down a prediction about the person in 5, 10 and 15 years. The paper is then folded so that the next person can make his or her predictions without looking at previous predictions. The predictions should be positive and should reflect positive qualities about the person in question. Ultimately, all participants end up with a piece of paper with everyone else's predictions about them. Thus, the game offers participants a multiplicity of positive predictions about their future. The game concludes with a discussion of whether participants would have made similar predictions about themselves, if anything came as a surprise, and whether or not participants are inspired to realize certain predictions (Jones 1998, pp. 164–5). The game is basically about encouraging employees to toy with their own images of the future, and when the future becomes contingent so does the present. If an alternative future is recognized as desirable it becomes a premise for the present and changes the present space for action. A future is always a future in relation to a present. However, the game also shows that the present can be defined as the present of the future.

Another game that deals with employees' projections of themselves in time is called "My novel life". It is about identifying life events that influence adult life. Participants are given 15–20 minutes to write a story about their life from birth to death. First, they are asked to recall and describe four or five events in their past and how they feel about them. Then, they are asked to look into the future and predict three or four events in their lives. They are asked to describe these and express why they feel that these events will happen to them. Once all participants have finished their story, they are divided into groups of three where they are invited to share and discuss each other's stories. Possible discussion questions could be: "How have those earlier events affected your life as an adult? Have these events affected your feelings about yourself and others? How do your imagined future events compare with past events? How do past events differ from your predicted future?" (Scannell et al. 1998, p. 213). This game plays with the past of the present and the future of the past in order to demonstrate to employees that future possibilities become frozen by the stories they tell about their past.

However, it is not only employees' self-images that freeze the future. Employees can also freeze each other in unmoving pictures of who each other is and what kind of resource they represent. Some games address these kinds of freezes. A few of these target diversity and multiplicity in the workplace. If the organization and its employees do not value diversity, human resources are overlooked which might potentially benefit the organization. The self-development of the individual employee does not only depend on his or her imagination but also on the way others imagine that person, including the ability of others to see someone as a resource outside their familiar context. While many of the games take as their point of departure predefined categories such as gender or ethnicity, their

Person who has served meals in a soup kitchen	Person who has milked a cow	Person who knows how to do regression analysis	Person who has more than one set of stepsiblings or stepchildren	Person who has attended a "Take Back the Night" rally
--------------------	---------------------	------------------------	-------------------------	--------------------------
Person who has overcome a disability	A single parent	Person who has shared a home meal with a family of a different race	Person who has lived more than five years in a town of less than 2000	Person who is first college grad in his or her nuclear family
--------------------	---------------------	------------------------	-----------------------	--------------------------
Person who knows someone who uses foodstamps	Person who has prayed at a mosque	Person who speaks two or more languages	Person who has done bungy jumping	Person who has played a wheelchair sport
--------------------	---------------------	------------------------	-----------------------	--------------------------
Person born in an Asian country	Person who has dated someone of a different race	A single child	Male with paid child care experience	Person who has run for political office
--------------------	---------------------	------------------------	-----------------------	--------------------------
Person who rode a city bus to or from work or school	Female who has worked on a construction site	Person who has lived in another country for two or more years	Person who has two or more living grandparents	Person who has attended a Bar or Bat Mitzvah
--------------------	---------------------	------------------------	-----------------------	--------------------------

Source: Kaagan (1999, p. 147).

Figure 3.15 Diversity bingo card

goal is to create a multiplicity of diversity categories. One of these games is called "Diversity bingo". The objective of the game is described as follows: "Diversity Bingo invites participants to understand the extent to which they themselves stereotype others solely on the basis of superficial characteristics. It also introduces members of a group to the dimensions of diversity that exist within the group" (Kaagan 1999, p. 146). The first part of the game is about designing bingo cards and diversity categories. The second part is about guessing the people in the group. A bingo card might look like that shown in Figure 3.15.

Another diversity game is called "Differences" and is described as follows: "I am always amazed and confused about the fact that we are all different in so many different ways. I use Differences to provoke people into realizing that diversity goes beyond just racial or ethnic differences" (Thiagarajan 2006, p. 209). The "flow" of the game goes like this: First, the partial sentence "I am a. . ." is written on the board. Participants are then invited to complete the sentence in their minds in order to describe what distinguishes them from everyone else. After that, they write down the sentence on a piece of paper. This is repeated ten times so that everyone has ten phrases that describe themselves. The lists are then all placed on the table and participants pick somebody else's list. They are given the following worksheet listing categories of differences. Participants are then asked to sort the phrases according to the categories and to discuss how the phrases fit the different categories. Subsequently, they discuss what characterizes the most popular and less popular categories of difference. Finally, they are asked if there are phrases that do not match any category, and, if so, to create new categories for these phrases. A category of difference sheet might look like the example given in Figure 3.16.

It is important, however, that the focus on diversity and other people's unique characteristics does not come to impede the forming of new partnerships within the organization and the ability to see shared values. Therefore, many games focus on the creation of partnerships. The game "So much in common" is designed to show that people have more in common than they think and to create a collective team identity. Participants are given a printed sheet of paper (see Figure 3.17) and they are asked to get together in groups of two. The object of the conversation is to find things that the two people have in common. The two people write down these things on their piece of paper. Participants are given 2–3 minutes for this conversation. Then everyone gets a new partner and the procedure is repeated a few times. The game concludes with a shared discussion guided by the following questions: "1. How many of you found that you had more than 15 things in common? 2. What unusual shared characteristics did you find? 3. How did you arrive at these shared characteristics? 4. Is it likely that we will reach the same results in most situations, that is, that we share much more in common than we think? 5. What does this mean for us as a team? For a diverse working group?" (Newstrom and Scannell 1998, p. 25).

Finally, there are quite a few role-switching games, which allow employees to experience, through play, how the world appears to someone else. This is particularly apparent in games that address management roles. The game "Leadership advice" takes as its point of departure management role models taken from work, family life, sports, and so on. Participants

1. Activity level (couch potato)

2. Association membership (Mensa member)

3. Astrological sign (Aries)

4. Belief (pro-life proponent)

5. Birth order (first born)

6. Ethnicity (Hispanic)

7. Gender (woman)

8. Interests (mystery-story reader)

9. Marital status (divorced woman)

10. Personal characteristics (impatient person)

11. Personality type (introvert)

12. Social class (underprivileged)

13. Socioeconomic status (yuppie)

14. Thinking style (analytical)

Figure 3.16   Categories of differences

Commonality Exercise

List the things you find in common with three other people in the workshop

Name:	Name:	Name:
1.	1.	1.
2.	2.	2.
3.	3.	3.
4.	4.	4.
...	...	...

Figure 3.17   So much in common

choose a role model and write down his or her name. They are then asked to assume the role they believe characterizes their role model and, based on this, provide advice to an imagined young manager. Subsequently, participants exchange role model cards and go on to play someone else's role model. The game develops gradually by using the results from previous stages as an object of game and reflection. First, role models are chosen, then advice is given, then roles are switched, then advice is compared, and so on (Thiagarajan 2006, pp. 173–5). Gradually, the game creates not only particular advice, but also a range of perspectives based on which advice can be given and a set of reflections on the perspectives and the advice given.

As we have seen, an entire semantics has developed around such employee games. The games are almost all about self-creation, about creating oneself and one's destiny as social relations, self-relations and self-discovery. The games cut across distinctions between self/other and us/them, and the games are not simply about defining oneself, but about managing these distinctions in a variety of folded-in forms. It is a question of playing oneself forth and establishing the self as a playing self, which is never fully defined. This self, then, is meant to play both with itself and about itself. Some games are about supporting the formation of self-images. The relationship between self and other is thus re-entered into itself. One achieves a self by relating to a multiplicity of self-images. These self-images thus become "oneself as the other for oneself". Other games form images of the other and the self becomes the negation of these images. Still other games are designed to have the group of participants create images of each person, so that the self is played forth in the reflection of others' images of the individual participant. Similarly with the us/them distinction in teambuilding games, which are both about imagining "the others" in relation to which one becomes an "us" and about "the others" in "ourselves"; that is, how a team defines some as being outside. This means that we end up with a range of re-entries such as the self of the self, the self's other, the other's other, and so on. Organization, membership and personality are constituted through play (See Andersen 2009 for further analysis).

The Form of Play

Throughout this semantic development, organizational systems explore possibilities for coding the membership of self-enrollment as play. Basically, it means the creation of a language for a particular playful realization of the membership of self-enrollment. A playful realization of self-enrollment is one in which the problem of self-enrollment finds a specific solution, where the employee can be assigned responsibility for her self-inclusion into the organization in a particular way. This particular way is concerned with the employee who voluntarily participates in a variety of games designed to define the organization's social relations, which the self-relations of the individual member literally gambles with. Whereas the language of love contains the risk of routinizing anticipation, and the risk that social relations end up in fixed mutual expectations and notions about possible partnerships, the game semantics is precisely directed at the softening of relations that appear to be frozen, and this pertains to both social relations and self-relations. Communication relevancy here means to participate in play and to accept (and enjoy) being played with. Thus, what the semantic of play proposes is a codification of the membership of self-enrollment in the language of play. I will present a brief description of play as a form of communication before returning to the question of its implications for membership as play.

As early as 1936, in his book *Homo Ludens*, Johan Huizinga described play as an independent cultural form, which cannot be reduced to other forms. The first part of the book explores the question of whether play can be understood as an aspect of other forms: "The more we try to mark off the form we call 'play' from other forms apparently related to it, the more the absolute independence of the play-concept stands out" (Huizinga 1971, p. 6). Play, says Huizinga, is fundamentally characterized by being superfluous (Huizinga 1971, p. 8). What he is saying is precisely that the meaning of play originates in play itself. It is not a function of another form. It is not an obligation.

While Huizinga observes play as a cultural form, Bateson sees play as a specific form of communication, which always involves meta-communication about whether or not the act of speaking is indeed play. For Bateson, play represents a particular form of communication marked by a particular paradox, which is continually unfolded in play. He describes this paradox rather precisely. Bateson begins by noting that play always involves meta-communication about the fact that "this is play". Therefore, a form-logical characteristic of any act of play is its ongoing communication about itself as play. Play continually communicates that "this is play" or asks "is this play?"

In Bateson's further formal definition of play he explores the nature of the distinction that the statement "this is play" draws. He first suggests: "Expanded, the statement 'This is play' looks something like this: 'These actions in which we now engage do not denote what those actions *for which they stand* would denote'" (Bateson 2000, p. 180). When children play-fight, they continually draw up a distinction between play-fighting and fighting, and this distinction is made by the notion that a marked strike signifies the strike but does not signify that which a strike would signify. Bateson's final and more formally precise formulation is: "These actions in which we now engage, do not denote what would be denoted by those actions which these actions denote" (Bateson 2000, p. 180).

This way of defining play, however, contains an inherent paradox or condition of impossibility. This paradox has to do with the difficulty in play of delimiting itself: "This is play" sets a frame for the act of play, an inside and an outside of play, which says "pay attention to what is inside and do not pay attention to what is outside" (Bateson 2000, pp. 184–5). The inherent paradox consists in the fact that the frame cannot escape its part in the act of play since the frame is precisely defined in the game by virtue of the question "Is this play?" Play makes up its own rules, but as soon as play begins to play with its rules, it also plays with its frame and it becomes clear where the game ends. To return to the example of play-fighting, one could say that the strike, which is not a strike, is not always easily recognizable. Play-fighting has the potential to quickly turn into fighting, where strikes denote what they usually denote. Play-fighting continually explores what marks the marked strike, and this establishes the game and its rules. Play plays, but it also continually puts its own constitution to the test. Only in play can it be determined whether play is play, which means whether to continue or discontinue the game.

Articulated in Luhmann's form-analytical discourse, we might propose that play is a form of communication as the unity of the difference between "These actions in which we now engage do not denote what those actions for which they stand would denote" and "These actions in which we now engage, denote what these actions denote." Play always defines its outside as "These actions in which we now engage, denote what these actions denote." The outside represents that with which one can play but which play cannot be. Play has to always be continued on the inside of the difference in order to continue to be play. However, the problem for play is that this difference is not given and is often difficult to establish. Therefore, we see a so-called re-entry of the difference where the difference becomes a part of its own unity. In order to have play, one has to play, so to speak, with the difference between play and non-play, which means that the incompleteness of the form of play both ensures and threatens the continuation of play. That can be formalized as shown in Figure 3.18.

As already mentioned, the outside of the distinction represents that which can be played with but which play cannot be. From within play, the outside represents the reality where linguistic figures of representation apply and where signs and actions mean what they say. Someone who puts out fires is a firefighter and does not simply play firefighter. Play plays with the representational figures of the outside but has to stay on

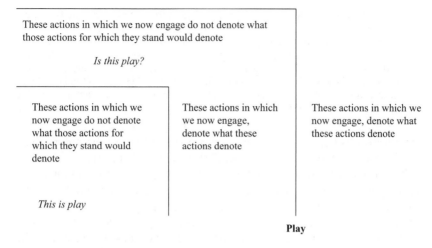

These actions in which we now engage do not denote what those actions for which they stand would denote

Is this play?

| These actions in which we now engage do not denote what those actions for which they stand would denote | These actions in which we now engage, denote what these actions denote | These actions in which we now engage, denote what these actions denote |

This is play

Play

Figure 3.18   The form of play

the inside where representation, signs and actions are always assigned the status of *as if*. Play plays with signs, representation and actions through signs, representation and actions, which only point to the meaning these carry in "real life" and do not apply in play.

Thus, play represents a distinct communicative doubling machine. Play doubles the world so that we have a world of play and a real world, and the doubling takes place on the side of the play. Dirk Baecker formulates it in this way: "In play, socialness is constituted by ways of reflection onto itself as the other side of itself. In play, socialness is experienced as what it is, namely as contingent, roughly meaning that it is neither necessary nor impossible, or again, given yet changeable. Play in general reveals the form of the social by which the play infects the world (Baecker 1999, p. 103). Play represents a communicative sociality, which is characterized by its doubling of this sociality so that the contingency of the social reality becomes visible. In 1955 at one of the renowned Macy conferences, Bateson reflected on this dynamic: "It is not the learning of a particular style that you are playing at, but the fact of a stylistic flexibility and the fact that the choice of style or role is related to the frame and context of behavior. And play itself is a category of behavior, classified by context in some way" (Bateson 1955, p. 149). According to Bateson we always play with categories, lines or frames, and one can only play with something one knows. In one of his examples, a child plays archbishop:

> The child is playing at being archbishop. I am not interested in the fact that he learns how to be an archbishop from playing the role; but that he learns that

there is such a thing as a role. He learns or acquires a new view, partly flexible and partly rigid, which is introduced into life when he realizes that behavior can, in a sense, be set to a logical type or to a style (. . .) Play is one of the ways in which we learn what the "not" object is. That is what I meant when I said we do not learn specific roles when playing an archbishop. We learn something about the whole structuring of the frame of "not" objects (. . .) One can learn about a line which will be between archbishop and "not archbishop", or play that line. (Bateson 1955, pp. 149–52)

Play brings to light communicative distinctions: "(Play) discovers where the lines are and learns to cross them" (Bateson 1955, p. 151).

This obviously makes specific demands on potential communication participants. Someone is only relevant to the communication to the extent that he or she is willing to play along, and to play along also means to double oneself as player and as one's personality outside the game. As a player, one has to be prepared not only to observe the contingency of the world but to see oneself as contingent. The "playing self" puts "the real self" in parenthesis, and that makes it possible to freely act out different roles in play without being held responsible at the end of the game. I only pretended to be Darth Vader. However, pretending to be Darth Vader, that is, pretending to be someone else, opens up a new perspective on the self: perhaps I could be a bit more like Darth Vader? One can play with oneself and thereby learn to see the contingency of the manifestation of one's self.

Play can only be defined from within. Only play itself can answer the question "is this play?" Huizinga notes that one cannot be ordered to play. Bateson's example makes a similar point about play as treatment. According to Bateson, a doctor may prescribe play to a patient by asking him or her to play golf or do something creative. But that changes the message of play: "If it is prescribed, it cannot conceivably be play (. . .) Prescription can only be effective after the patient has forgotten that it was a prescription" (Bateson 1955, pp. 221, 227).

Imagination is the symbolic medium for play as a communication form. Every act of play shapes imagination and the more the imagination is shaped through play, the more imagination there is. A single act of play is unable to exhaust the imagination as medium. Play has to always gamble something by dissolving a given into contingency. Play thrives on the tension inherent in gambling a given. It energizes play. And in play, imagination is construed as the source of imagining contingency. In that sense, "seriousness" does not stand in opposition to play. Play has to always be serious about the management and creation of tensions. Otherwise play falls victim to boredom and loses its energy. In other words, from the perspective of play, imagination is a medium that can be used to explore not only the actually possible but also the conceivably possible and perhaps even the inconceivably impossible. One uses one's imagination when seeking to go beyond the limit of what is possible. Or employing Luhmann's form-logical discourse, we might say that imagination is the symbolic medium, which not only makes use of a distinction and divides the world into a marked and an unmarked space but also explores the boundary between the marked state and the unmarked state, that is, the boundary between the state of difference and the state of indifference (Spencer-Brown 1969). This exploration, of course, relies on numerous new distinctions seeking to be marked as "borderline". I do not claim that imagination actually explores the "state of indifference". Or in other words: Play plays with meaninglessness but can only do so in a meaningful way. In this way, imagination as communication medium resembles the medium of "faith" in the religious communication system. The code of religion is immanence/transcendence and also explores the boundary between the state of difference and the state of indifference through questions about given human conditions such as death (transcendence) and mutable human conditions, for example, how we live towards death (immanence). In the religious system, this exploration happens without a doubling of the world, which is why religion, despite similarities, still stands in opposition to play. Religion explores the limit for knowing and addressing necessity, which is a given even if we do not like it. Play explores the same limit but with a view to exposing contingency and going beyond the possible (it is interesting to note here that the literary genre of "Fantasy" has become the object of religious studies as a particular form of religious expression).

Playful Self-Enrollment

Through the coding of self-enrollment in the form of play and imagination as symbolic medium, we end up with an employee capable of playing with herself and with social relations within the organization. I have tried to illustrate this in Figure 3.19.

When the membership of self-enrollment becomes codified by imagination as the medium of play it means that the communicative rules of play come to determine membership. When play is the form and imagination the medium, the employee is expected to both participate in available organizational games and also make herself and her social relations available as the object of play. These are the membership criteria when self-enrollment is codified through play. And in that way, play becomes a solution to some of the problems that arise from the pedagogical and passionate membership.

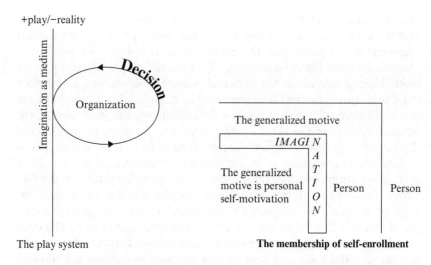

The play system   **The membership of self-enrollment**

Figure 3.19   The formation of the medium of play through self-enrollment

With the code of play, self-enrollment becomes something one plays forth. One plays that one is included and plays with the act of playing that one is included. From the perspective of play, one is included because one plays. And if one plays, one is expected to gamble oneself and forget oneself through acts of play. However, the playful membership is also one in which one plays with the notion of inclusion, and in this game it is not only the self that is explored but also the contingency of membership. The playful membership effects a potentialization of selves and a potentialization of different memberships, that is, a surplus of possible connections and ways to self-enroll. In other words, in the playful membership one plays with different ways of being a member and this is the way in which one becomes a member. Thus, the playful membership puts the very idea of membership in question and multiplies and virtualizes it rather than clarifying it.

Voluntariness is the basic premise of play. One cannot be ordered to play. Or at least no acts of play result from an order to play. Thus, in the formation of play through self-enrollment one is free to enter the game, but once one enters the game it is difficult to get out without being a bad play-mate. The games are basically designed in a way so that they appear voluntary but become increasingly binding as the game develops. The games suddenly change with the interjection of seemingly innocent questions such as: "Do any of the other participants' images of the future appeal to you? And what will you do to ensure that this image of the future becomes a possible realizable future?" Play shifts imperceptibly into the register of binding premise with the characteristic of decision despite the fact that moments earlier it was just a game. If someone wants to get out, she is seen as a bad playmate or as someone who has engaged in "false play" as Roos et al. condemningly note in an article based on case studies of play in an organization. They conclude that not all employees play along as they should: "Play, as a process, is by definition voluntary (. . .) participation in adult play is a choice that must be made by each individual. Absent this choice, a kind of ersatz or false play can emerge" (Roos et al. 2004, p. 561). Ken Jones writes in similar terms: "Participants in simulation must also play their roles. They must not become wreckers. They must not play the clown. Doing so would reduce the simulation to sabotage" (Jones 2002, p. xix). The fact that play is based on voluntary participation translates into the expectation that participants should choose to play and should consider their choice voluntary. It is an expectation that employees in any case observe their participation as voluntary and therefore renounce the possibility of employing external references in the play communication, which would install an authority outside the game. One has to at least play *as if* it is voluntary.

Play entails a demand for total dedication similar to the demand for engagement in love communication, but in a way that to some extent is even more unconditional. In love communication, one has to anticipate the other's need so that the expressive side of the communication becomes so dominant that all signs are read from the perspective of the distinction she loves me/loves me not. However, love does not exclude a certain distanced strategic perspective on one's self-expression. There is an inherent strategic question built into all love communication about how to express oneself in order to remain lovable. This is different in play. The doubling of oneself into one's self and one's playing self precisely serves the purpose of allowing someone to leave their self outside the game in order to better fully dedicate the playing self without reservation. As Hans-Georg Gadamer says in *Truth and Method*:

> "Play" (. . .) is not tied to any goal which would bring it to an end (. . .) The movement which is play has no goal which brings it to an end; rather it renews itself in constant repetition. The movement backwards and forwards is obviously so central for the definition of a game that it is not important who and what performs this movement. The movement of play as such has, as it were, no substrate. (Gadamer 1985, p. 93)

Hence, what is special about play is that it originates in itself, which also means that play cannot be controlled by the intentions of its players. Play frees itself from subjective intentions underlying it. Paraphrasing Gadamer, a criterion for inclusion for communication participants is that they forget themselves in play: "Play fulfils its purpose only if the player loses himself in his play" (Gadamer 1985, p. 92). Serious play means to forget oneself in play and to accept the primacy of the game over the players: "All playing is a being-played. The attraction of a game, the fascination it exerts, consists precisely in the fact that the game tends to master the players" (Gadamer 1985, p. 95). In an organization, this is simultaneously a serious machine of exclusion, which not only establishes "the private" as irrelevant to the communication, but also establishes the work and work roles of employees as irrelevant to the communication unless play decides to play with these relations, in which case they are only relevant on the self-created terms defined by play. We might say that play institutes a rather violent prohibition on self-reality. An example could be a game that addresses one's image of the future in which colleagues and managers literally play with one's future. One is encouraged to play along and is only considered a good playmate to the extent that one does not make use of references to reality such as: "I don't feel like doing that", "my experience tells me. . ." or "that is not possible because. . ." One is required to offer one's unconditional participation in the game including an unconditional faith in the fact that what we play has nothing to do with real life. We experiment through play with possibilities for alternative manifestations of the social. We use our imagination and we require of participants that they are confident that nothing happens to "real work" while we are playing with it. We are expected to believe that the virtual world and the real world remain distinct, and even though we play around with work constellations in the office, this does not mean that I necessarily have to switch teams once the game is over. This can be pretty difficult to believe. Sandelands, who argues in favor of more play in organizations, expects play to be "an encompassing dynamic of love that fully engages those it touches" (Sandelands 2010, p. 80). Quoting again from Pat Kane's *The Play Ethic*, the conception of the ideal relation between play and engagement is that play "opens up the infinite possibilities arising from full engagement of heart, body and soul" (Kane 2004, p. 89). That seems like a lot to expect of employees.

Whereas pedagogy's solution to the question of adaptation and change is to invite employees to understand their competencies and to answer supervised questions about their own strengths, weaknesses and learning objectives, play plays with the very notion of competency. In pedagogy, lifelong learning is the solution to the idea of adaptation to adaptability. Play can even make contingent our definitions of competency and qualifications. Moreover, play can stimulate employees' ability to imagine themselves as someone and something else. When playing, it is the imagination, not talent or willpower, which marks the ultimate limit for self-development. And this makes it possible to view imagination in terms of economics as a scarce resource. If one is incapable of imagining an alternative future, it makes no difference that one has will power, engagement and competence for competence development.

Imagination as a scarce resource pertains not only to the self-relation but also to collegial partnership relations. It is also about including imagination in the workplace relationship. Play may increase the organization's human resources by improving employees' abilities to imagine each other; that is, increase employees' possibilities to observe each other as knowledge resources and collaborators. The link between the play semantics and the love semantics is explicitly articulated in parts of the play semantics, not least in Sandelands' work with organizational change. Sandelands' basic position is that play strengthens and develops love: "Play is founded upon love" (Sandelands 2010, p.77). Hence, the point of departure is the organization as love and partnership relations among employees. And play is assigned a special function: "Play is a way that love grows and develops" (Sandelands 2010, p.77). This happens by introducing imagination into the love relationship: "Play is the form that love takes at the boundary between fantasy and reality where new social arrangements arise to take the place of old social arrangements" (Sandelands 2010, p.72). Sandelands sums up: "Play is new love being born or an existing love being renewed" (Sandelands 2010, p.80). And Pate Kane writes: "People at play are more present, more engaged, more passionate and better performers" (Kane 2004, p.84).

Love's solution to adaptation to change is an employee who anticipates the organization's needs. Play may add here the possibility to play with existing and alternative relations. We can play with the very notion of organizational needs. We can play with the meaning of projects, with the concept of team, with what unites us and separates us so that we might again anticipate the organization's needs without falling back on old routines.

But how are we to perceive of the opening provided by the playful membership? How far-reaching is it? Do we not basically play at one seminar but forget all about it the next day? There are at least three possibilities and it remains an empirical question which of them applies when.

1. PLAY AS EMPLOYEES' RESPITE FROM THEMSELVES

Employee games may provide an opening in the membership through which new possibilities can be played forth. One takes a break from oneself during which one is given the chance to assume a different virtual self. One takes a break from the relationships at work, in teams, projects, and so on. It is a break through which contingency becomes apparent in relation to alternative relationships with other colleagues. There might be speed-dating games, which flirt with ideas about opening up new work relations and where new sides of supposedly familiar colleagues are revealed. Then the game ends. The double world of play returns to being just one. Perhaps one has achieved a new work relation or a new notion of how to further evolve.

2.   PLAY AS THE PERMANENT DOUBLING OF EMPLOYEE AND MEMBERSHIP

The second possibility is a doubling of membership. A person is essentially constantly involved in more than one membership, one of which is a virtual playing membership and one of which a "real" membership, which sometimes is a formal membership, other times a membership of self-enrollment or a passionate membership. The employee's fantasies about herself and her social relations are constantly stimulated through a flow of new games within the organization. These can be organized differently, perhaps as a recurring element at meetings, perhaps as permanent HRM programs with games at meetings, football during breaks, breakfast and social games on the first Friday of every month. Games that constantly produce new virtual possibilities for self-enrollment. Perhaps even independent fun programs, something that has already become popular in England.

3.   PLAY AS GENERALIZED PERSPECTIVE, WHICH CAN BE APPLIED TO ANYTHING

The third possibility is the most radical. Here, play is an always readily available possibility, which need not be organized by means of specific games. Play is present as a permanent latent form, at all times available for communication as a way to explore the otherwise possible. This implies never knowing exactly which world one belongs to at all times. Reality and virtuality can at any moment cross into each other. And the same applies to the self: Does one play someone else? Does one play playing someone else? Or does one play that one does not play? Or does one simply not play? This can only be known retrospectively. Not until one looks back at a given situation is it possible to decide whether it assumed the status of play or some other form of reality. In this third option, one can always assume a playful perspective on communication that otherwise did not encourage play with the result that what is communicated changes.

An example could be my own workplace, The Copenhagen Business School. In 2009, a meeting in the Academic Council started out with a game of role play. After the game was over, participants were divided into groups who were instructed to discuss the future of the Academic Council: What needed more emphasis? What did not work? What should be initiated and finalized? Was the group work a continuation of the role play game? Or was it decision communication? No one had said that play-time was over. But the group work had not been marked as a game. Its status could only be decided retrospectively by the one who assumed the authority to call it play or decision.

CONCLUSION: THE MULTIPLICITY OF SELF-ENROLLMENT

I began by stating that organizations are fundamentally based on a principle of exclusion according to which people are only included if they have been granted membership in the organization through an organizational decision. Membership is the unity of the difference generalized motive/person. A decision about membership is on the one hand a decision about generalized motives and on the other hand, a decision about linking a particular person to this motive. Generalized motives are organizationally motivated motives, which are formulated in general terms and therefore go beyond the personal and situational. Thus, membership entails a zone of indifference between organization and individual, allowing the individual to maintain her own motives for being in the organization, which are irrelevant to the organization.

I then went on to argue that the notion of adaptation to adaptability fundamentally challenges the traditional membership. The question of inclusion and exclusion in the organization is displaced and turns into a question of how the organization can take responsibility for the individual employee taking responsibility for her own inclusion in the organization, which is, at the same time, constantly transforming itself into something else.

My thesis was that membership evolves in the direction of the membership of self-enrollment. The membership of self-enrollment copies and re-enters the traditional membership distinction between generalized motive and person into itself on the motive side of the difference. On the one hand, this means that the distinction between generalized motive and person is maintained. On the other hand, however, the generalized motive becomes personalized, and this installs self-enrollment as a fundamentally paradoxical figure in the organization. The generalized motive is now defined as personal self-motivation. That is, the generalized motive establishes an expectation that the person who becomes associated with the organization independently defines the generalized motive, which serves as a binding obligation for the person as if the motive were motivated by the organization. The organizational motive becomes the employee's personal motivation. The expectation is that the person is personally motivated to motivate herself as if her motivation was that of the organization.

The traditional membership typically links up with the legal system and its medium, which is "existing law". This results in a decision about membership colored by the code right/wrong, and in effect the organization becomes a formal organization constituted through formal membership, which serves to decide if someone is a legitimate member of the organization and the particular rights and responsibilities that follow. However, only with great difficulty is it possible for the law to serve as medium for the membership of self-enrollment. It makes only limited sense to formulate personal self-motivation as obligation. Therefore, organizations begin to look for new media through which they may assume responsibility for their employees taking responsibility for their own self-enrollment in the organizations.

Pedagogy, love and play represent three different strategies for the deparadoxification of the paradox of self-enrollment. I have shown the way that pedagogy, love and play make themselves available as different media for the membership of self-enrollment and how these three media each create a problem of excess in the membership of self-enrollment, which keeps the organizational search and generation of new semantic deparadoxification strategies alive. Pedagogy defined itself as the answer to ways for employees to constantly develop themselves from the perspective of workplace relevance but lacked a language for the definition of the organization's needs. Love precisely defined itself as the answer to ways for employees to anticipate the organization's needs without the organization having to formulate such needs. The language of love, in turn, ran the risk of effecting a merging of employees with the organization, and hence play became the answer to how to incorporate a greater level of imagination into the relationship.

I have tried to sum up the three codifications of the form, function and effects of the membership of self-enrollment in Table 3.2.

In all three codifications of the membership of self-enrollment communication goes into a mode of reflection and is emptied of content:

Table 3.2 *The form, function and effects of the membership of self-enrollment*

Code	Form	Function	Effects
Right/wrong	Formal membership granted through organizational decision	Fixation of expectations for employee expectations	Constitution of organizational memory Zone of indifference Exclusion of the personal
Better/worse in terms of learning	Self-enrolment through continual self-development. One is included because one constantly seeks to make oneself relevant to the organization in flux	Selection based on ability to self-select	Self-infantalization Self-correction of personality Economizing with one's talent
Loved/not loved	Self-enrolment through anticipation. One is included because one makes oneself lovable and has installed the organization as one's significant other	Renounce and lighten organizational communication by leaving it to employees to anticipate the organization's needs through a highly personal relationship with the organization	Continual struggle to make oneself loved Zone of intensity Stress as an effect of no defined limit to the production of expectations Over-inclusion
Play/reality	Self-enrolment through play. One plays with the notion of being a member and thus becomes a member	The making visible of social contingency in employees' self-relation and in all social relations within the organization	Forgetting of self Denial of reality The virtualization and multiplication of membership

- In the pedagogical membership, the aim is not to learn something specific but about being learning.
- In the intimate membership, the aim is not to love a specific person or to be loved for a particular quality but to be loving and lovable.
- Finally, in the playful membership the aim is not to play a specific game but to play that one plays and to be playful and forget oneself in play.

These are three different ways to unfold the logic of transience and transform it into a regime. As I mentioned in Chapter 2, the central tenet of transience is that organizations increasingly seek to suspend decisions' character of decision in order to support adaptability so that one can always be something else. Undecidability becomes a decision program. In the logic of transience, order is not simply generated from noise. The concern is whether there is enough noise to generate order from. From this perspective, self-enrollment is a membership decision that suspends itself. Self-enrollment is a way to both make and defer a decision about membership. Pedagogy, love and play are three ways in which to suspend this suspension. Pedagogy through self-development, love through anticipation and play through the multiplication and virtualization of membership. They represent three different ways to manage and maintain the transience of membership.

In effect we end up with an enormous systemic mass of incommensurably coded clusters of expectations, each of which articulates the self and subjectivity differently:

- The learning self.
- The loving self.
- The playing self.

These all make demands on an employee's existence. They are accumulated and heterogeneous expectations pertaining to existence. Employees are expected to simultaneously create themselves as a learning self, a loving self and a playing self, all in the image of an organization in constant flux.

4. Management of authentic feelings: the trembling organization

When is somebody authentic? A great many employees frame questions like this to themselves, and so do a great many organizations and leaders regarding their employee relations. That question is urgent because the difference between being a member and not being a member of an organization to a greater extent is left to each employee's own self-enrollment. This creates a fundamental insecurity in organizations regarding the authenticity of the employee's own self-enrollment. Is she truthful now? Does she mean what she says? Is this a case of genuine engagement? I can see that she is making an effort to work with commitment and engagement, but does she really understand what we are doing here? And the employee is asking similar questions: Am I really happy being here? Is it the work I love or is it my colleagues? Can I be the one I want to be when I am in this organization and in this job? Therefore, am I genuine and authentic in my own membership? It enables the observation of emotions and the management of emotions as a key issue for organizations in the transient regime. Often this is discussed as the emotionalization of organizing (Sieben and Wettergren 2010).

The conception of employee relations in terms of pedagogy, passion and play means that personal emotions become relevant to organizational communication. The primacy of self-enrollment makes the organization dependent upon the individual's personal engagement but also upon the extent to which interactive relations are conducive to the individual's engagement. This is, as this chapter shows, by no means a simple issue since it concerns both how increasing organizational complexity adds to the irritability of psychic systems and how organizations are increasingly dependent upon the way in which psychic systems handle this irritation. The issue is further complicated by the fact that psychic systems are non-communicable and that the authenticity of emotions cannot be represented in organizational communication. Organizations engage with the non-communicable and seek to develop a language for the management of that which necessarily escapes them. Personal feelings are considered relevant to the communication but cannot be communicated.

In the membership of self-enrollment, inclusion and exclusion become a question over which the organization does not have full control. In terms of communication theory, inclusion can be defined as communication relevance and exclusion as communication irrelevance. Inclusion is never full inclusion. Only a fraction of the person in question is considered relevant to the communication. Any act of inclusion, therefore, is also an act of exclusion because inclusion/exclusion does not only concern whether someone is included but also how they are included in the communication. In a formal membership, the organization can decide on communication relevance by establishing the general motive that defines the criteria for communication relevance and by deciding whether to hire or fire someone, where firing someone results in complete communication irrelevance. In the membership of self-enrollment, inclusion and exclusion become self-inclusion and self-exclusion. In the pedagogical codification of self-enrollment, self-inclusion is a question of making one's work relevant in terms of competences. Self-exclusion comes to mean the de-selection of oneself as the effect of insufficient pedagogical capacity for inclusion. In the highly intimate codification of self-enrollment, self-inclusion is about showing one's engagement through the anticipation of the organization's needs. Self-exclusion happens when someone is unable to demonstrate their engagement and therefore can no longer be observed as the organization's significant other. In the playful codification of self-enrollment, self-inclusion is a question of one's full dedication to play. Self-exclusion happens when someone is incapable of forgetting themselves through play and neglects reality.

This raises a series of questions, both for organizations' self-relation and for the structural coupling between organizational systems and psychic systems. How to manage its dependency on the ability and will of the individual to effect inclusion and exclusion becomes an urgent question for the organization. If the organization is to avoid reverting back to the formal membership, how can it find control equivalencies that might compensate the loss of the control of issues of inclusion and exclusion? This chapter is about how the management of emotions in some organizations becomes articulated as control equivalent. Making themselves sensitive to the emotional realities of their employees becomes a theme for some organizations.

The question of how to perceive the relationship between organization and emotion, however, is by no means a new theme. It is inherent in the formal membership form, with the difference between role and person and between the organization's own decided motives and the personal motives of employees. This difference is constituent for organizational systems, even as a re-entered difference in the membership of self-enrollment. This distinction defines personal emotions as located outside the organization.

Max Weber had already emphasized this in the 1920s in a series of articles, later compiled in the book *Economy and Society*, and many others have subsequently noted this. In his theory about bureaucracy, Weber writes: "Bureaucracy develops the more perfectly, the more it is 'dehumanized', the more completely it succeeds in eliminating from official business love, hatred, and all purely personal, irrational, and emotional elements which escape calculation. This is appraised as its special virtue by capitalism" (Weber 2003, p. 83; Weber 1978 [1922], p. 975). For Weber, it was a notion of organization, which was neutral and without passion. To exclude emotions from the organizational field meant to focus on objectivity, to guarantee citizens that their cases reflected pure objectivity removed from personal emotions and the status of social workers. The bureaucracy should be calculable to its environment.

This is not to say that Weber was a complete stranger to the notion of "management of emotions". A rational organization can indeed relate to emotional content. Thus, emotions become a disciplinary tool subject to the organizational goal. Discipline, says Weber, is an objective element at the disposal of any power that reflects on its services (Weber 2003, p. 158). Discipline presupposed "the individual's integration into an inescapable, inexorable mechanism" (Weber 2003, p. 159). This discipline can also include the disciplining of emotions: "Enthusiasm and unreserved emotion may, of course, have a place in discipline (. . .) leadership uses emotional means of all sorts" (Weber 2003, p. 159). What is important, says Weber, is "first, that everything is rationally calculated, especially those seemingly imponderable and irrational emotional factors – in principle, at least, calculable in the same manner as the yields of coal and iron deposits. Secondly, devotion is normally impersonal, oriented toward a purpose, a common cause, a rationally intended goal, not a person as such, however personally tinged devotion may be in the case of a fascinating leader" (Weber 2003, p. 159).

In Weber, the organization is responsible for rational disciplining of personal emotional issues. Weber speaks from the perspective of the formal membership form, where appealing to emotions can be perceived as an element of employees' subjection to the general motives of the organization. It does not mean that personal emotions have become relevant as precisely personal. Emotions can only be relevant as means to reach organizational goals.

Today we see a new literature about organization and emotions. A subsection of this literature even proposes that we speak of an "affective turn" not unlike the "linguistic turn" of the 1980s (Fineman 1993, 2006, 2010; Massumi 2002; Clough 2007). Despite the fact that many of the critics who write about the affective turn make frequent references to Foucault, very few of these question the affective turn genealogically. Foucault pointed out that the truth about madness is not to be found in madness itself but in the history of madness. This history, Foucault showed, was also the history of the origins of modern reason. Madness arises and develops as the constitutive other side of reason. The proponents of the affective turn fail to look into the genesis of their own object of inquiry. They prefer to establish it as ontologically given and make themselves immune to genealogical criticism by claiming that affect and emotions are pre-linguistic and therefore escape any epistemological genealogy. There are studies of the history of affect in research in relation to organizations such as, for example, Howard Weis and Arthur Brief's "Affect at work: a historical perspective" (2001), but they often limit themselves to a study of how the research came to discover its object and gradually came to the mature insights of today. The affective turn presents itself as a turn within sociology and psychology, having discovered an object which was always there, but which has been invisible for us because we have been blinded by a certain concept of reason. It seems to me like too much of a coincidence that the affective turn happens precisely at the moment when the organization needs it. What interests me is not whether we are able to establish a pre-linguistic phenomenon, which we can refer to as affection, feelings or emotions. What interests me are the implications it has for organizational conditions of possibility that feelings, affection and emotions become a semantic reservoir, available to decision communication.

In order to stay focused on the organizational implications, it seems crucial to me not to buy into the heavy ontology about emotions in the so-called affective turn. I will carry on the systems-theoretical line of inquiry and observe how organizations observe emotions and what the implications are for them. Here, I perceive the semantic analytical strategy as equivalent to Foucault's knowledge archaeology and genealogy (Andersen 2003b).

THE SYSTEMS THEORETICAL TAKE ON EMOTIONS AND THEIR INCOMMUNICABILITY

Luhmann distinguishes between different self-referential autopoietical systems, including living systems, psychic systems and social systems. Living systems are cells, the brain, the organism and nervous systems. Luhmann describes their operation as life. It is through life that these systems create themselves. Psychic systems are another form of systems where the autopoietical operations are made up of thoughts and sensations. Social systems are societal systems, organizations and interactions. Their autopoietical operation is communication.

Luhmann describes the autopoietical systems as operatively closed: "Everything that is used by the system as a unit is produced as a unit by the system itself. This applies to elements, processes, boundaries, and other structures, and last but not least, to the unity of the system itself. Autopoietic systems, then, are sovereign with respect to the constitution of identities and differences" (Luhmann 1990a, p. 3). Why is this important? It is important here because of the current discussions about where the phenomenon of emotions belongs. Does it belong to the brain, consciousness or social systems? Branches of the social sciences would argue that emotions are a social construction. Branches within brain research would say that it is chemistry, and so on. I do not want to join this debate but will instead describe the answer provided by systems theory and the analytical possibility it suggests.

The central premise is that a system cannot define the elements of another system. Social systems cannot produce emotions as an element in a psychic system. Similarly, different biological systems such as the brain or the central nervous system cannot produce emotions within the psychic system. If we are to describe emotions, we have to pick our systems reference, and our description of emotions cannot then be transferred to a description that has a different systems reference. Luhmann himself chooses to describe emotions with reference to the psychic system, which makes the conditions under which he makes his statements exceedingly clear. Emotions, for Luhmann, are the continuation by other means of the autopoiesis of the psychic system. I will return to this point.

Poul Stenner, who is also a systems theoretician, suggests that we start by admitting that biological, psychic and social systems create elements, which can each be called "emotions", but that these elements are not at all alike. The point of departure is that biological, psychic and social systems function as parasites on one another. They are operationally closed but may create structural couplings through irritation: "Nevertheless, consciousness, for instance, can irritate or otherwise stimulate the system of communication that is its environment. Likewise organic activity can irritate consciousness (. . .) In this sense, we abstractly conceive of consciousness as having parasite organic life, and of communication as having parasite consciousness" (Stenner 2004, p. 167). He suggests that emotions create a structural coupling between the organic and consciousness: "Emotion can be thought of as biological means of generating a distinctly psychological level of functioning that is precisely no longer understandable as organic process. For the sake of clarity, we might refer to emotions in their organic manifestation as *affects*. On a psychic level, different affects take the form of distinct subjective forms of consciousness (emotions)" (Stenner 2004, p. 169). It is productive to be aware that the systems irritate one another. However, the distinction between feelings, emotion and affect has only a limited scope if one wants to be sociologically clear about the validity of one's statement. The distinction feelings/emotions/affect is a distinction in communication. I prefer clarity to vague complexity because the latter makes it exceedingly difficult to distinguish between first and second-order observations, undermining the ability to observe.

Luhmann himself assigns emotions only to the psychic system. The psychic system generates meaning by linking thoughts to other thoughts. Its continued existence relies on its ability to link thoughts to already existing thoughts. If thoughts do not provide possibilities for new thoughts, the system's autopoiesis comes under threat. You have meatloaf for dinner, which is your father's favorite meal, and think about telling him about it before remembering that he has died. How to continue the line of thought? Thoughts present themselves and yet cannot be thought. You are biking down the street thinking about everything you need to get done. Suddenly a plastic bag gets stuck in your wheel, you fall off your bike, sense that you have broken something, and the horizon of thoughts that happened a minute ago no longer provides possibilities for continued linking. Recursive linking of thoughts to thoughts becomes difficult. A third example: After a long period of unemployment you have success with an application and are offered the job you had hoped to get. Your existing horizon of daily routines disappears and a new and unknown one emerges. The "old" horizon no longer provides possibilities for linking since the new premise is a daily work schedule. However, the "new" horizon is also not particularly easy to link up to since you are not sure what to expect of your colleagues, job, and so on. Perhaps this causes your mind to "race". The point is that emotions represent a continuation of thoughts whose continuation becomes endangered (positively and negatively): "Emotions arise and grip body and consciousness when the autopoiesis of consciousness is in danger" (Luhmann 1995d, p. 274).

We might take this to mean that emotions represent the psychic system's response to external threats and problems. However, this is very far from Luhmann's point: "Emotions are not representations that refer to the environment but *internal* adaptations to *internal* problem situations in the psychic system that concern the ongoing production of the system's elements by the system's elements" (Luhmann 1995d, p. 274). The question of whether the new job produces a feeling of happiness or anxiety depends entirely on how the psychic system responds to the new situation, which has to do with expectations, and so on. The psychic system responds exclusively to its own operations – not operations in its environment.

Emotions are an internally produced element in the autopoiesis of the psychic system.

The important point is that "emotions are more than interpreted biochemistry – they are the psychic system's self-interpretation with regard to whether its operation can continue" (Luhmann 1995c, p. 274). According to Luhmann, emotions protect the autopoiesis of the psychic system: "In terms of their function, emotions can be compared to immune systems; they seem to assume an immunizing role for the psychic system" (Luhmann 1995c, p. 274). Thus, emotions unburden the system of consciousness and allow it to generate vague and scattered meaning (Fuchs 2004).

Steven Fineman, who is currently the foremost agenda-setting thinker of "the emotional organization", makes a distinction between feeling and emotion according to which emotions express social affect and feelings express internal individual affect. Similarly, Luhmann discusses the relationship between communication about emotions and emotions as psychic operation:

> The well-known variety of distinct emotions comes about only secondarily, only through cognitive and linguistic interpretation; thus it is socially conditioned, like the constitution of all complexity in psychic systems. This holds even more for everything one could designate a "culture of emotions"; for refinements of the occasions and the forms of expression in which emotions take shape. Such transformations serve, on the one hand, to control emotions socially but, on the other, are burdened with problems of authenticity. Anyone who can say what he is suffering already finds himself no longer entirely in the situation he would like to express. Thus special problems of incommunicability come into being – not of the emotions per se, but of their authenticity – which affect social systems and may burden psychic ones. (Luhmann 1995c, p. 275)

Several issues relate to this: (1) emotions are interpreted. Thoughts connect with emotions and, in order to do so, make use of social categories and communicatively generated concepts, (2) although social systems provide concepts and semantics for the interpretation of emotions, they do not constitute emotions qua conscious operations. Interpretation of emotions is not an emotional operation, (3) emotions are incommunicable because the psychic system as such is incommunicable: "We start out from the assumption that consciousness cannot communicate itself because every communication is always already autopoietic components of a social system" (Luhmann 2001, p. 21). But also because any interpretation, message about, and naming of an emotion shifts the condition of the psychic system. Incommunicability is then not simply a question of lacking language for the thing someone wants to express, it is also not a question of emotions surfacing faster than someone is able to express them. Incommunicability means that the experience of meaning is lost at the moment it is spoken (Luhmann 1998, p. 123). When seeking to communicate emotions, the very distinction between information and message collapses because the message itself is seen as information. An employee says "I am stressed" and this message is itself considered information because we look for signs in the very form of the message that may indicate whether the person is indeed stressed or not (shaky voice, looks pale, and so on). So the message does not only deliver information but is read as information in itself. This becomes problematic, particularly in highly intimate communication where we expect authenticity.

So far, I have defined two questions within the context of my study of how organizations evaluate the relevance of emotions. One concerns the development of a semantic of emotions available to organizational communication. How does a culture of emotions evolve in modern organizations? Are one or more semantics available to organizations and how does each of them frame ways in which organizations can address and thematize emotions? The other question is the fundamental incommunicability of emotions. How do organizations manage this? Is it something they consider? Or are they fundamentally blind to the fact that they have made themselves dependent upon operations to which they have no access, cannot observe, communicate, or manage? Have they developed different strategies for the communicative management of the incommunicable?

Even though social and psychic systems are mutually closed and cannot link up with each other's operations, they can still be linked. Luhmann uses the term interpenetration to speak to this issue. Interpenetration refers to when social and psychic systems make their own complexity available to each other (Luhmann 1995c, p. 213). Luhmann writes: "The interpenetrating systems remain environments for each other. This means that the complexity each system makes available is an incomprehensible complexity – that is, disorder – for the receiving system. Thus one could say that psychic systems supply social systems with adequate disorder and vice versa" (Luhmann 1995c, p. 214). We might ask the question, then, of how social systems produce noise for psychic systems and vice versa?

Beat Thommen and Alexander Wettstein have attempted to illustrate this as shown in Figure 4.1.

Social systems make noise in relation to psychic systems by forming expectations of them. But expectations can assume many different forms and, in relation to the emotional operations of the psychic systems, Luhmann distinguishes between expectation and claim. According to Luhmann, expectations can be condensed down to claims when the psychic system has the experience of being struck by an expectation and takes it upon itself as a self-obligation, which can either be fulfilled or disappointed. The transition from expectation to claim "increases the chance and the

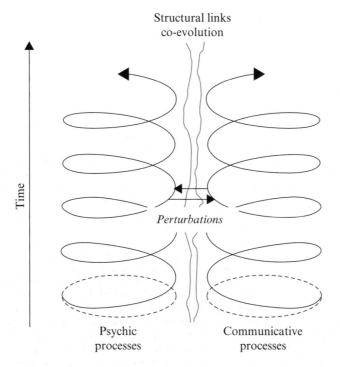

Structural links
co-evolution

Time

Perturbations

Psychic
processes

Communicative
processes

Source: Thommen and Wettstein (2010, p. 229).

*Figure 4.1   Structural couplings and coevolution between psychic and
social systems*

danger that emotion will form" (Luhmann 1995c, p. 269). Emotions, in
turn, can be dampened by the downgrading of claims to pure expectation.

   The distinction expectation/claim and the awareness of the possibility of
different formal condensations of expectations into psychic systems allow
us to begin to develop a set of premises for a present diagnostics about the
relationship between social and psychic systems. As Luhmann says: "The
consideration of social systems' psychic relevance for the emotional and
linguistic domain [. . .] could offer a starting point for investigations of the
psychic consequences and, above all, the burdens of reflection posed by
modern individualism" (Luhmann 1995c, p. 275).

   Luhmann goes on to ask:

   what occurs psychologically when *individually* grounded claims are increasingly *socially* legitimated and when the social order finally incites individuals
   to put forward even their individuality as a claim – as the claim to recognition

and as the claim to promoting what makes one happy (. . .) But how is it possible, and how does it come about that an individual can ground a claim to individuality – can, so to speak, claim the *droit de seigneur, "tel est mon plaisir"*? (Luhmann 1995c, p. 269)

Luhmann goes on to reflect on the modern conditions for individuals' self-relation:

We had said that expectations organize episodes of autopoietic existence and claims reintegrate such episodes in the psychic system. For one thing, this implies that, if claims cannot be made routine, the individual is increasingly subject to the individual's own emotions. Thus modern society is more endangered by emotionality than one usually thinks. For another, individuals are encouraged to talk about themselves and their problems. If one accepts that an individual can justify claims not just by merit but by individuality alone, then the individual must provide self-description. The blindly progressing autopoiesis of consciousness is insufficient for this; it must be "identified" as a point of reference for statements – that is, it must be capable of being handled as a difference from something else. This, however, is possible in the psychic system only as the performance of autopoiesis – that is, as episodes that can be terminated and transcended, with fluid boundaries, the possibility of being perturbed or distracted, and so on. The individual is forced to produce reflections and self-presentations (which can never be "accurate"). One encounters difficulties in doing this, looks for assistance, and develops the additional claim to a comprehensible, if not therapeutic, treatment of one's claims. This last claim to assistance in grounding claims is so absurd that it is as easy to accept as to reject (. . .) Contrary to the Freudian psychology of sublimation, the suppressed universal does not return to consciousness in an improved state, but in a worsened one, as sickness. (Luhmann 1995c, pp. 270–1)

Although Luhmann does not speak here of modern work and the shift in membership form to self-enrollment, his ideas clearly resonate across differences. It is time to try to clarify a few of our theses. Let us look back at the last chapter from the perspective I have tried to frame here. We will begin with the form of self-enrollment.

In self-enrollment, the organization's generalized motive was defined as personal self-motivation as if one was motivated by the organization. This definition of motivation constitutes a re-entry of the distinction role/person on the role side of the distinction. The question is what kinds of expectations can be produced for the psychic system within this form? Expectation or claims? And can the management of these become routine or not? I argue that the form fundamentally opens up for the production of particularly double-bound expectations and claims. A re-entry does not mean that the "first" distinction disappears. Self-enrollment as re-entry constitutes a simultaneous operation of both the distinction personal self-motivation/person and the distinction role/person, and means that these two different forms are considered equal to each other. Self-enrollment is at once non-formal membership and formal membership. We have a non-personal claim for personal motivation, and we have a routine expectation about non-routine. It is an expectation that one both subjects oneself to the formal membership and becomes a subject within a hierarchy while also rejecting subjection and finding one's own personal motivation for joining the organization. Thus, the form of self-enrollment communicates the double-bound expectation: "Do as I say!" – "Be independent!"

Susanne Ekman explores this paradox in her dissertation where she sees it as a double-bind between hierarchy and authenticity. Managers communicate to their employees that they should be free and authentic while still performing on time and subjecting themselves to their responsibilities. Employees take on this double-bound expectation in a claim for limitless freedom from the organization. They want boundaries but want to define them on their own. And on the other hand there is the claim for constant appreciation and recognition from the management. Employees expect the manager to both stay away and be constantly present (Ekman 2012).

Moreover, the thesis could be that the production of expectations in the form of self-enrollment varies depending on the medium, that is, on whether the communication is pedagogical, highly intimate or playful. In order to address this more precisely we need to explore the more recent history of organizational semantics of emotions, including whether and how the transition from formal membership to the membership of self-enrollment calls for the development of other organizational semantics of emotions.

THE HISTORY OF ORGANIZATIONAL SEMANTICS OF EMOTIONS

Below I will inquire into how varieties of semantics of emotions for organizational communication developed from 1950 until the present. My basic thesis is that the organizational semantics about emotions follows the shifts in the membership form. The membership form defines the fundamental organizational question of the relationship between organization and employee and hence is also the generator of what organizations consider it meaningful to communicate about. From this follows a distinction between emotions as they are articulated in the formal membership and emotions as they are articulated in the membership of self-enrollment. Thus, I see it as meaningful to distinguish between two different phases in the development of the semantics of emotions, one from 1950 until 1980 and one from 1980 until today (see Table 4.1).

Table 4.1   Table of questions

Phase	Form	Question	Codes
1950–80	Formal membership	Emotions and mental atmosphere represents a limit to the performativity of power	Primarily power Secondarily care and pedagogy
1980–present	Self-enrollment	Self-enrollment is fundamentally intimate. Emotions signify the authenticity and intensity of self-enrollment	Primarily love Secondarily pedagogy, play, care

I begin my analysis in 1950. The sources I use are primarily articles taken from international management journals, particularly the *Harvard Business Review*. I have emphasized journals and books which can be said to focus on a semantics of practice. The focus is the articulation of emotions in the description of the relationship organization/employee. There exist organizational semantics about emotions that focus on areas other than employee relations, primarily with regard to consumer culture and specific professions. Consumer culture and advertisement represent an independent field of study in the context of emotions. The same applies to what has been termed "emotion work", which includes care professions, education of children, police responsibility for safety, and so on. This field has its own specific history pertaining to emotions as an aspect of the description of professions. These fall outside the scope of my analysis.

THE SEMANTICS OF EMOTIONS OF THE FORMAL MEMBERSHIP: EMOTIONS AS THE LIMIT OF POWER

I refer to the first phase as "the semantics of emotions in the formal membership". This phase runs through to the end of the 1980s, at which point it becomes clear that other questions come to organize the articulation of emotions. I have chosen to begin this phase in 1950, which is an entirely arbitrary beginning, established simply because this is where my archive begins. My sense is that I could have extended the first phase back to the 1920s, to the rise of the human relations movement. But this is only a sense and not something I have explored further.

The formation of semantics from 1950–80 provides concepts for three different articulations by communication systems of emotions in organizations. The three systems are power, pedagogy and care.

As I have already mentioned, the formal membership is codified legally. That means that the relationship between role and person can be expressed legally through notions of formal duties and rights. However, the formal membership also constitutes an organization whose decisions are codified through power and which divides employees into superiors and subordinates. The relationship between law and power in the formal organization is worthy of extensive discussion but put simply, modern power presupposes the absence of force, and the law's designation of employee rights places a limit on power, which power perceives as productive because it is the foundation of power's ability to distinguish between power-superior and power-inferior. Power presupposes that power-inferiors are free to manage themselves and from that perspective, the law contributes by assigning individual rights to employees.

Luhmann claims that the modern form of power has the character of a communicative code, which divides the world into power-superiority (+) and power-inferiority (−), where the first represents power's positive motivating value (how to gain and exercise power) and the latter represents the reflective value of power (what do they want with me and how did I end up in this position? But also, what do I want with power?). Communication that employs power as form can only link up with one of the two sides. Power is not power-superiority or inferiority but precisely the relationship between them. Power is the unity of power-superiority and power-inferiority.

Power-superiority is not the same as force and cannot be achieved through force. Rather, power presupposes precisely the absence of force. No relationship between power-superiority and power-interiority is possible without the exclusion of force. Modern power is constituted on the ability of the power-superior to shift complexity onto power-inferiors who have to tolerate and manage this complexity through continual interpretations of the intentions of the power-superior. The exercise of power takes place when the power-inferior reflects on the will of the power-superior and disciplines herself in relation to this interpretation. The power-superior may express a wish and assign the employee a task, but this task typically remains somewhat indeterminate. The task is complex. The power-inferior has to independently figure out what the specific task consists of and how to solve it. This is how complexity is shifted onto the power-inferior. The power-inferior is only rarely informed about the specifics of the task. Thus, power is only realized once the power-inferior, because of the experience of uncertainty, interprets the intentions of the power-superior.

The precondition of this shift of complexity is the absence of force. Force leaves the power-inferior without the possibility to choose between different actions and without the possibility to interpret the intentions of the power-superior. Luhmann puts it like this: "Power arises under the condition of *double contingency* on both sides of the relation. This means that for *the person who has power* as well as for the *person who is subordinate to it* the relation must be so defined that *both* could act otherwise. Thus in this sense: doubly double contingency" (Luhmann 1990c, p. 156). In less ambiguous terms, this means that power presupposes the freedom of the power-inferior. If power-inferiors are not free, they cannot discipline themselves through the interpretation of the wishes of the power-superior. Modern power, in other words, is based on self-management and the freedom of the subject: "Power increases with freedom on both sides" (Luhmann 1979, p. 113). On this point, Luhmann is in perfect alignment with Michel Foucault, who writes: "One must observe also that there cannot be relations of power unless the subject is free. If one or the other were completely at the disposition of the other and became his thing, an object on which he can exercise an infinite an unlimited violence, there would not be relations of power. In order to exercise a relation of power, there must be on both sides at least a certain form of liberty" (Foucault 1988, p. 12).

Power is exercised when the power-inferior experiences uncertainty about the power-superior and self-manages based on interpretations of the possible intentions of the power-superior. Thus, power presupposes the freedom of the power-inferior. Power consists in managing the freedoms of others. Thus, the greater the capacity for self-management in the power-inferior, the greater the overall potential for power. Force represents the outside of power. Through the use of force, power is complete in its elimination of freedom as such. Modern power is non-force. Force has to always be present as the alternative to power in the form of sanctions, but as soon as the power-superior makes use of sanctions, it causes the complexity to shift back onto the power-superior, who is then forced to admit to his intentions. As Luhmann writes: "Power, therefore, comes to an end if the exercise of this possibility can be forced. The exercise of physical violence is not an application of power but an expression of its failure – or, at best, a presentation of the considered possibility *of being able* to apply sanctions repeatedly" (Luhmann 1990c, p. 158).

Figure 4.2 shows that power represents the unity of power-superiority and power-inferiority and that force serves as the constitutive outside of power. Force is necessary as an unrealizable possibility. Without the possibility of force as negative sanction the operative difference between power-superiority and power-inferiority would fall away. However, any crossing

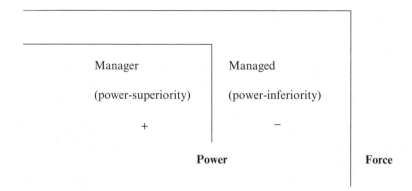

Figure 4.2   The form of power

of the distinction from power to force will also cancel out the difference between power-superiority and power-inferiority. In other words, force represents a necessary impossibility for the constitution of communicative power relations.

In the same way that Weber claimed that discipline works best in organizations that focus on objectivity and purposefulness through the exclusion of the emotional, one may conclude that emotions do not become defined as relevant to communication when communicating through the code of power in which managers are installed as power-superior and employees as power-inferior.

Nonetheless, it remains a fact that emotions have become articulated precisely from the perspective of power since the early 1950s. Elizabeth Jennings and Francis Jennings' article "Making human relations work" from 1951 employs a chain of causality according to which emotional atmosphere affects individual emotions in employees, which again affects their behavior and efficiency in the organizational relations of authority:

> Environment is not just the physical plant and surroundings; it is also the mental and emotional atmosphere inside the plant (. . .) It is the total of all the invisible contributions of voice, clothing, gesture, word, report of report which every morning are behind every bench and desk, every ledger and typewriter, every wheel and tool in organization. And every individual reacts according to the way his experience in his environment makes him feel. If he feels comfortable, mentally and physically, he will react favorable; if he is uncomfortable, his reaction will be unfavorable. (Jennings and Jennings 1951, p. 30)

The question raised is about the impact of emotions on the performativity of power. "The emotional atmosphere" is articulated as decisive for employees' ability to productively self-manage through interpretations of

the intentions of the power-superior. This produces power communication, which reflects on emotions as a form of limit to the performativity
of power.

Let us take a look at the way in which Jennings and Jennings go on to
develop this question. They argue that fear can undermine the emotional
atmosphere: "The tension which arise as a result of these value conflicts
may take many forms – any one of which tends to limit the productivity of the worker as a human personality, and more often than not his
actual output of work as well. Principally they show up as fear emotions" (Jennings and Jennings 1951, p. 33). They then go on to distinguish
between different kinds of fear, including "fear of authority", "fear of
being themselves" and "fear of being different". Their basic assumption
is that workers orient themselves towards authorities and want to please
them, but that there are often many different authorities who need pleas-
ing at work and outside of work. In effect, Jennings and Jennings speak
of the split self: "The worker has to split himself into several selves" in
order to "get along with everybody" (Jennings and Jennings 1951, p. 34).
This game generates fear of being oneself: "The worker fears expressing
and being himself. Instead of expressing his personal feelings and beliefs
in the job situation, the worker says what he believes the management
and his boss want him to say" (Jennings and Jennings 1951, p. 34). The
point here is that power itself may undermine power if the power-inferior
is too focused on the wishes of the power-superior: "This fear of being
one's self is carried into every situation in which the worker is involved. It
becomes a fear of making mistakes, a fear of admitting ignorance, a fear
of conflict" (Jennings and Jennings 1951, p. 36). Thus, power may itself
threaten the freedom and contingency that constitute its conditions of possibility. If power generates fear, the distinction between power-superiority
and power-inferiority is abolished and is transformed into force and the
employee relationship into an object relation. This happens when employees do not consider themselves free to self-manage. Moreover, Jennings
and Jennings speak about the fear of standing out from the group: "Many
workers would rather remain secure in their group association than put
to test the personal discomforts, the ridicule, the isolation which attend
development" (Jennings and Jennings 1951, p. 36). This kind of atmosphere causes employees to treat each other poorly and the individual to
take "every opportunity to reduce the person to what he feels is his own
level of accomplishment. With gossip, insinuation, or seemingly playful
pranks he endeavors to place the co-worker in an unfavorable or ridiculous position" (Jennings and Jennings 1951, p. 37). Fear becomes a mechanism, which destroys the possibility for power communication to perform
by destroying the conditions of individual self-management.

Jennings and Jennings place the responsibility for the emotional atmosphere on mangers. Certain management attitudes may stimulate a fearful
atmosphere. They speak of "blame games" but also argue that empty
appreciation and praise can have unproductive effects:

> At the best, most of us feel slightly uncomfortable when we are praised, unless
> our need for approval is acute. And as for the obviously superior-inferior kind
> of praise, if we are not immediately concerned with the implied blame (from
> what blame did the praise arise?), we are likely to wonder what there was in our
> attitudes which indicated a need for praise. (Jennings and Jennings 1951, p. 40)

The point is that "unless we feel within ourselves that we are (or are not)
doing a satisfactory job, we can become so dependent upon praise from
the person in authority that we have to have it in order to sustain performance" (Jennings and Jennings 1951, p. 40). Real authority is valued over
false authority. False authority is "the blame-praise technique, and all that
goes with it (. . .) But real authority evolves from competences; and competences, in turn, from tested experience" (Jennings and Jennings 1951,
p. 41). Jennings and Jennings do not only hold managers responsible for
managing but also for ensuring and maintaining the distinction between
superior/inferior lest the distinction collapses into force. Some forms of
management (false authority) destroy the performativity of power by
undermining the conditions for the inferior's self-management, while
other forms of management (true authority) support the inferior's self-
management and stimulate performance.

This highlights yet another issue for Jennings and Jennings. In order
for a manager to achieve real authority, she has to be self-analytical:
"Management will be willing to analyse and alter their own attitudes and
behavior" (Jennings and Jennings 1951, p. 47). It is a question of creating
an environment, which supports "self-esteem, recognition and appreciation, the respect of others, a social life, and assurance of economic security" (Jennings and Jennings 1951, p. 50). Thus, the ability of managers to
self-analyze their own attitudes is seen as a precondition for the creation
of a mental atmosphere in which authority performs most effectively. In
order for the power-superior to exercise power in relation to the power-
inferior, the superior has to exercise power over herself and commit herself
to true authority, which supports the best mental atmosphere.

The set of questions formulated here by Jennings and Jennings is
repeated in varying forms in subsequent years. In 1959, Davis Sirota
studied the relationship between employee frustration and effective management of employees. The basic assumption being that management
produces frustration in employees and that the level of frustration decides
whether or not management is effective. The feeling of frustration,

thus, is articulated as a form of noise that the management continually produces for the individual employee. He proposed two hypotheses: "Hypothesis 1. Moderately frustrated employees will have the greatest amount of information about management, satisfied employees somewhat less, while highly frustrated employees will have the least information (. . .) Hypothesis 2. The most highly frustrated employees will have the greatest amount of hostility towards management and the supervisor, the moderately frustrates less, and the satisfied the least" (Sirota 1959, pp. 274–5). Hence, the ideal is not for employees to feel no frustration. Moderate levels of frustration can increase performance levels.

In 1960, Robert Katz compared the employee to a steam kettle. When the kettle functions efficiently, the employee can be managed efficiently. If pressure goes up disproportionately because of blocked spouts, no amount of external motivation will work:

> I find it useful to think about motivation as if a person were like a steam kettle with three spouts – one representing his need of affiliation and acceptance; the second his needs for reciprocal influence or recognition; and third representing his need for self-direction or self-esteem (. . .) If one or more of these spouts is blocked by conditions perceived to be beyond his control, such blockage is viewed as reactivation of the individual's safety needs. This way of thinking allows us to view the blockage as thwarting the individual's natural development, and causing him to perceive the blocker (management, the company, the union, or work associates) as arbitrary or unfair (Katz 1960, pp. 93–4)

With this, Katz defines employees' internal motivation, including their emotions and relations, as a decisive factor for management's ability to be effective; the effect of external motivation is seen as dependent upon internal motivation, which makes it imperative to reject a mechanical understanding of authority (Katz 1960, p. 98). The manager is assigned responsibility for emphasizing employees' internal and emotional motivation, or at least for not undermining internal motivation since this would cause the preconditions of power to break down. Management must be sensitive to how it is perceived from the perspective of the power-inferior. Katz's metaphor is beautifully illustrated in the *Harvard Business Review* (see Figure 4.3).

John Huberman discusses the possibilities for discipline without punishment. His main point is that discipline presupposes employee self-respect and respect for superiors: "Self-respect is probably the most potent motivator" (Huberman 1964, p. 66). Emotions are referred to here as capable of ruining someone's feeling of self-respect and thus the possibility of discipline. Fear produces anger and "anger results in negativism or other undesirable attitudes" (Huberman 1964, p. 66). Fear

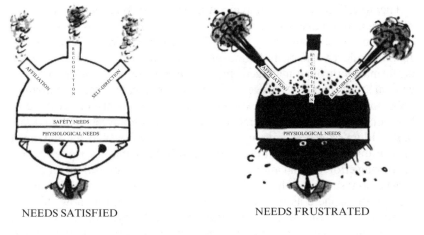

NEEDS SATISFIED   NEEDS FRUSTRATED

Source: Katz (1960, p. 98).

Figure 4.3   The mental steam kettle

is generated as "public shaming, threats of punishment, or actual pun-ishment operate in a negative direction" (Huberman 1964, p. 66). Once again, we see this figure where certain forms of power undermine the preconditions of power and therefore also its performativity. Emotions such as fear and anger are a symptom of the dysfunctional exercising of power.

As we have seen, the internal motivation of employees and their emo-tional attitude to work is repeatedly articulated as crucial to the performa-tivity of power, and this led Gordon Dilts to ask: "How can I change the attitude of employees to make them more productive" (Dilts 1966, p. 5). Thus, employees' emotions are no longer simply a symptom of functional or dysfunctional exercise of power but become a management objec-tive. Dilts focuses on the notion of "Business Climate", which includes "the total complex of facts, beliefs, and feelings within which attitudes develop" (Dilts 1966, p. 6). He describes the objective of the manager like this: "The supervisor must work with the people in his unit, individu-ally and collectively, toward development of an atmosphere of trust and confidence. Out of this atmosphere can grow the feeling of security which is indispensable to high moral" (Dilts 1966, p. 6), and high moral means "high motivation to produce" (Dilts 1966: 8). It is not a question of man-aging the individual's emotions. The idea is to manage what Dilts refers to as "atmosphere", which then establishes growth conditions for individual emotions.

The question about managing atmosphere produces the desire to measure it and make it visible, which subsequently develops into the phenomenon we all know today as satisfaction surveys. While Jennings and Jennings address the mental atmosphere of a company as crucial to work performance through management, Fred Blum similarly talks about "the general atmosphere": "This general atmosphere created by the company's policy and executives is an expression of a basic underlying attitude of trust on the part of management towards the employees" (Blum 1958, p. 79). Blum's agenda is to make this atmosphere visible by making it measurable in order that it can subsequently be managed. He terms this measuring effort "social audit", which is basically a proposal for employee satisfaction surveys. Thus, whereas Jennings and Jennings define the mental atmosphere as relevant to management, the effort now shifts to an attempt to define atmosphere as an observable object of management. Another article sets out to measure employee satisfaction and morale and justifies the necessity of such measuring like this: "Management needs to recognize what psychologists have long reported: that what the employee believes to be true and significant is for him what is true, and he may feel many grievances, real or imagined, to be much more important than management would ever suspect (Glennon et al. 1960, p. 106). The book *The Motivation to Work* explores a range of different attitudes to work and their effect on work performance. The book asks employees the following question: "Did these feelings affect the way you did your job?" The book distinguishes between the impact of negative and positive emotions on the speed and quality of work, mental health, stress, and job changes (Herzberg et al. 1967, pp. 51–119). Lyman Porter and Edward Lawler ask a number of questions that concern the measuring and management of employee attitudes: "What kind of attitudes are important to measure? What interpretations should be put on the results of attitude studies? For example, is high job satisfaction good? Does information on job satisfaction tell anything about motivation" (Porter and Lawler 1968, p. 118). This discussion is ongoing today and provides enough material for a separate book. My point in this context is simple: the articulation of employee emotions as the precondition of the performativity of power spawns a debate about the visibility of emotions, which becomes operationalized as satisfaction surveys.

Some people involved in this debate worry that the focus on employee emotions and satisfaction might lead to a much too harmony-oriented organization. Chris Argyris, for example, argues against the "'let's love them' schools of human relation". He claims that an employee friendly management philosophy only works under stable conditions. When organizations are under pressure to create growth, expansion and efficiency, the "being nice" policies break down (Argyris 1960). Similarly, David Ewing points to tension as a productive element in organizations. He warns against a harmony-centered management perspective, focused on the minimization of friction amongst individuals. Tension, according to Ewing, can be both healthy and unhealthy. Healthy tension produces manageable but irreducible contingency for employees. Frictionless environments result in static organizations. Healthy tension can result in learning, development and creative problem solution skills. Healthy tensions include innate organizational value conflicts between profit and collective, friendliness and direct management, self-interest and organizational interest. Such conflicts create productive tensions that widen employees' space for action and provide possibilities for development and maturation: "He had to see that the drive to dominate and control, important as it was, conflicted with another important value – the need to be a better teamplayer. These conflicting values could not be brought together in one man's perspective without tension. Tension was thus the price of a more mature, complicated, sophisticated approach to life" (Ewing 1964, p. 76). Here, the management perspective is to make tensions visible in order to make them productive for the organization. A similar line of argument is proposed by Kelly who writes: "Perfect organizational health is not freedom from conflict. On the contrary, if properly handled, conflict can lead to more effective and appropriate adjustments" (Kelly 1970, p. 104). "Hence the way conflict is managed – rather than suppressed, ignored, or avoided – contributes significantly to a company's effectiveness" (Kelly 1970, p. 105). "Conflict is endemic, inevitable, and necessary to organizational life and always involves some testing of the power situation" (Kelly 1970, p. 106). Aggression, too, is recognized as a positive emotion.

Emotional Maturity as Competence

In power as form, emotions are articulated as the limit of power and the manager is assigned responsibility for maintaining the distinction between power-superiority and power-inferiority in order to ensure that the power-inferior may self-manage on the basis of self-esteem and self-respect. However, there are limits to how well someone, in the language of power, can deal with the formulated problems. As I will discuss next, this leads to the incorporation of pedagogy and care in organizations to help solve the question of performativity of power. I will first discuss the way in which emotions become articulated in terms of pedagogy within the scope defined by the question of power communication.

As mentioned in the chapter on the pedagogization of the employee, pedagogy as communication form employs the binary code better/worse in terms of learning (Luhmann 1989, pp. 100–106). Everything in peda-gogical communication is observed through this lens. Everything is per-ceived with a view to perfecting the child/student in relation to learning objectives. It is a corrective code according to which one can either link up with the code's positive preference value, for example, by considering how to improve a student in relation to learning objectives, or link up with the code's reflexive side, for example, by reflecting on reasons for lack of improvement despite the employment of the most current pedagogical methods.

Power communication makes the manager responsible for taking responsibility for the performativity of power. Pedagogical communica-tion observes power communication and initiates a communication about the manager's emotional competencies. As early as 1951, Roethlisberger pointed to sensitivity to emotions as a significant supervision competence in teaching human relations. He defines sensitivity as "feelings upon feelings" (Roethlisberger 1951, p. 56). Around the same time, Robert McMurry articulated emotional maturity as an issue of competence and screening in the context of management recruitment. An emotionally disturbed chief executive officer (CEO) can have a disastrous effect on an organization. Here, the pedagogical lens is applied not in order to educate managers with respect to emotional competencies but in order to test and select on the basis of emotional competencies. It is a question of avoid-ing neurotic and emotionally immature managers or, if the damage has already been done, to help them mature through education and therapy (McMurry 1951).

In an article from 1953, Roethlisberger frames "listening to employees' feelings" as an important communicative competence. Without the ability to listen to other people's feelings, communication risks breaking down (Roethlisberger 1953). So the precondition for managers to exercise what we refer to as true authority is learning to listen to the feelings of their subordinates. Frederic Randall invokes the same logic when he asks: What can management do to stimulate the emotional atmosphere of creativity? The basic notion is that emotional atmosphere is "made up of the thoughts and feelings affecting a group's operation (. . .) It is largely a result of poli-cies and procedures which have become established (. . .) Consequently, if management wants to stimulate creativity, it must be prepared to recog-nize facts and feelings which may or may not have been planned" (Randall 1955, p. 124). In 1955, we see a distinction between three different kinds of administrative skills: (1) technical skills, (2) human skills and (3) concep-tual skills. Robert Katz identifies emotions as an aspect of the so-called "human skills". Having self-insight as a manager is defined as understand-ing the utility and limits of emotions (Katz 1955, p. 34).

In 1958, Hrand Saxenian discussed administrative and management skills and pointed out that it is not enough for managers to be technically competent and intelligent. In addition, administrators and managers need emotional maturity: "Technical competence, intelligence and drive are not enough; he also needs the emotional maturity to deal constructively with others while coping with the pressures created by the problems confronting him. Indeed, the degree of his maturity in dealing with others while under pressure is crucial; it determines to a great extent the amount of administrative responsibility which he can handle effectively" (Saxenian 1958, p. 56). He goes on to distinguish between different emotional skills that should be taught. These include "the ability to love", "the ability to face reality" and "the ability to relate to others".

Jennings and Jennings see managers' self-analysis of their own attitudes as necessary for their involvement in creating a mental atmosphere in which authority performs most successfully. Hrand Saxenian continues this logic but adds a pedagogical perspective by arguing that managers' self-analysis can be tested and shaped through education. Emotional maturity becomes articulated as a management skill necessary for managers to perform as authorities: "A man's emotional maturity determines his ability to work effectively by himself and with others while under pressure; and this ability, in turn, is a basic requirement for line administration" (Saxenian 1958, p. 56). Technical skills and intelligence are not considered sufficient: "He also needs the emotional maturity to deal constructively with others while coping with pressures created by problems confronting him. Indeed, the degree of his maturity in dealing with others while under pressure is crucial; it determines to a great extent the amount of administrative responsibility which he can handle effectively" (Saxenian 1958, p. 56). It becomes a question of operationalizing the concept of "emotional maturity" and developing a training program for generating maturity. The most explicit formulation of emotional maturity is "the extent to which he expresses his own feelings and convictions, balanced with consideration for the thoughts and feelings of others, without being threatened by the expression of feeling, either his own or others" (Saxenian 1958, p. 56).

Employees Have Feelings, Too: The Care Perspective

Like pedagogy, care communication is invited into and observed by power communication as a solution to the problem of the performativity of power. In care communication, the symbolically generalized medium is *care* and the code is *to help/not help*. When a client appeals to the care system, the system can land the appeal on either the help or no help

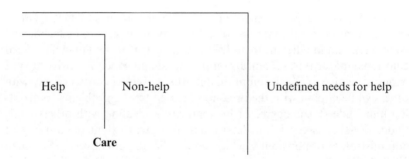

Figure 4.4   The form of care

side of the difference. Care communication alone can judge whether or not there is a need for help and the precondition for this decision is a diagnosis of the problem. That also means that the reservoir of possible diagnoses in the care system determines the production of needs for help. And the definition of diagnosis is, of course, an internal element within the care system. From the perspective of the care system, problems in the environment are undefined until the care system has established a diagnosis, meaning whether and how there is a need for care. The problems presented by a client in the system's environment are considered undefined needs for help. No action can be applied to them. The undefined need for help can be transformed through internal diagnosing of the system's communication to a defined need for help or a defined non-need for help. From this point, the care system can then intervene methodically (Moe 1998; Cour 2002). Thus, problems do not exist in advance as care problems in the system's environment. The system produces the problems it responds to, and its capacity to produce problems depends on the possibility of diagnosing. Moreover, the care system may increase its communicative capacity for reflection by effecting a re-entry in the system of the code help/no help. This allows the care system to communicate about forms of help as non-help. The system can choose to not provide help in relation to a diagnosed need for help if it believes that the help may have an adverse effect, for example, by ultimately clientizing the client. This makes it possible for the care system to indefinitely nuance and differentiate its internal operations through distinctions, for example, between help/non-help, and help/self-help. Care as form can be illustrated as shown in Figure 4.4.

In 1959, Leo Perlis introduced employee feelings and emotional health as the object of care in an article with the shocking title, "Workers have emotions". Its basic assumption is that emotional health represents the USA's biggest health problem. Perlis writes: "It is my guess that *every-*

body has emotions – employees, citizens and – employers" (Perlis 1959, p. 1434). His main message is that companies need to take responsibility for the emotional health of their employees: "Management should recognize that an employee is not a machine, that he does have emotions, that he is a human being with a great many personal problems that may not necessarily be related to his job in the plant but which are influenced by the attitude of the company and the behavior of its supervisory personnel" (Perlis 1959, p. 1435).

The question, then, is how to define the care perspective if managers are expected to care for the feelings of their employees. In 1967, Harry Levinson asked what a manager should do if the problem an employee presents him with is personal. His first advice to managers is that it is indeed alright to have compassion but that it remains important for managers to maintain a sense of objectivity. A compassionate manager needs to be able to distinguish between personal problems that he can help solve and problems that he cannot. Moreover, he needs to acknowledge that the person in question is the only one who can ultimately solve her personal problems. The manager's role consists of being the objective part. The person seeking help cannot see clearly because of his or her emotional state: "Emotion makes it hard for them to see and deal with their own problems objectively. If the man in the middle loses his objectivity, then he cannot help either" (Levinson 1967, p. 67). Thus, emotion complicates the response to personal emotional problems. It does not make it any easier that emotionally agitated people find it difficult to articulate their true feelings, whereas for the objective manager it "is essential to get from what is said to what is meant and deal with it constructively" (Levinson 1967, p. 67). Levinson concludes the article by saying that certain employees make a habit of sharing personal problems with their managers. In such cases, it is important to remember that "the job is still the basis for the person's relationship with the organization" (Levinson 1967, p. 68) and that managers are not omnipotent: "You will make mistakes; everybody does" (Levinson 1967, p. 69). The article was accompanied by the illustration reproduced in Figure 4.5.

In a subsequent article from 1972, Harry Levinson argues that organizations need to also take responsibility for employees' feelings of loss during organizational change: "In an era of increasingly rapid organisational change – when people feel more and more alienated and alone and management strive with increasing frustration to sustain identification with the organization, loyalty, and interest in the task – it becomes imperative to look ever more closely at how these two separate needs of the individual and the organization can be welded into a common purpose from which individual, organization, and society

Source:　Levinson (1967, p. 68).

Figure 4.5　Employee appeals to a much too emotionally involved manager

all profit (. . .) All organizations increasingly will have to evaluate the human cost of loss and change" (Levinson 1972, p. 88). The assumption is that experiences of loss have psychological effects, including "mixed feelings of deprivation, helplessness, sorrow and anger" (Levinson 1972, p. 80). Experiences of loss in organizations can be triggered by organizational changes where people are moved, work processes change, or during mergers. If managers were more aware of such experiences of loss they would, according to Levinson, not only be better equipped to help employees overcome their loss but also "foster a closer, more effective working relationship between the organization and its members" (Levinson 1972, p. 81).

Conclusion

Emotions do indeed find articulation within the form of the formal membership but, as we have seen, in a particular way. It is not so much a question of generating specific emotions that the organizations consider positive as it is a question of avoiding emotions that are considered dysfunctional in relation to the performativity of power.

Indeed, the performativity of power is what dominates this discussion. Certain forms of exercise of power provoke an emotional response in the power-inferior whose self-management is weakened and at worst

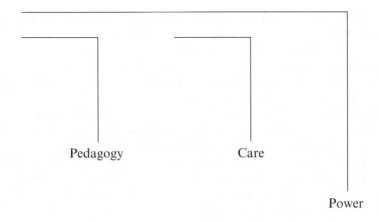

Pedagogy   Care

Power

Figure 4.6   Power works as a hegemonic parasite on pedagogy and care as
a way to avoid dysfunctional emotion

causes the abolishment of the distinction between power-superiority and
power-inferiority, objectifies the employee, and results in the use of force.
Thus, in the code of power, emotion becomes articulated as a relevant
limit of power. The problem defined by power communication can only
to a limited extent be addressed through power communication, and the
power perspective sees pedagogy and care as services for the management
of the challenge of power communication. This results in a pedagogical
and care-based communication about emotion, but the constant reference point for this communication is the question defined by power
communication. In that sense, we might describe this phase as power's
hegemony over pedagogy and care in the question of employee emotion.
Power communication works as a parasite on pedagogy and care, which
during this phase never develop their own autopoiesis in the form of independent questions, themes, and so on. I have illustrated this relationship
in Figure 4.6.

How was the incommunicability of emotion handled? I think we can
say that during this phase the incommunicability of emotion does not
present a major challenge because individual emotions never become a
management object, even when emotion is addressed.

In the code of power, individual emotions are seen as an effect of a
collective atmosphere, which becomes the object of management. This
renders the authenticity of individual emotions irrelevant to management
efforts. The focus is to create an image of the collective atmosphere. This
image is generated through satisfaction surveys. Degrees of satisfaction come to indicate employees' inner motivation and emotions. The

discussion almost never articulates a problem of authenticity between survey and actual feelings. Employees' experience of the world is considered authentic reality, and these experiences can be aggregated in surveys of groups of employees. The central effort is to find an image that represents the atmosphere. If an individual survey is not authentic, this is only a problem if it skews the general image.

In the code of pedagogy, the focus becomes managers' sensitivity to employees. The interest is not directed towards the self-relation of the individual employee but towards managers' emotional maturity, which is considered crucial for good management as the ability to be sensitive to employee emotion. This results in an unarticulated question about the organization's sensitivity to managers' "feelings upon feelings". From the perspective of pedagogy, this question becomes objectified in two ways. The first is about the development of impersonal tests of emotional skills as a way to screen managers. The other is about operationalizing emotional maturity through training programs in emotional skills such as listening. Both methods decouple the organization from problems regarding the incommunicability of emotion. This makes it possible to simultaneously consider emotion relevant to the organization and the authenticity of individual emotion irrelevant.

Finally, the care perspective takes employee emotion seriously as a question of care. Emotion is seen as an indication of a problem and therefore not the problem itself. The organization encounters employees' problems through emotional expression, but the manager's job is not to address the emotions but the problem that is assumed to underlie the emotions. The manager, on the one hand, may communicate compassion, but compassion should not obstruct the objective care perspective, whose objective it is to see beyond the expression of emotion in order to identify a problem. Although emotions do indeed indicate a problem, the problem is not observed through the emotions, which is why the authenticity of the emotion does not become a central focus. Emotion and emotional communication is seen as an obstacle to objective identification and resolution of the problem. Or again: the personal feelings of employees are considered relevant to the organization but the authenticity of these feelings irrelevant.

Accordingly, we see during this phase the creation of a semantics within the form of the formal membership, which simultaneously articulates the relevance of emotion without making the organization and its decision power dependent upon the emotional life of the individual employee. During this phase, the emotional semantics is primarily a semantics of self-reflection within the organization, which addresses ways for the organization to manage its boundaries.

THE EMOTIONAL SEMANTICS OF SELF-ENROLLMENT: EMOTION AS INCOMPREHENSIBLE HYPER-REALITY

The membership of self-enrollment produces an entirely different semantics of emotion. In the membership form of self-enrollment organizations view themselves as fundamentally dependent upon the operations of the psychic systems, and the relationship between employees' self-presentation in the organizations and their inner self-relation becomes a thematic. In the language of power, the question is no longer about the self-reflexivity of power, that is, the self-relation of power and the power-superior. The question of the performativity of power shifts from the power-superior to the power-inferior. The performativity of power is now seen as relying on the power-inferior's ability to self-manage. The code of power becomes double so that the power-inferior is expected to relate to herself through the lens of power. The employee's self-relation becomes split into superior/ inferior, and performativity is seen to rely on this distinction. Thus, from the perspective of the power-superior, the challenge is to have the power to empower the power-inferior. The question becomes how to manage in a way that supports self-management. Power communication only has very limited capacity to develop a language for this problem. We might speak of power's powerlessness vis-à-vis the question of empowerment. If nothing else, we note that the articulation of employee emotion in the self-enrollment phase takes place in languages other than that of power. Power shifts. From the 1980s, emotion has been primarily articulated by means of the communication forms of love, pedagogy, care and play. I will begin with the emotional semantics of love because it appears significantly more defining and hegemonic for the entire issue than the other discourses.

The Desire for the Authentic Membership: The Love Perspective

When self-enrollment is coded passionately, one becomes a member, as we have already discussed, by anticipating the needs of the organization and seeking thereby to win the love of the organization. The code of love is loved/not loved (as I discussed in Chapter 3). In love communication, the partner is defined as the significant other that everything revolves around. In modern romantic love, the desire is to be loved for who you are, not money or status. The anticipation of the other's needs is precisely an indication that you see the other person. If you cannot recognize yourself in the other's anticipation of your needs, you begin to doubt whether you are loved for who you are. Modern love communication is self-referential: Love because of love and love for love: "It involves loving oneself as the one who loves and is loved, and also loving the other as one who loves and is loved" (Luhmann 2010, p. 34). Love communication: "intensifies the capacity to enjoy feeling but also the potential to suffer on the account of feelings" (Luhmann 2010, p. 35). Love communication sustains the ideal of immediacy: "The entire experience of the partner should be an experience shared in common. Each partner should tell the other what they experience every day, each should tell the other all about their problems and resolve them through a joint effort. There should be no 'facades'" (Luhmann 2010, p. 9). Thus, there is always a question of authenticity in love communication. Literary critic Edgar Landgraf puts it like this:

> In love, we wish to express ourselves authentically and find ourselves acknowledged and appreciated for who we are (. . .) While the quest for self-validation has broadened the standards for acceptable romantic interactions, the reliance on "authenticity" has increased. Lovers today are expected to adhere to an ideal of communication that emphasizes genuineness, truthfulness, and originality. Although it is rarely contemplated whether authenticity is indeed desirable or even possible, for the purpose of self-validation it appears to be indispensable. (Landgraf 2004, p. 29)

This is particularly true when two people express their feelings for each other in love communication. It is expected and demanded that articulations of feelings are authentic. That applies both to the person expressing the feeling and the one it is addressed to. Thus, precisely in love communication, the incommunicability of emotion constitutes a central challenge. That is, how does one know that the significant other indeed loves one, and, in turn, how does one find certainty about one's own feelings for the significant other (Luhmann 1998, p. 70). About the history of this question, Luhmann writes: "Medieval knight had to prove himself by overcoming danger through heroic deeds and by realizing the ideal of knighthood. In the seventeenth century, in contrast, the lover was called upon to prove his love as lover (. . .) Thus the process of love was switched over to autodrive, and had to continually recharge its own batteries" (Luhmann 1998, p. 70). In this process, feelings function as catalyst without fundamentally solving the problem of authenticity.

We see a similar logic in the love semantics of self-enrollment. Emotion is not simply articulated as the limit of power or as the indication of a problem or condition beyond emotions. Emotion is articulated as that around which everything revolves, as that which creates the organization for better or worse. An example is the book *Passion at Work* from 1998, written by marketing professional Kevin Thomson. His basic assumption is that "one of the strongest emotions of all is PASSION. It is a motivator which drives us in incredible limits" (Thomson 1998b, p. 3). For Thomson passion is the single most important quality in an employee: "When the passion is gone, people either quit from believing in their job and go, or even worse, they 'quit' and stay. We're left with people with no enthusiasm or excitement for what they do" (Thomson 1998b, p. 4). Thomson's point is: "Our emotions are what drive us and our organizations to incredible feats. Let them loose!" (Thomson 1998b, p. 6).

In a similar book entitled *Emotional Capital*, passion is not only a human resource management (HRM) issue but also a characteristic of society:

> Capitalism as we know it would be better described as "emotional capitalism". And this is what makes us all emotional capitalists – our success comes from our hearts and our heads and our will to make business succeed (. . .) The bottom line: emotional capital is the stuff of dreams. It is energy, drive and commitment invested and held in hearts of everyone connected with business. Emotional capital is expressed not in terms of data, process or guides, but in such wonderful, emotive words as passion and obsession. (Thomson 1998a, p. 13)

Thus, for Thomson emotions represent the most significant management object: "Emotions are entwined with everything an organization does and produces; in its products, services, brands and identity. And it is the hearts and minds of everyone in that company that creates its personality. Emotional capital therefore involves the responses of employees to the company brand *and* their feelings about the company as a whole" (Thomson 1998a, p. 22). Here, the organization does not exist outside the emotional relations that constitute it. Passion basically becomes an organizational ontology. It becomes crucial for an organization to create itself as the significant other of its employees (and customers): "In today's society employees are no longer willing to be part of a rigid, unfeeling bureaucracy. People want to work in organizations they like, and are like them. Customers want to buy from organizations they like, and are like them. This is the real essence of corporate personality" (Thomson 1998a, p. 25). Through this lens, organizations are ascribed emotions as well: "Companies are living entities with emotions just below the surface – and not necessarily good ones." Seeing the organization and its relations as emotional realities makes it necessary to work from a register of emotions. Thomson distinguishes between ten dynamic emotions and ten deadly emotions in organizations. The categorization of these emotions simultaneously functions as an observational tool for management who can use them to ask about existing emotions and how to improve them. I have tried to sum up his categorization in Table 4.2 (Thomson 1998a, pp. 23–4).

On this basis, it becomes important to recognize the emotions that surround the organization, including the individual employee's feelings

Table 4.2   Thomson's typology of dynamic and deadly emotions

Ten dynamic emotions	Ten deadly emotions
Obsession	Fear
Challenge	Anger
Passion	Apathy
Commitment	Stress
Determination	Hostility
Delight	Anxiety
Love	Envy
Pride	Greed
Desire	Selfishness
Trust	Hatred

towards the organization. Is it love or envy, passion or apathy? Certain emotions need promotion and recognition. Others are considered deadly for the organization.

Richard Chang's book *The Passion at Work* is in line with this idea and argues that, "passion is the single most powerful competitive advantage an organization can claim in building its success (. . .) The passion-driven organization inspires its employees, invigorates its customers, and reaps the benefits of their shared enthusiasm in its success" (Chang 2001, p. 5). Chang develops what he refers to as a "Passion Scale" where organizations can test themselves and find out if they score high or low on passion. In addition, he provides a model for interpretation that allows an organization to understand its level of performance depending on the emotions that exist in the organization. The interpretation model is shown in Figure 4.7.

On the Y axis we find the organization's performance, which depends on the level of passion. The farther out one gets on the X axis, the more clearly the organization is represented by emotions of pure passion such as enthusiasm and excitement (Chang 2001, p. 27).

The question of the authenticity of employee emotions is also articulated by Dennis K. Mumby and Linda Putnam in several articles from the beginning of the 1990s. Writing from the perspective of a feminist management critique rather than marketing, I am sure they would decline the company I am placing them in here with people like Patrick Thomson. However, precisely because they seem so far removed from the rhetoric of marketing, their semantics interests me in this context. In the article "The politics of emotion: a feminist reading of bounded rationality", Mumby and Putnam introduce the concept of "work feelings" as a counter concept

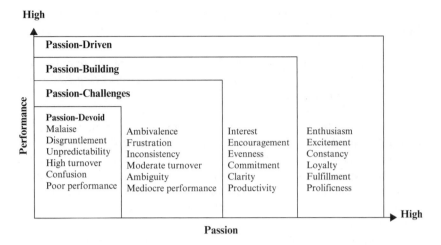

Figure 4.7   Interpretation model for the passion scale

to "emotional labor". They define emotional labor as organizational instrumental subjection of expression, for example, in organizational programs for how service employees are expected to smile and speak to customers. Here, emotions represent aspects of a professional role. Work feelings, by contrast, refer to the emotions that emerge in the ongoing work process and in social activities beyond the organization's control (Mumby and Putnam 1992, p. 477). On the one hand, their feminist critique is directed at Herbert Simone's theory of "bounded rationality" and, on the other hand, at the general practice of "emotional labor". They criticize the theory of bounded rationality for conceiving of emotions as the limit of rationality (Mumby and Putnam 1992, p. 471). Instead, Mumby and Putnam want to see emotions as a rationality that works for the organization. However, they do not seek to praise any attempt to incorporate emotions into the organization. Emotional labor represents a flawed way of thinking the relationship between organization and emotion. They criticize proponents of emotional labor for instrumentalizing and commodifying emotions (Mumby and Putnam 1992, p. 472).

Emotional labor "refers to the way individuals change or manage emotions to make them appropriate or consistent with a situation, a role, or an expected organizational behavior" (Mumby and Putnam 1992, p. 472). Emotional labor refers to those aspects of care or service work which prescribe specific emotional behavior and expression in employees, for example, smiling or speaking in a soft voice. Here, emotions serve "instrumental goals and task functions" (Mumby and Putnam 1992, p. 472). This is the traditional understanding of rationality. According to Mumby and Putnam, what is problematic about emotional labor is that it alienates employees from their identity. In this context, they quote the following statement from Ferguson: "Like prostitutes, flight attendants often estrange themselves from their work as a defense against being swallowed by it, only to suffer from a sense of being false, mechanical, no longer an integrated self" (Mumby and Putnam 1992, p. 472).

It is difficult to imagine a stronger and more unambiguous rejection of emotional labor. The alternative is called "bounded emotionality". It is perceived as a liberating utopia for future organizing. Let me describe the expectations linked to bounded emotionality. Instead of expectations about satisfying others based on standards and rules, they articulate an expectation about *tolerating ambiguity*. Here, the employee is required to work based on a desire to connect and to develop relations. It is a question of supporting a structure that allows for divergent positions among organizational members. Hierarchy is replaced by *heterarchy and a fluid social order* in which goals and values are flexible and unpredictability a fundamental condition. There are no fixed roles that members can assume. They must take responsibility and care for one another: "Nested in an environment of caring, members balance the demands of differing values, goals, and relationships to make the group a place where all members feel comfortable and achieve their individual aims" (Mumby and Putnam 1992, p. 475). The objective, thus, is to recognize the needs of others and those of the organization and to balance these. In order to achieve such balance, one cannot exclude personal identity as in a traditional hierarchy. Instead, the organization is to create norms, which "strive to preserve the *integrated self-identity* of organization members" (Mumby and Putnam 1992, p. 476). Such expectations transcend a relationship defined by obligation and enable a passionate relationship between organization and member. The self-relationship of the individual member is articulated as entirely relevant to the organization. Finally, the organization is emphasized as a *community* of employees: "a sense of community is vital to the maintenance of integrated self-identities" (Mumby and Putnam 1992, p. 476). Rigid descriptions of different professions do not work in such an organization: "The needs of the person or the relational context would guide feeling rules, rather than the occupational identity" (Mumby and Putnam 1992, p. 477).

Mumby and Putnam sum up their notion of bounded emotionality in a concept of "work feelings", which is defined in antagonistic contradistinction to feelings in emotional labor. In emotional labor, feelings are controlled by the organization, they are commodified and instrumentally motivated. Work feelings, on the other hand, are spontaneous and express connectedness. Work feelings are the product of a dialogical process in which employees are mutually responsive: "These work feelings are *spontaneous and emergent*; they are not directed to particular instrumental goals, but rather are outgrowths of relationships and interpretive schemes (. . .) they encourage *interrelatedness* and mutual understanding (. . .) They aid in 'bounding' emotions because a person uses these emotions to recognize the other person's subjectivity and to promote responsiveness to others (. . .) Employees form a dialogical relationship" (Mumby and Putnam 1992, pp. 477–8). The basic notion of work feelings is the search for an alternative to formal expectations, an alternative in which expectations and obligations are not unilaterally controlled and regulated by the organization but spring from employees' emotional attention to each other and each other's needs. In a subsequent article, Putnam and Mumby (1993, p. 52) sum up the sentiment in this way: "Work feelings (. . .) contribute to the building of community by forming a bond of interrelatedness." Work feelings are perceived to be the authentic expression of the employee's real feelings and identity.

It is interesting that Mumby and Putnam on the one hand reject feelings as an organized and decided aspect of a professional role. Instead, utopia is defined as the effort to allow for the relationship between role and person to develop through spontaneous emotional interrelatedness, which is to say from within the social relation and interaction rather than through external organizational force. What they articulate here is an expectation about and call for passion as the medium of membership. Moreover, they insist that organizations need to make it possible for the individual organization to re-emerge as "a bond of interrelatedness" constituted by the authentic work feelings of employees. Although these expectations are explicitly directed at organizations and the creation of possibilities for having work feelings, Mumby and Putnam's expectational semantics ultimately also includes the employees themselves: Either an employee recognizes her feelings as "work feelings", which gives her integrity and self-identity, or her feelings are unauthentic. This causes alienation and the commodification of feelings (as in prostitutes). Thus, we have both the notion of the authentic organization and the authentic employee, at one with their feelings and the expression of them.

Shaul Fox and Yair Amichai-Hamburger define a more practical set of questions about how to enable employees to give to the organization, including how to create the organization as a place for employees to invest their emotions and how the organization can tap into employee passion. The basic assumption is that emotion and change are linked: "Emotions are very important in transformational leadership. Emotion must be taken into account when building a leadership vision. If not, it is unlikely that the vision will win the support of the workforce" (Fox and Amichai-Hamburger 2001, 87). The challenge is: "How to tap the emotional components of human behavior?" (Fox and Amichai-Hamburger 2001, p. 87). A program focusing on change, therefore, should be based on tension and anticipation. It is a question of appealing to engagement and positive emotions in employees. The organization needs to found itself on the metaphor about the organization as family and partnership: "The Organization must also see itself as having a warm, open relationship between its management and employees" (Fox and Amichai-Hamburger 2001, p. 88). In order for it to function properly, the management has to recognize employee emotions. The technology for this is to listen in a loving manner: "Listening to people's hopes and dreams, encouraging them to express their fears and doubts, and enabling them to present their visions of the future of the organization may lead them to feel that management is attentive to their concerns and respectful of their feelings" (Fox and Amichai-Hamburger 2001, p. 90). John T. Kotter writes in a similar terrain in his distinction between three steps in change management: (1) see, (2) feel, (3) change. Speaking of step (2), he says: "The visualizations awaken feelings that facilitate useful change or ease feelings that are getting in the way. Urgency, optimism, or faint may go up. Anger, complacency, cynicism, or fear may go down" (Kotter 2002, p. 10). Gerard Seijts and Grace O'Farrell continue this line of thinking in their article "Engage the heart", which is about allowing employees to engage emotionally and passionately in the organization. They begin like this: "Reason and logic may be fine, but when it comes to winning commitment to organizational change the fact alone won't win people over (. . .) Employees also need to be fired up by leaders who recognize that both the heart and the mind mater" (Seijts and O'Farrell 2003, p. 1). Commitment to change only happens through the engagement of individuals' emotions and feelings: the "Individual has to 'see' and 'feel' the message" (Seijts and O'Farrell 2003, p. 3) and they go on: "Continue to show people the need for change and make them feel the need for change (. . .) Engaging both the head and the heart helps transform individuals and organizations" (Seijts and O'Farrell 2003, p. 5).

In this way the love semantics articulate emotion in relation to the question of authentic self-enrollment. The employee's relationship with the organization must spring from within as authentic engagement. Thus, in this semantics organizations come to rely entirely on their employees' authentic feelings for the organization. The sought after engagement is not supposed to be external, instrumental and commodified but spontaneous, relational and expressive of the self-identity of the individual employee. The organization wants to be loved for what it is, and this makes it dependent upon the authentic engagement of its employees. The implicit and explicit expressions of emotion become signs of either the absence or presence of engagement, which is why it becomes so important for employees to be given the opportunity to express their true feelings. Management becomes a continual appeal to emotion, the creation of possibility for engagement and the recognition of employee emotion.

SENTIMENTAL EDUCATION: TAKING RESPONSIBILITY FOR ONE'S EMOTIONS

From the late 1990s, we can trace a semantics about employee emotions. This semantics takes its program from the love semantics but applies a pedagogical disciplinary perspective to emotions. One needs to learn to take responsibility for one's emotions. Authenticity is not a value in itself. One should not necessarily express negative emotions whether or not they are true. The aim is to support positive emotions through the building of emotional competences in managers and employees. With Flaubert, we might say that it is a question of "Sentimental Education" (2010 [1857]).

Montgomery wrote in 1985 that employee anger might develop in workplaces where employees are not allowed to express their anger (for example, if the manager is the source of the anger). It does not suffice to simply deny the anger. Instead, employees need to be helped to assume responsibility for their own emotions: "Begin to accept and assume ownership for your anger" (Montgomery 1985, p. 22). However, doing so requires special skills.

Fifteen years later, this question was reopened by Elena Antonacopoulou and Yiannis Gabriel (2001) who made a distinction between emotions as cultural and feelings as individual. Feelings become separated from their social manifestation and the social manifestation cannot simply be seen to represent feelings authentically. This distinction makes it possible to view emotions as something than can be acquired and cultivated. Elena Antonacopoulou and Yiannis Gabriel's perspective is that employees need to learn positive emotions, which then support organizational change: "Learning about one's emotions provides a useful starting point for recognising what causes these emotions and how they may be worked on, reconciled with and corrected. This in itself is the first step to freedom – moving out – to a new state of acting, behaving, being" (Antonacopoulou and Gabriel 2001, p. 445). Learning about emotionality liberates employees so that they are no longer victims of their feelings. They go on to argue that, "learning, at its highest, has a liberation quality, defeating ignorance, fear and superstition, unleashing potential and developing new ideas and outlooks. It can stimulate emotions of hope, love and solidarity as well as desire for a better order" (Antonacopoulou and Gabriel 2001, p. 445). Thus, the basic assumption is that the authentic expression of one's feelings does not necessarily effect hope, love, and solidarity. Knowing about emotionality and its effects creates better conditions for love. They argue that managers of organizational change typically focus on negative feelings such as opposition and fear but that organizational change can be better supported by teaching employees positive emotions.

Daniel Goleman, who became a major name within this field, believes that the modern organization must strive to constitute a partnership among employees and between management and employees. He identifies emotional intelligence as the condition of such a partnership and as a skill to be learned (for a Foucaultian analysis of the discourse on emotional intelligence, see Hughes 2010). His point of departure is a particular understanding of commitment: "The essence of commitment is making our goals and those of our organization one and the same. Commitment is emotional: We feel a strong attachment to our group's goals when they resonate strongly with our own" (Goleman 1998, p. 119). Based on this concept, he develops a concept of organizational citizenship: "The committed are the model citizens of any organization. They go the extra mile. And like pebbles in a pond, committed workers send ripples of good feeling throughout an organization (. . .) Organizational commitment grows from such emotional bonding" (Goleman 1998, p. 120). In contradistinction to model citizens, Goleman speaks of "disaffected people" who "are most prone to using the resources of the organization solely for their own benefit" (Goleman 1998, p. 121). He refers to the organization of model citizens as "the organizational marriage" and the relationship between manager and employees as "the vertical couple" (Goleman 1998, pp. 212–13). And as in every marriage: "If both do well emotionally – if they form a relationship of trust and rapport, understanding and inspired effort – their performance will shine. But if things go emotionally awry, the relationship can become a nightmare and their performance a series of minor and major disasters" (Goleman 1998, p. 213). Goleman elaborates:

> Virtually everyone who has a superior is part of at least one vertical "couple"; every boss forms such a bond with each subordinate. Such vertical couples are a basic unit of organizational life, something akin to human molecules that interact to form the latticework of relationship that *is* the organization. And while vertical couples have all the emotional overlay that power and compliance bring to a relationship, peer couples – our relationships with coworkers – have a parallel emotional component, something akin to the pleasures, jealousies, and rivalries of siblings. If there is anywhere that emotional intelligence needs to enter an organization, it is at this most basic level. Building collaborative and

fruitful relationships begins with the couples we are part of at work. (Goleman 1998, p. 215)

Like in other relationships, "our passions operate here also" (Goleman 1998, p. 287). "The good news is that emotional intelligence can be learned (. . .) At the individual level, elements of emotional intelligence can be identified, assessed, and upgraded. At the group level, it means fine-tuning the interpersonal dynamics that make groups smarter. At the organizational level, it means revising the value hierarchy to make emotional intelligence a priority – in the concrete terms of hiring, training and development, performance evaluation, and promotions" (Goleman 1998, p. 315). Goleman defines emotional intelligence like this: "Emotional intelligence refers to *the capacity for recognizing our own feelings and those of others, for motivating ourselves, and for managing emotions well in ourselves and in our relationships*" (Goleman 1998, p. 317). He differentiates between five basic competencies: self-awareness, self-regulation, motivation, empathy and social skills (Goleman 1998, p. 318).

What this amounts to is a pedagogical semantics about emotions as skills, which can be acquired through education and training and which makes it possible to handle the problem of authenticity in a cultivated and disciplined way. Emotions need to be educated. The pedagogical semantics contain a notion of a self, capable of splitting itself first into feelings (operations) and emotions (expression) and then into desirable and undesirable emotions. One has to learn to assume responsibility for one's emotional expression. Pedagogy does not supply an answer to how to be authentic and honest and how to distinguish honesty and dishonesty in someone else. Its solution seems to be training for professional dishonesty.

CARE AND COLLEGIAL COMPASSION

In addition, we see the development of a new care semantics, which no longer sees emotions as the sign of underlying problems but manages emotions as they appear. This care semantics relates to the negative emotions that are produced in organizations as the side effect of passionate work.

Peter Frost contributes to this development. His starting point is the passionate organization in which self-enrollment is codified in a highly intimate way: "And as people are increasingly invested in their work rather than in their personal lives or communities, organizations more and more become the stages where people's hopes and expectations play out. Indeed, the modern work organization has become a zone where life is increasingly lived for full meaning – encompassing the full spectrum of human emotions and experiences" (Frost 2003, p. 102). However, Frost's take on this organization is clearly that of care. He writes himself up against Goleman like this: "While Goleman's early work, at least, focuses on positive effects of high emotional intelligence, what became most salient to me (. . .) was that contagion could be positive *or* negative, and the emotions experienced by one person might also be *absorbed* by the person who attempts to help" (Frost 2003, p. 4).

Frost is interested in how to manage the many negative emotions that develop in organizations in which employees invest themselves fully and how negative emotions can spread throughout the organization from person to person. He speaks of emotional pain: "Pain thus can provide a powerful lens into organizational life that leaders can use to tease out the roots of many kinds of vexing organizational problems" (Frost 2003, p. 216). The organization must care for the pain, which can arise when employees invest themselves fully, and he sees the emotional pain of employees and managers as a form of toxification of the organization: "We live in times where there is much pain and suffering in and around organizations. There is much to be learned about toxicity in organizations and how best to handle it" (Frost 2003, p. 226).

Organizations have to be built in a way so that they can manage emotional toxicity: "Organizations that want to stay healthy need to learn to handle such toxicity effectively" (Frost 2003, p. 9). Frost points to seven deadly toxins: "INtention, INcompetence, INfidelity, INsensitivity, INtrusion, INstitutional forces, INevitability" (Frost 2003, p. 36). The individual employee can become toxic and thus become a toxin for the organization: "Over time, a single employee can do any or all of these kinds of things, fostering a workplace that is unhappy indeed, because employees who are uncivil are toxic"; "Toxicity is produced when an individual's attitude or an organization's policies, or both, fail to take into account the emotional attachment people have to their contributions to work" (Frost 2003, pp. 51, 56).

The solution to the growing toxicity problem is the compassionate organization:

> The compassionate organization – sees a clear link between the emotional health of employees and the organization's bottom line – recognizes and rewards managers who are good toxin handlers – hires for attitude as well as technical skill – maintains a fair-minded workplace, recognizing the direct connection between consistent values such as loyalty, responsibility, and initiative, and the health of the organization overall – has intervention strategies in place for times of distress or change (. . .) – Build a company culture that values compassion and community as beneficial to productivity and to people. (Frost 2003, p. 28)

A central concern for the compassionate organization is to have toxin handlers. The way I understand it, any employee and manager can, in principle, function as toxin handlers. Anyone can assume responsibility for the organization's handling of pain and toxicity. Frost et al. speak of the organization as one that must care for its employees' mutual care for one another; that is, care for care. Thus, the code of help becomes doubled as help for self-help. Compassion represents the central form of care: "We identify compassion as comprised of three interrelated elements: noticing another's suffering, feeling empathy for the other's pain, and responding to the suffering in some way" (Frost et al. 2006, p. 846). Compassion is seen as interpersonal work, which includes listening and the creation of a space for pain. It is not just management that needs to listen. Rather, management is responsible for helping employees listen to one another: "Pain in organizations can often be overlooked or misinterpreted unless the listener actively engages empathically and commits to listen for emotions in the message that those in pain allow themselves to send" (Frost et al. 2006, p. 850).

The toxin handler names the role of compassion: "The work of toxin handlers is about responding compassionately to pain in their organization in order to either minimize or prevent it, identify it, contain it, remove it, or find ways for people to live with it constructively (. . .) They focus on the emotional needs of individuals and on the emotional linkages and relationships within organizations" (Frost 2003, p. 62). Frost asserts that a toxin handler is responsible for "listening, holding space for healing, buffering pain extricating others from painful situations, transforming pain" (Frost 2003, p. 63). Listening to pain also means to create human bonds within the organization: "Listening with compassion to someone else's pain, providing a moment of human connection" (Frost 2003, p. 63). As a listener, the toxin handler also becomes a pain manager: "As listeners, then, pain managers provide consideration and attention that allow the person in pain to feel heard, respected, and helped" (Frost 2003, p. 66).

This notion of listening as the management of toxins creates a particular variation of the question of inclusion/exclusion. When the toxin handler listens to the toxic and pained employee, the employee is considered emotionally excluded, perhaps self-excluded. Painful emotions signify that the employee does not feel appreciated and respected. Listening does not simply lead to inclusion but rather to the organization's ability to contain the excluded. The organization needs to be able to contain pain. This produces a re-entry of the distinction inclusion/exclusion so the excluded becomes included as excluded. So while the pain-stricken employee has not successfully self-enrolled, the effort on the part of the organization to "contain" the pain indicates a recognition of the enrollment effort. The one who does not feel loved is recognized and her love pains observed, and she thus becomes included in a compassionate collective.

Toxin handlers need to be able to read and anticipate the other's emotions: "She can visualize and feel the anger, fear, or demoralization that derogatory statements or actions would trigger if they were directed at people personally. The handler is often particularly quick at recognizing such situations and stepping in to serve as a buffer" (Frost 2003, p. 71). Compassion can help those in pain reconnect with their work and recreate their sense of worth. Compassion might even transform the individual's self-relation: compassionate acts "can help transform people's sense of themselves, change the way they relate to their colleagues, and shape the way they view their organizations" (Frost et al. 2006, p. 850). The inclusion of the excluded can lead to the employee's self-inclusion.

Frost et al. further emphasize ways in which compassion stories may contribute to the creation of membership identities: "As compassion stories are shared in organizations, they help people make sense of who they are within a context" (Frost et al. 2006, p. 853). In this perspective, compassion represents a form of storytelling help, which simultaneously functions as a collectivization technology in relation to the individualized self-inclusion (Frost et al. 2006, p. 854).

However, the work of toxin is not without its dangers. Toxin handlers can be infected by the pain they see and allow it to overwhelm them (Frost 2003, p. 90): "The people who handle the emotional pain of others might themselves be vulnerable to that very same pain. In effect, handling emotional toxins can be as hazardous as working with physical toxins" (Frost 2003, p. 4). Again, we see the metaphor of contagion, which indicates that the individual's pain is relevant to the organization. Feelings of pain cannot be isolated. Therefore, toxin handlers have to be treated with compassion themselves, not least because toxin handlers can be affected by the suffering because they come to depend upon the emotions generated through the work of toxin:

> Handlers for their part, bring some of this suffering on themselves. They get careless about their own well-being. They pay more attention to others than to themselves. They become consumed with worry about whether they are doing the right thing. They become addicted to the "fix" that helping other people can deliver. These tendencies will feed any predisposition to aid others in exchange for gratitude or friendship. The handler can be lured into a seductive spiral from providing balanced and clearheaded support to feeding the handler's personal need to be a "savior". (Frost 2003, p. 105)

Ultimately, a toxin handler can become a toxic employee and a toxin for the organization: "Handlers of toxins can become so infected with other's pain that they, in a real sense, become 'toxic' themselves, and begin inflicting pain on others" (Frost 2003, p. 8).

This care perspective leads to specific management requirements:

> The basic skills that compassionate managers employ are to: Read emotional cues and anticipate their effects in work situations, Keep people connected. They make a habit of engaging in "human moments" with their colleagues and their staff, Empathize with those who are hurt and listen to them with care, Act to alleviate the suffering of others, Mobilize people to deal with their pain and to get their lives back on track, Build a team environment where acting compassionately toward others is encouraged and rewarded. (Frost 2003, pp. 24–5)

These are significant demands about being sensitive to employee emotions, particularly since the employee's suffering might be a result of the relationship with the manager. Peter Frost believes that managers have to acknowledge the way in which they may have a part in the suffering and hence toxicity of employees: "Good leaders recognize the discomfort they create and construct ways to dissipate toxicity" (Frost 2003, p. 49). Therefore, managers need to be a kind of super toxin handlers: "Leaders who are effective handlers of pain draw on their own emotional competencies, that is, their self-awareness of what they are feeling in a given circumstance; their self-management skills, or their ability to manage those feelings; their social awareness, or sensitivity to what others are feeling; and their relationship management, or their ability to work through emotional issues with others" (Frost 2003, p. 171).

This amounts to a care semantics, which identifies painful emotions in employees as both an individual and an organizational issue. Emotions do not *signify* a problem but represent an iconic problem of toxicity in themselves. Listening to and recognizing emotion, thus, is a form of diagnosing. Care does not only relate to the manager's care for the individual employee but care for the mutual care among employees. In this way, care is defined as a generalized form of existence. Employees become subjectivized as care-giving toxin handlers. This semantics views the organization as strongly dependent upon employee emotions and as having to organize compassion as the response to the presence of suffering.

Authenticity becomes an important question but not in the same way as in the love-codified semantics. It is not a question of finding proof of love. Instead, it is a question of listening to what cannot be heard. The toxin handler is assigned the role of listening to the suffering of employees, allowing space for this suffering, feeling the pain of employees and showing it through compassion. The task of the toxin handler is to "listen for emotions in the message"; that is, to hear non-communicated emotions and pain. Moreover, the toxin handler must communicate the emotions of non-communicated emotion back to the employee so that the employee feels listened to, respected and helped. This doubles the problem of authenticity and the challenge of the communication of the non-communicable. Communicating one's listening constitutes the compassionate and detoxifying act.

This semantics also generates organizational expectations about pain. The perspective of pain expects pain. Pain becomes the flipside of emotional engagement. Pain does not constitute engagement but bears witness to it, that is, as rejected or misrecognized engagement. Thus, in a strange way, pain is assigned value. Pain becomes a sign of authenticity, which stands in for love. And which is perhaps considered more authentic and direct than love declarations.

THE EMOTIONAL SEMANTICS OF PLAY

Finally, today we see the emergence of a play semantics, which articulates emotion as relevant to the organization. As described in Chapter 3, as communication form, play divides the world into play and reality. We see a play semantics about emotions, which suggests that emotion is something we should play with.

Only in the last ten years has there been a development of such an organizational semantics of play with a focus on the relationship between play and emotion. In the semantics, the problem of authenticity becomes ubiquitous and relates to the notion of total dedication. In 2000, Pat Kane, who wrote a 2005 book about the ethics of play, wrote: "So to call yourself a 'player', rather than a 'worker', is to immediately widen your conception of who you are and what you might be capable of doing. It is to dedicate yourself to realising your full human potential; to be active, not passive" (Kane 2000). I discussed in Chapter 3 how this discourse is both radical and comprehensive. This applies to the articulation of emotions as well:

> The play ethic is what happens when the values of play become the foundation of a whole way of life. It turns us into more militant producers and more discriminating consumers. It causes us to reprioritise the affairs of our hearts, to upgrade the quality of our emotional and social relationships. It makes us more activist in our politics, but less traditional in their expression. And most of all, the play ethic forces us to think deeply about how we should pursue our pleasures – and how we reconcile that with our social duties. So, just like the work ethic, the play ethic is a set of feelings and principles. (Kane 2000)

We see a vitalist idea about emotional self-realization through a playful approach to the world. If one is seriously playing, playful feelings are not only required in specific instances of play but at all times as a general approach, a worldview, which should apply everywhere. According to Kane, to call oneself a player implies being constantly playing and dedicated to play: "Play as the exercise of human freedom and self-fulfillment, from birth to death" (Kane 2000). He sums up his perspective on the relationship between play and emotion in this sentence: "And the roots of our happiness, surely, lie deep in our playful selves" (Kane 2000).

Leslie Yerke's book, *Fun Work*, presents a somewhat less radical perspective, although the demand for dedication and authenticity is the same. The preface reads: "Fun-loving, passionate people are just going to make better leaders than nonsense, unenthusiastic types who have no place for a bit of foolishness in their lives" (Yerkes 2007, p. xi). Yerkes goes on to say: "True fun is not something you choose to do, it is something you choose to be" (Yerkes 2007, p. 11). There is no possible exteriority in a playful approach to work since playful is something one IS, a mode of being. Playing allows the individual to become identical with itself, it abolishes every split in the self and creates wholeness: "To bring your full, fun self to your work relationships, remove the layers of grudges and betrayals that insulate your heart. When your heart joins your head and hands in work, you will have released one of the most powerful forces in your life – the energy of your whole being" (Yerkes 2007, p. 43). "Fun is losing your self in the work" (Yerkes 2007, p. 224).

Accordingly, play becomes the form that fulfills the passionate membership and solves love's problem of authenticity: "The best conduit to our heart is fun. Fun makes work enjoyable, it makes us love what we do. Fun connects to love through the heart. When we enjoy what we do, we say we love our job. When our job is 'labor of love', it's less work and more fun. The more our work is fun, the more we love our work (. . .) Be authentic. Bring your heart" (Yerkes 2007, p. 175). Fun eliminates the doubt that relates to the code of love. Whereas love always creates uncertainty about whether I am loved for who I am and whether I love the other for who they are, and therefore creates doubt as to the authenticity of expressions such as "I love you", Yerkes' claim is that play demands authenticity without creating such doubts: "Authenticity cannot be learned, it cannot be faked" (Yerkes 2007, p. 109). Yerkes quotes a mid-level manager: "Fun is having passion for your work and linking up with your colleagues" (Yerkes 2007, p. 142). Yerkes also talks about loving management: "Offer love and encouragement. The more you give the more you get. Make it your priority to support; seek out those who need it" (Yerkes 2007, p. 218).

However, being authentic and playing requires inner balance: "Before you can be authentic, you have to be in balance (. . .) Balance is the conscious effort to choose what you put to your plate, to select the right complement of activities that will combine to produce a desired outcome. It is the ability to keep both the big picture and the details in focus at the same time. Balance is flexibility to change a plan and seize the spontaneous moment that promises to enhance your intended result" (Yerkes 2007, p. 123).

Balance begins with self-relation, with insight into one's own needs and emotions, and extends into a balance between work and play:

> The ideal balance of fun and work can be achieved when all individuals understand the boundaries of the work "playing field". Boundaries are not meant to constrain or inhabit individual contribution but rather to allow talented and well-intentioned team members to have as much autonomy as possible within the bounds of responsible fun/work (. . .) High control is the "dark force" when it comes to the Principles of fun/work. Issues of control can crush or strangle the natural energy that gives life to invention, productivity and prosperity (. . .) The more expansive the boundaries, the more room there is for fun to exist and then to grow. (Yerkes 2007, p. 93)

He quotes Renate Rottinger from La Venezia Café: "I don't want to be limited, I want to work on things that make me feel good" (Yerkes 2007, p. 96). Thus, authenticity requires inner balance, which is just another way to express authenticity, and inner balance further presupposes a balanced boundary between fun and work, which is only balanced if defined from within play in an expansive (not controlling) movement; that is, yet another authentic definition of boundary. Boundaries drawn from a different place than that of the playing self are not authentic but controlling and destructive. Fun and play are claimed to be the solution to the authenticity challenge of love but end in a tautology; authentic because authentic.

Moreover, authenticity is defined not only in terms of the social dimension but also the temporal dimension. Authenticity is perceived as pure presence in the now: "Capitalize on the spontaneous (. . .) Fun doesn't happen according to schedule. It isn't something we plan. Fun grows in a culture that fosters its existence; it springs automatically from the proper environment. Don't inhibit its existence by scheduling too tight; allow room for it to breathe and grow" (Yerkes 2007, p. 45). Fun is spontaneous, but at the same time, the argument is that fun performs: "We suffer from the lack of integration of fun and work" (Yerkes 2007, p. xiii). "Work needs fun" (Yerkes 2007, p. 5). "We are beginning to discover that fun belongs with work. It is my premise that fun and work naturally go together. That fun works and works pay off better when it is fun (. . .) When fun is integrated with work instead of segmented from work, the resultant fusion creates energy; it cements relationships between co-workers and between workers and company. When fun is integrated into work, it fosters creativity and results in improved performance" (Yerkes 2007, p. 8). This creates a strange paradoxical figure, which subjects itself to the demand for performativity and thus directs itself purposefully towards the future while insisting that performance is enhanced through absolute presence, that is, by disregarding and suspending future performance demands.

Certain emotions, however, function as a threat to play. Feelings of stress are considered a threat to play and authenticity: "Stress is the enemy. It reduces your capacity for engaging your fun self" (Yerkes 2007, p. 28). Fear is another emotion, which is seen as a threat to play:

> Fear and fun are opposite ends of a continuum. Fear comes from low trust; fun comes from high trust. When we have high trust, we have fun; when we have fun, there is high trust (. . .) Fear is often the thing that stands between us and what we want most. Fear creates a reaction that makes our desire elusive. What we want most is coated with our own fear. To reach our goals, we must trust in our ability to achieve them and not be put off by the fear that goals naturally elicit. When we have fun, we have trust; trust must replace fear and allows us to have fun. To have trust, you have to believe in the future and have fun in the present. (Yerkes 2007, p. 75).

It is important to note that stress and fear are emotions that point to a dependency upon an environment.

When recruiting employees, the organization should take a playful approach. Yerkes quotes a statement by an American airline company: "We want new employees to understand that work should be fun; that it's okay to jump and scream and have fun at work (. . .) We hire nice people, then we create an environment that is fun (. . .) We are looking for liberated, fun-loving people" (Yerkes 2007, p. 49). The same company also writes: "Having fun is what gets us through the day and having fun is what separates us from other dull carriers" (Yerkes 2007, p. 52).

As I mentioned in Chapter 3, Lloyd Sandelands formulates a particular relationship between organizational change, love, and play: "Change in organizations is best taken in the spirit of love that is play. As change calls to love, the greatest changes call to the greatest love of the divine in which all things are possible" (Sandelands 2010, p. 71).

This means that change is contingent upon certain emotions: "Play is the form that love takes at the boundary between fantasy and reality where new social arrangements arise to take the place of old social arrangement (. . .) play is to know not by analysis via mind and reason, but by intuition via body and feeling" (Sandelands 2010, p. 72). Feelings for play become constitutive for organizational change, and this perspective draws in particular on Csikszentmihalyi's concept of flow: "Flow denotes the holistic sensation present when we act with total involvement.

It is the kind of feeling after which one nostalgically says 'that was fun', or 'that was enjoyable' (Csikszentmihalyi in Sandelands 2010, p. 74). The feeling of total engagement is thus emphasized as that which creates play. In total engagement, the self is abolished and merges with the collective (which is why play is seen as the most profound and authentic form of love). Sandelands speaks of "selflessness": "In play, the boundaries that usually isolate one person from another – the identities that distinguish them as individuals – are overcome by the life of community" (Sandelands 2010, p. 76). Play is simply founded on love: "Play is a way that love grows and develops (. . .) Born of love, play is the second moment of social life. It is love's bloom of creation at the boundary of unseriousness (fantasy) and seriousness (reality) wherein new social arrangements arise to take the place of old arrangements" (Sandelands 2010, p. 77). Furthermore, play's feeling of total engagement is seen as equivalent with feelings of being human and fully alive: "In play we come to community fully human and fully alive" (Sandelands 2010, p. 78). Sandelands continues his chain of equivalencies and speaks of "the feelings of play" as the feeling of "being in it with others", "feeling of growth", "feeling of rhythm" and about "feeling of undergoing, of movement on the way to an unknown and undecided resolution" (Sandelands 2010, p. 79). He sums up play as "a feeling of social life" and points out that "although the feelings are felt in person, they are not personal" (Sandelands 2010, p. 79). Thus, feelings relate not only to the psychic system but also to the social. Play becomes the identification of the feeling of "the deepest vitality of human community" (Sandelands 2010, p. 81) and thus also effects "the deepest and most lasting change" (Sandelands 2010, p. 82). This is truly a radical figure of authenticity since it insists on the simultaneous identity with oneself and with the significant other. The individual has become one with the social.

Play as form divides reality into a reality of play and a real reality. From the perspective of play, the real reality is where the order of signs applies. I have discussed and described the emergence of a semantics that concerns emotions in play and how this is linked to a certain claim for authenticity in play. However, emotions are also seen as belonging to the "serious" world outside of play. As such, emotions become available to play. And authenticity is once again a central question. Play does not merely play with reality. It is considered to be part of reality. Alana Jones writes: "When they play a game, they have to act that way. The game is real. It shows what the participant really does. If there is a problem, you can address the behaviors as they occur. You don't have to talk about a past that is gone or a speculative future" (Jones 1998, p. 2). Similarly, Ken Jones, in his book *Emotional Games for Training*, argues that games can produce spontaneous feelings, which can then be examined in debriefings:

"Only the scenario is simulated – the thoughts, emotions and actions are real. Thus the events generate real self-awareness, real empathy and real understanding" (Jones 2002, p. x). The game is reality and creates reality in the form of personalities, social relations and temporal and cognitive perspectives on the world. Playing emotional games means that the emotions generated by the game are authentic as opposed to those emotions, which the game sees as applying in the real world. In the real world, many game designers argue, the emotion is no longer there when you speak of it. Emotional talk in the real word is burdened by problems of authenticity. The game, however, does not have this problem. The simulations of the game are considered authentic.

There is a wide range of games about handling emotions. In addition to Ken Jones' book, we could mention Epstein's (2000) book about stress-relief games which contains recipes for games with titles such as "The anti-boredom game", which is about slowing things down through positive planning, "The turtle technique" which deals with constructive withdrawing, and "Within you, without you" about exploring the body and its surroundings. Another book is Mary Scannell's *The Big Book of Conflict Resolution Games* (2010), which includes games that build trust, cooperation, communication and enhance employees' emotional intelligence. The game "The turtle technique" asks participants to sit in a relaxed pose while the organizer reads the following text:

> The stressors are all around you – a supervisor making demands, customers complaining, and co-workers driving you crazy – and you need to go away. Fortunately, you've still got some primitive turtle genes hidden somewhere in the recesses of your chromosomes, and now the time has come to turn those genes on. All around you, a great, green shell is forming. It's as beautiful and ornate as it is hard and impregnable. Slowly, you bring your head, arms and legs into that great shell. It's dark and warm and comfortable and comforting, this great shell. You feel secure and warm within its confines. The world around you is gone. You hear your breathing, and you feel calm and secure in the comforting darkness of your primitive home. You wait, and enjoy, and listen to the dark silence . . . You are at peace . . . Finally, you feel ready to emerge, back into the light. Slowly, gradually, you extend your arms and legs out into the world, and finally, triumphantly, confidently, calmly, you extend your head back into reality. The stressors are there, but you feel refreshed, renewed, and in control. (Epstein 2000, pp. 169–70)

Subsequently, participants are encouraged to collectively reflect on whether or not they often feel the need to escape, what they do when this happens, whether the turtle made them able to withdraw, and so on. The game is described as a "guided imagery exercise". A different game is called "Let's face it." It is about playing with the way we express emotion through facial expressions. Participants are divided into groups of four–ten people. Everyone is asked to write down emotions on a piece of paper, fold it and hand it to the facilitator. Then they all draw a note from the facilitator. Participants now take turns trying to express the feeling on their note by only using facial expressions, and the other participants try to guess the expression and the feeling it represents. At the end, everyone participates in a discussion of the meaning of facial expressions for the communication of emotions, of which feelings were easy to understand and misunderstand, and so on (Scannell 2010, pp. 189–90).

Thus, in addition to a semantics of love, pedagogy and care that relate to emotions, we also see a semantics of play about emotions. Like the semantics of love, this semantics centers on the question of authenticity.

RECAP

I have sought to explore the semantic history of the relationship between organization and emotions in the context of organizational member-ship from 1950 until the present. I do not claim to have written a fully comprehensive conceptual history since my archive is too narrow for such a purpose. However, I do claim that the scope of my archive is wide enough to show how the emergence of self-enrollment produces a radically new semantics of emotions and to indicate some of the organizational implications of this.

I have shown the development since the 1950s of a semantics of emo-tions defined by the formal membership form. This is primarily about the performativity of power communication. The limit of power is the power-inferior's power over herself, and I have discussed how certain forms of power exercise weakens the self-management of the subordinate. This finds expression in fear, lack of self-esteem, poor mental atmosphere. Care and pedagogy become the solution to power's performativity issues. Emotions become articulated as relevant to the organization in this period. Emotions affect the emotional atmosphere, which affects the per-formativity of power. But the emotions of the individual employee never become significant. And it is not considered a real problem that emotions are non-communicable.

This changes from the mid 1980s. Over the course of the subsequent 30 years emotions became articulated radically differently in the form of self-enrollment in the language of love, pedagogy, care and play. The dominant issue became one of authenticity even though the question is raised differently in different communication forms. It seems as if love communication constitutes the organizational problem of authenticity, and pedagogy, care and play provide the language for how to solve it. The result, however, appears less as a solution and more as a continual elaboration on the problem.

In love communication, the problem of authenticity is both a question of how to trust one's own love for the significant other and whether the significant other really loves one for who one is. And this, of course, pertains to all organizational relations: organization/employee, employee/ employee, manager/employee, and so on. Love communication produces doubt regarding the authenticity of love declarations. Is the expulsion of engagement now expressing a genuine commitment? Is the initiative truly felt or is it simply expressing a strategic hypocrisy? On the whole is the self-enrollment really full and complete?

With pedagogy, we are given a language for the education of emotions. One has to learn to assume responsibility for one's emotions. Positive expression of emotions is considered more responsible and constructive for engagement than negative expression. The notion that emotional expression can be learned might be seen to short-circuit the question of authenticity. But as Luhmann writes: "Sincerity and authenticity cannot be communicated; but if others cannot know his sincerity, the individual will feel unable to trust himself. The same problem arises in love affairs. Whoever tries to convince another of his love becomes insincere by attempting to do so. The only escape seems to be a profession of insincerity" (Luhmann 1986, p.315). *Positive pedagogy becomes a profession of insincerity*, which merely pushes the problem of authenticity around without solving it. The pedagogical language about the sentimental intelligence is first and foremost about being professional and disciplined in emotional expressions. Authenticity is coded in a program of politeness, which is expected to turn on in the "genuine authenticity".

The language of care shifts the question of authenticity so that unrecognized love and painful emotions become interpreted as more authentic than positive emotions such as being loved or recognized. The language of care says: "we need to also take negative emotions seriously". The language of care wants to allow room for pain as the effect of passionate work, but the result is that expressions of pain are ascribed greater trustworthiness than other expressions. One is recognized as an emotional and authentic person through the expression of frustration, pain, stress and dissatisfaction rather than more positive declarations. Here we rely more on self-enrollment, when absent, when it takes a tragic form or when the employee exercises resistance in her own self-enrollment. Resistance is considered more genuine than going along.

The language of play appears to have finally solved the problem with its claim that authenticity cannot be faked. Play requires full and complete dedication to the game, which eliminates any question of authenticity. One forgets oneself through play. Content and form become one in play. One is one with what one plays. Play only contains authenticity. The paradox, however, is that one is only considered authentic as long as one plays and disregards "the real reality". It is not possible to fake in games, but one is therefore only authentic as long as one fakes (plays). Only when one is playing self-enrollment can we be sure that the self-enrollment is genuine.

It becomes clear that employee emotions are far from a given entity but are highly dependent upon the observer, that is, dependent upon the communicative code through which they are observed (as also Fineman 2006, p. 688). Each semantic has its category system for emotions. Each semantic has its notion of when an emotion is genuine. Authentication claims are obviously depending on the semantic reservoir of concepts and distinctions for observation. Semantics upon semantics are developed in the effort to define the question of authenticity in an organizationally manageable way. However, every introduction of a new language for this question causes the problem to simply expand and hence also the organization's reliance upon the inaccessible emotions of its employees. Each introduction of a new language increases the level of organizational uncontrollability. The problem of the emotions of the individual employee multiplies.

Below I have tried to sum up the organization's different possibilities for thematizing and articulating emotion. There is a differentiation of the possibilities for speaking of emotions but without an increase in the possibilities for communicating emotions. And the more languages, the more obvious the arbitrary nature of organizational ascription of emotion (see Table 4.3).

The emergence of multiple emotional discourses also increases the amount of emotional signs. As Landgraf writes about romantic love communication: "The rhetoric of sensibility and immediacy increasingly realizes the impossibility of safely communicating true intentions or feeling (. . .) Tears, speechlessness, fainting or, in writing, exclamation marks, ellipses, and hyphens come to communicate incommunicability. Unfortunately, all of these communicative strategies are also open to imitation and simulation. Communicating speechlessness quickly becomes another commonplace, another rhetorical strategy that cannot guarantee authenticity and inwardness" (Landgraf 2002, p. 171). Similarly, we see in modern organization an interest in communicated non-communication. Managers and employees must learn to decode each other's body language, voices, gestures, and so on. And the organization tries to communicate love non-linguistically through bodily equivalents such as architecture and material structures. The organization creates playrooms, cozy corners, homey architecture, and so on, and expects these things to create an

Table 4.3 The poly-contextuality of emotion

Membership form	Power	Care	Pedagogy	Love	Play
Formal membership	Emotion is articulated as the limit of power	Emotion can be an indication of a problem requiring an objective perspective, which disregards emotion	Emotion is seen as a mental management skill. If managers are mentally immature or emotionally blunted they destroy the performativity of power	Minus	Minus
Membership of self-enrollment	Minus	The organization must care for the mutual care of employees. Painful emotions are seen as something negative, which needs to be met with compassion	Emotions become split into feelings and emotions (expression). Feelings need to be trained to allow the individual to assume responsibility for her emotional expressions	Emotion is seen as a sign of authenticity. Everything is about whether or not the individual's self-enrollment is a sign of real engagement	In play, one needs to be one with one's emotions. Authenticity means to become one with the game and forget oneself. One is not oneself until one forgets oneself

atmosphere. Christian Borch speaks about "organizational atmospheres" (Borch 2009). And the organization tries to capture and interpret the narratives that travel around in the organization and create other narratives that mimic the poetry: It is through the holes, the blind spots, the untold within the told that the organization believes it can express itself with authenticity. Emphasis is on non-communicated communication.

We might suggest that the result of this is *the trembling organization*, which grows increasingly uncertain of everything that happens because what is important is that which is not communicated or cannot be communicated. It is an organization, which gives more credence to the non-communicated noise that accompanies any communication rather than the communication itself: The noise is seen as authentic and communication as unauthentic. When employees speak at performance reviews about their perspective on how things are going and how they are feeling the manager listens not for information in the communication but for the noise that surrounds the communication. The employee said she was pleased with the work, but how was she actually sitting on the chair? If the manager informs an employee that she has made a mistake, the employee listens to the information in the manager's communication. However, if the manager praises the employee for her work, the employee listens to the noise that surrounds the information. What is she trying to gain by giving praise? Why now? Should I worry? What is the unspoken "but" that his praise suggests? Why did he not smile when he said it? Why was he so quickly out of the room again? When there are meetings with employees managers might not simply listen to what the employees actually say, but also observe the "mood" and "energy" in the room. The manager might not concentrate as much on concrete proposals, as in "the good process", and even in meetings with the opposition, acidity, anger and criticism can be considered signs of a "good and powerful engagement". The trembling organization is one which is always uncertain of its support and always busy with its support. Have the employees now seriously stepped in? How deeply does their self-enrollment stick? It also produces, of course, difficulties regarding how an employee has to address the organization. How is it possible for us to address and participate in communication when we already expect that nobody will listen to the information in the message, but only to the silent message in the form of the message? What happens when at the beginning of the communication one already expects that what one is saying is not heard for what it is? That the listener only listens for the same implicit signs and signals. The trembling organization shows a particular paranoid drag, where the undesirable condition is considered more likely than the wanted one.

One form of noise in this context might be silence (Luhmann 1994a, pp. 25–37). Silence, first of all as a rejection to questions regarding authenticity: Are you happy here? Are you fully engaged in your work? We know now that any positive answer to these questions carries with its difficulties. But silence as a rejection to connection is tricky too. It will be observed in the communication through a difference between speaking and silence, and silence will be a counter-image that communication projects into its environment, a mirror where communications come to see that what is not said is not said. It might be a risky strategy for the employee as well.

With self-enrollment as membership form, organizational systems come to depend upon the emotions of their employees, and this dependency assumes a different form depending on the code and semantics through which these emotions are observed. However, the different perspectives do not mutually exclude one another. The trembling organization is a polyphonic organization, capable of addressing emotion from shifting perspectives. Luhmann makes the following general observation about the relationship between society and psychic systems: "As the complexity of communicative possibilities increases, the psychic irritability of society also increases" (Luhmann 2001, p. 25). Likewise, we might argue that, with the differentiation of the semantics of emotions in relation to organizational systems, the psychic irritability of organizational systems increases significantly. The formal membership established a zone of indifference between organization and employee, which not only protected the employee from organizational meddling, but also protected the organization against too much psychic irritation, too much interpenetration between organization and the psychic systems. The many emotional languages and the increasing burden of the question of authenticity intensify the noise within the structural couplings between organization and employees qua psychic systems (see also Luhmann 1995b, p. 89). This noise might very well threaten the organizational autopoiesis by requiring a large amount of attention. "The little demons" and "the ghosts of undecidability" (from Chapter 2), as follows with any decision, seem to get exceedingly good conditions.

Obviously, coupling works both ways. The question of authenticity is not exclusive to the organization. The organization shares this problem with its employees whose credibility and sincerity also come under threat. The fact that authenticity is no longer simply a communicative expectation but a requirement that the individual employee recognizes and takes on as her own has serious effects for the psychic system's ability to continue its autopoiesis. The acceptance by the employee of the need to develop an authentic self-relationship places her in an impossible situation. Fundamentally speaking, a psychic system cannot have an authentic self-relation. That would require the ability of the psychic system to represent itself; however, as Landgraf notes: "The self, in order to indicate (think) itself, must make itself different from itself to be able to do so (. . .) The self must draw a distinction, must split itself, and both be and not be itself to 'be' itself, must both know and not know itself to 'know' itself" (Landgraf 2002, p. 160).

With the emergence of romantic love, literature takes up the problem of self-authenticity, for example, in Johan Wolfgang von Goethe's novel *The Sorrows of Young Werther* (2008 [1774]). Landgraf sees the novel as Goethe's warning against accepting authenticity as a personal obligation: "Are we not to read Werther as a warning against attempts to find self-validation outside the social order?" (Landgraf 2002, p. 171). And he continues: "When Werther stages the ultimate act of 'free' self-fashioning, he reiterates the paradoxical structure of any attempt to truly or fully self-form a self: it has to do away with itself to ascertain itself" (Landgraf 2002, p. 172). *The Sorrows of Young Werther* is about a sensitive young man who becomes hopelessly smitten with the lively Lotte who, however, is already engaged to a somewhat dull and correct civil servant. The novel ends with Werther's suicide. However, before reaching the end, we witness, through his diary, a man who only feels alive through intense affect. He achieves this state of mind through his love for Lotte. Lotte gives his life authenticity by bringing him into a state of affect. He naturally begins to doubt both his own feelings for her and her feelings for him. For a long time, he tries to convince himself that it is not important whether or not his love is reciprocated. But as time goes by, he develops a need for her recognition. He longs for it. However, each time he receives it, it still is not enough. It is too concrete, and not at all the total recognition of, his "whole" self that he desires. Similarly, he has only contempt for Lotte's love for the civil servant and the latter's non-authentic and rather practical lifestyle. And gradually his options run out. An obvious analogy is to wonder what possibilities are left for employees if they take on the organization's expectations as demands. What kind of space does one leave for oneself in relation to managers and colleagues once one takes on authenticity as requirement? (For a solid fieldwork study on this topic, see Ekman 2012.)

However, the result does not have to be as tragic as in *The Sorrows of Young Werther*. Instead, we can try to imagine a strategification of the authenticity claim. Rather than seeking convergence between mask and person, the result could be greater strategic distance. We arrive, then, at the employee who does not simply self-reflect and ask about self-identity but has accumulated a significant repertoire of not necessarily coherent self-narratives, which, when used in the right situation, can perform authenticity without essentializing the self. That is, an employee who seeks out affect in the different communicative possibilities within the organization and chooses self-narrative depending on the intensity made possible by the narrative. Thus an orientation towards the contexts with a high level of pulse and energy (a high level of interpenetration between social and psychic systems), and so we take upon us the identity which fits for this particular party.

5. Managing interpenetration and intensity

In the previous chapter I described feelings as three different types of operations: as diffuse thought in the psychic systems, affection in the biological systems and emotional expressions in the social systems. I argued that biological systems, psychic systems and social systems cannot be reduced to one another, nor do they determine each other. Instead, they play a crucial role as each other's environments. In my historical analysis, the body temporarily moved into the background. It was not so much that it was totally absent, but I chose not to underline the bodily references in order that the analysis did not become too complex. The focus was the disruptions between social systems and psychic systems. I investigated how authentic feelings became a way to recognize self-enrollment, and how this created specific organizational challenges.

I will now include the body and biological systems as system references. I will argue that not only the employee's feelings become constructed as an object for management. The interpenetrations between bodies, psychic and social systems emerge as management subjects. It becomes a target for the organization to create intensity between body, psychic and sociality, because this intensity represents a potentiality resource for the organization. My question is: How do references to the body work in the communication about emotions and membership? What meaning is assigned to bodies and bodies' relations to each other when emotional authenticity becomes a membership criterion?

My thesis is that the play-semantic proposes a management form that aims to maximize interpenetration between social and psychic systems, between psychic systems and between body and consciousness in order to create potentiality of self-enrollment. As an example, the game "speed-dating" potentializes possible partnership formations between employees and simultaneously incorporates the body as an element in self-enrollment. Speed-dating does this by creating indefinite complexity, determined by employees through their mutual interaction. It is about creating a *zone of intense interpenetration* between the organization and psychic systems, inter-human interpenetration and the interpenetration between psyche and body.

INTERPENETRATION

First I will briefly elaborate what systems theory understands by interpenetration. Interpenetration is a key concept in systems theory, which offers a way to describe relations between systems with different autopoiesis – such as life (in biological systems), consciousness (in psychic systems) and communication (in social systems) without classical figures of causality or determination. Feeling hunger, thinking of one's hunger and talking about it are not the same thing. The question is: How is it possible to describe relations between autopoietic systems that operate radically differently? The basic idea in the theory of autopoiesis is that it is the system itself that creates the elements it consists of. One system cannot determine another system's elements. Neither life nor communication determines the elements of consciousness. This means that occurrences in biological systems such as cells, brain or the hormone system simply cannot cause any adverse effects in the psychic system, or vice versa. It also means that biology cannot be described simply as the limit of consciousness. On the other hand, we all know there are connections. Without biology there is no consciousness. How can such connections be described alternatively, without resulting in reductionism, whether as biologism or social constructivism? Systems theory offers an alternative.

Luhmann proposes the concept "penetration": "We speak of 'penetration' if a system makes its own complexity (and its own indeterminacy, contingency and pressure to select) available for constructing another system" (Luhmann 1995d, 213). In other words, penetration is when the system observes or relates to a complexity that another system makes available. When we sit in a train across from a person talking on a cell phone, we cannot help making sense of the small fraction of the conversation to which we have access. The person on the phone does not decide what we think. It is also wrong to say that he or she is the cause of our thoughts – even if we think of what the person is talking about. A complexity is made available in the form of indefinite statements, and it is our own consciousness that is attributing meaning to this complexity by directing attention to it and by trying to determine it by associating thoughts. This is a causal relation; both are elements of our own consciousness. It is our own expectations that condition the way we think about what we hear. Penetration could also be that the body produces an unusually large amount of adrenaline. To the awareness system this adrenaline represents a complexity, available and compelling our thoughts. The conscious system does not need to know about this availability of adrenalin, in the same way that we do not need to know about brain cells in order to think. As complexity, adrenaline is forcing the consciousness to select among thoughts and feelings, but not *specific* thoughts. These are determined only by consciousness itself. Depending on our experience or lack of experience with large amounts of adrenaline, our psychic system conditions its own reactions.

Interpretation is when penetration works both ways: "Accordingly, interpenetration exists when this occurs reciprocally, that is, when both systems enable each other by introducing their own already-constituted complexity into each other" (Luhmann 1995d, p. 213). Interpenetration is when the systems mutually make complexity available.

An obvious theoretical advantage of the concept of interpenetration, as opposed to simple causality, is that interpenetration is not perceived as the reduction by one system of another system's options. The point of systems theory is that interpenetration increases the freedom of all involved systems. Interpenetration increases the individualization of the systems. When interpenetration takes place between different systems, the autopoiesis of the individual systems is reinforced. For example, human beings become as complex as they are precisely because social systems develop language, culture and semantics, which then are made available to the psychic systems and thereby increase the level of complexity that can be handled intellectually (Luhmann 1995d, p. 224).

Luhmann reminds us what we can understand by complexity: "We recall that complexity means that a plurality of elements, here actions, can be linked only selectively. Thus complexity signifies the pressure to select. At the same time, this necessity is freedom, namely the freedom to condition selections differently" (Luhmann 1995d, p. 214). When systems interpenetrate they make complexity available to each other without exchanging structures. Each system defines its own conditions for how to relate to indefinite complexity. Interpenetrating systems therefore remain external environments for each other: "This means that the complexity each other makes available is an incomprehensible complexity – that is, disorder – for the receiving system" (Luhmann 1995d, p. 214).

Relating to the themes of this book, we can differentiate between three types of interpenetration: (1) interpenetration between psychic and social systems, (2) interpenetration between psychic and biological systems and (3) inter-human interpenetration between psychic systems.

Regarding the biological systems, it is important to note that the "human" refers to a patchwork of systems. The body is NOT seen as one system. The body is not a set of biological subsystems. The human as a "patchwork" of systems means that a wide range of systems, including the nervous system, the brain, the psychic system, the endocrine system and the cardiovascular system function as environments to one another and interpenetrate each other without constituting any unifying whole. There is no division between body and soul or something similar. Basically

Luhmann uses the concept "body" to describe how the social formulates ideas about the body's subjugation of consciousness: "What the body is for itself we do not know" (Luhmann 1995d, p. 245). If one were to formulate a basic systems theoretical concept of "body" it could probably draw on Michel Serres's book *The Five Senses* (2008), which empirically observes the body as traces of sense perceptions. The concept of "body" may in this respect be reserved for describing the connections and tracks that the psychic system builds to its environment of biological systems through the experience of sensation and interpenetration. The body then is not one you have, but one that continually comes to exist for the individual through the selection of options made available as an indefinite complexity of systems in the environment.

ARTICULATION OF INTERPENETRATION

If we revisit the previous chapter with a focus on interpenetration, we will see that the interpenetration of biology, psychology and social systems becomes a management object. It does not mean that interpenetration is actually managed, but only that it becomes a desired object of management. And this happens with the emergence of the self-enrollment configuration.

In the formal membership period there are only a few references to the body that relate to communication about emotions and membership. The body is mainly a reference point for gestures, which the manager must read when he diagnoses the employee's need for help. Tears are observed, for example, as signs of an emotional issue that must be objectivized in order for the manager to act.

The formal membership period also develops a concept of "mental atmosphere". The concept focuses on anything that affects employees' mental state but does not articulate any relationship between body, mind and sociality. Physical conditions, management practices and working conditions are seen only as external conditions, that is, employees' external environment.

With the transition to self-enrollment, the number of references to the body increases and interpenetration is articulated in different ways and to varying extents depending on the communication codification.

Body in Pedagogical Self-Enrollment

In the pedagogical communication, however, references to the body seem almost absent. Interpenetration is articulated as self-development with reference to the relevance for the workplace and thus includes only interpenetration between the psychic system and the social system. It is all about the psychic system's relevance to the social systems. Management of interpenetration can be seen as creating opportunities for the psychic system to relate to itself in a pedagogical way. In other words, interpenetration is about the self-discipline of the psychic system. This does not add anything new to my previous analyses in my book about the pedagogization of employees.

Body in Passionate Self-Enrollment

In communication codified through passion, there are also surprisingly few references to the body. These references are mainly about the ideal of "the whole person". The division between the impersonal and the personal, public and private, body and psyche is to be rescinded. But the semantics also enables intimacy as a bodily experienced phenomenon. Seijts and O'Farrell, for example, emphasize that the "individual has to 'see' and 'feel' the message" (Seijts and O'Farrell 2003, p. 3). In order to achieve a greater level of intimacy the relationship is expected to register on a bodily and sensuous level in addition to a visible register. An employee is only really dedicated when he/she can feel the dedication on his/her body, when he/she does not have to think "I'm dedicated". Thus, dedication comes to require a physical being. Fox and Amichai-Hamburger even ascribe bodily heat to the organization: "The organization must also see itself as having a warm, open relationship between its management and employees" (Fox and Amichai-Hamburger 2001, p. 88).

However, it is primarily inter-human interpenetration, which is articulated as intimacy and passion. Passionate communication is what mediates inter-human interpenetration. Management of interpenetration thus means to create opportunities for employees to anticipate the needs of each other and of the organization. One might even talk about management as meta-passion; *management becomes a question of anticipating anticipations.* The focus of management is to provide complexity in the form of a "loving/ affectionate atmosphere" (the warm organization), where employees are given the opportunity to discover each other and the organization as potential significant others. The role of management is to continually create opportunities for the eruption of passion between employees and managers.

Body in Caring Self-Enrollment

In the semantics of passion there seemed to be only a few but very central references to the body, whereas care communication incorporates many references to the body. References to the body are used primarily in communications about employees' suffering. Here the communications stress that employees are both psychical and physical, as for example in this quote by Frost: "We live in times where there is much pain and suffering in and around organizations. There is much to be learned about toxicity in organizations and how best to handle it" (Frost 2003, p. 226). These statements about "pain", "suffering" and "toxicity" make it clear that these are not only psychological feelings. The negative emotions associated with the work have also taken hold of the body and inflicted it with suffering.

Care comes to simultaneously mean caring for the body of "the other". "Noticing another's suffering, feeling empathy for the other's pain, and responding to the suffering in some way" (Frost et al. 2006, p. 846), including paying attention to the body of "the other": "listening, holding space for healing, buffering pain extricating others from painful situations, transforming pain" (Frost 2003, p. 63). The stage is set for employees to sense each other, rather than just communicate with each other. Interpenetration is then articulated as care for employees' mutual care – a care that includes both body and mind. Thus, the care semantic articulates both inter-human interpenetration and interpenetration between biology and psyche.

The care semantic presents us with another interpenetration problem which seems quite interesting. It concerns the concept of "infection"; the fact that pain and suffering can be spread among employees within the organization. The care workers are especially at risk of infection: "The people who handle the emotional pain of others might themselves be vulnerable to that very same pain. In effect, handling emotional toxins can be as hazardous as working with physical toxins" (Frost 2003, p. 4). In this way the care employee can also be a carrier of infection in the organization and spread the toxins throughout the entire organization: "Handlers of toxins can become so infected with other's pain that they, in a real sense, become 'toxic' themselves, and begin inflicting pain on others" (Frost 2003, p. 8). An employee's work-related disorders and pain may spread to others, whereby the organization itself is slowly poisoned. Here, the organization is being articulated as an *organic* collective rather than a social system. Infection spreads among employees, but not through communication!!! Infection is negative interpenetration occurring directly between bodies and between psychic systems without the mediation of communication. Management of interpenetration thus means to take care of the employee's care and develop an optic for the individual's pain, psychic as well as physical. Care is expected to include the relations among bodies, and hence cannot be reduced to communication alone. The care must attend to the suffering-effects related to uncontrollable and unwanted interpenetration between bodies and between psychic systems.

Body in Playful Self-Enrollment

In play-communication, references to the body are everywhere. Many of the sensations articulated in the play-semantic very clearly include the body, as when Jones writes: "Don't forget to have fun, laugh, and enjoy yourself while in the process of helping others learn more about themselves and the world around them (Jones 1998, p.17). To laugh, to have fun and experience enjoyment is difficult to imagine without a bodily/ psychical relationship. Kane simply talks about play as another "breath of life" (Kane 2004, p.319). Play is seen as fundamentally sensuous.

Furthermore, there is almost always a bodily element to the games being proposed. In the game "Barnyard", participants must make themselves known by using animal sounds (Forbes-Greene 1983, p.9). Other games include throwing balls to each other or drawing on each other's backs. Generally speaking, all management games seem to require physical/ bodily participation, as for example in the game "I like me because", where participants "are encouraged to relax, to not cross their arms, but sit with an 'open body position' [and] listen and express interest through body language" (Scannell et al. 1998, p.207). Emphasis is placed on the futility of simply enrolling in the communication. One must also participate with one's body. The body is the sign of full participation. The body must be invested in the game, which means that playing becomes more than just communication. Play also becomes interpenetration amongst bodies and between body and psyche.

Furthermore, the ideal of play seems precisely to be a fusion of the physical, social and psychological. When play is perceived as "flow", the physical/bodily, the social and the psychical come to represent one unit. As Yerkes says: "When your *heart* joins your *head* and *hands* in work, you will have released one of the most powerful forces in your life – the energy of your *whole being*" (Yerkes 2007, p.43). Or as Sandelands says: "play is to know not by analysis via mind and reason, but by intuition via body and feeling" (Sandelands 2010, p.72). Play seems precisely to articulate the essence of interpenetration as such. "In play we come to community fully human and fully alive" (Sandelands 2010, p.78). Sandelands continues his chain of equivalencies and speaks of "the feelings of play" as the feeling of "being in it with others", "feeling of growth", "feeling of rhythm" and about a "feeling of undergoing, of movement on the way to an unknown and undecided resolution" (Sandelands 2010, p.79). Here play only becomes play when the body, the psyche and the social unite.

In the play-semantic, interpenetration is articulated as the space where bodies, psychic systems and communication unite through play and tend to amalgamate. Management of interpenetration is about inviting the body, psyche and sociality to be united through play. Management then becomes a question of creating a playful atmosphere where employees are invited to invest both body and psyche in a search for organizational potentiality. Play becomes a technology for *interpenetration-intensification* (see Table 5.1).

SUMMARY

When we open the perspective to include the relevance of the body in the self-enrollment we can observe that management is not only about the relationship between organization systems and the individual psychic systems, but also about interpenetration between psychic systems, between psyche and body, and between bodies. I concluded the previous chapter with the observation that the zone of indifference between organization and employee seems to be replaced by a zone of intensity, and now we can see how a focus on inter-human interpenetration and interpenetration related to bodies can be used to increase this intensity.

To manage interpenetration is not to control the outcome of interpenetration. Classic conventional upbringing can be said to consist of an attempt to discipline the psyche's control of the body. It was about compliance related to a predetermined intentionality. Management of interpenetration seems in this context different, given that interpenetration as such is observed by the organization as a source of creation, including the source of membership creation. As Justine Pors points out, "noise" is currently seen as a resource for innovation (Pors 2011b). The play discourse seems a particularly vital discourse. Managing interpenetration is about *interpenetration-intensification* rather than about discipline in a traditional sense. It is about increasing the opportunities for the systems to make unlimited complexity available to each other. It is about management of potentiality (Juelskjær et al. 2011). And *management of potentiality means to create a zone of intense interpenetration between the organization, the interactions, the psychic systems and their bodies (biological systems), maximizing the production of social contingency and variation available to the organization.*

If we define management as the effort to reduce difference, then what we are talking about here designates a very special difference. If we identify formal bureaucracy with control and surveillance, we can say that this type of management is about reducing the difference between rules and

Table 5.1 Management of interpenetration

Communication form	Interpenetration	Body-reference	Management practice
Pedagogic	Focus on interpenetration between the psychic and the social system	Body references are almost absent	Management of interpenetration is about creating possibilities for the psychic system to relate to itself in a pedagogical way
Passion	Focus on inter-human interpenetration	Only a few body-references. Focus is primarily on the "whole being"	Management of interpenetration is about anticipating anticipations, including creating a passionate atmosphere where employees can meet each other as significant "others"
Care	Focus on both inter-human interpenetration and interpenetration between body and psyche	Many body-references. It is primarily about employee suffering as both physical and psychical, with metaphors of toxification	Management of interpenetration is about caring for the psyche as well as the body with a focus on the individual's suffering and infection
Play	Focus on interpenetration between the psychic system and the social system, inter-human interpenetration and interpenetration between body and psyche in the ideal of the body as well as the unity of psyche and sociality through play	A great number of body-references. Play is observed as inseparable from sensuousness and most play is about the sensuous	Management of interpenetration is about inviting employees to play. Play incorporates the body, the psyche and the social. Interpenetration is seen as a resource for the creation of possibilities. Thus, play is about increasing interpenetration. Play becomes a technology for *interpenetration-intensification*. To create a playful atmosphere

behavior, where the actual behavior must be disciplined according to the rules. The professional bureaucracy, by contrast, manages by aiming to reduce the difference between aim and means. The choice of means must be optimized in order to match the aims of the organization. *In management of potentiality – the difference to be reduced seems to be between potentiality and realization of possibilities* (see also Andersen 2008b, pp. 139–41). The realization of existing possibilities is considered less important than the potentialization of new possibilities. Realization must be subsumed to the logic of the virtual and potential. The creation of possibilities is put far above the realization of possibilities, and interpenetration becomes the *medium* for potentialization. Indefinite complexity ("noise" from psychic systems as well as from biological and social systems) has become valuable because it points towards a yet to be realized and not yet imagined potentiality of the organization (Pors 2011a, 2011b). Management of interpenetration is thus also potentiality-management.

Thus, management here becomes a matter of intensifying interpenetrations, autopoiesis and coupling between systems in order to increase potentiality; that is, connectivity, variations, mutations, indeterminacy and contingency. However, at the same time this form of management causes increased intensity to become an externality; that is, an uncontrolled effect. Management of potentiality via intensification of interpenetration means to value energetic operations in themselves.

6. Loving layoffs: the intimate strategies of the break-up

Where there is enrollment, there is sure to also be termination of membership. Until now my focus has been on the conditions for enrollment when membership becomes self-enrollment. Now, I am going to cut across the distinction and focus on conditions for termination of membership. My thesis is that shedding light on the termination of membership can provide essential insight into the membership of self-enrollment as such.

Zygmunt Bauman stresses the movement towards transient relationships in both love life and work life. In his book, *Society under Siege*, Bauman writes: "it is a facility of *dis*connection, of switching *off*, that sets apart the new brand of interpersonal relations" (Bauman 2002, p. 153). But perhaps it is not as simple as mere transience negating permanence. Many families, particularly with kids, who have lived through divorce, find out that the divorce does not simply abolish the relationship. One never fully regains one's previous independence. The relation cannot easily be shut down. Even following rather irreconcilable break-ups, the two people have to establish a decent relationship that can tolerate the dependencies (children) that remain.

My thesis here follows a similar logic in relation to organizational membership. Perhaps the love-codified organization runs into similar challenges with respect to the cancellation of membership as serial families?

In the film *Up in the Air* from 2009, one of the characters who has been fired by Ryan Bingman says: "I've heard that losing your job is like a death in the family but personally I feel more like the people I work with were my family and I died". Ryan is assigned a trainee. He asks her: "What is it you think we do here?" She answers: "We prepare the newly-unemployed for the emotional and physical hurdles of job hunting, while minimizing legal blowback." He answers: "That's what we're selling. It's not what we're doing", and he goes on to explain what it is they are doing: "We are here to make limbo tolerable, to ferry wounded souls across the river of dread until the point where hope is dimly visible. And then stop the boat, shove 'em in the water and make 'em swim."

We should remember that the membership of self-enrollment constitutes a form of doubling of the formal membership. The formal membership does not disappear because of self-enrollment. This also means that there is a coexistence of two forms of inclusion and exclusion; the formal form of inclusion and exclusion, and the self-inclusion and self-exclusion of self-enrollment, which I have previously discussed. The two forms are obviously linked and one of the most significant links in this context is that when the formal organization observes the absence of self-inclusion, this becomes a criterion for a formal dismissal. Thus, today we will often hear a manager say: "We have given her so many possibilities. She has not accepted them. Now it is our duty to let her go." Self-exclusion in the code of love leads to firing in the code of law.

My point of entry is the semantics of layoffs. I argue that, in addition to the legal semantics about the correct way to fire someone, we see the emergence of a semantics about layoffs with love parallel to the modern professional divorce semantics. This semantics does not suggest that firing someone is a loving act, but it relates strategically to the break-up as precisely an emotional break, that is, it is a semantics that recognizes the fact that the employee's relationship with the organization can have the intimate characteristics of a partnership.

When self-enrollment shapes passion as a medium, we see a structural coupling of the organizational system and the love system, which colors the elements of the organizational system and draws paradoxes from the love systems over into the organization. From the perspective of the form of decision, the love system's construction of a semantics of the break-up can be observed (productively misunderstood) as a semantics of firing. In other words, my thesis is that the double membership – formal and self-enrolled – also produces a double figure of layoffs – the formal layoff, which is coded legally, and a highly intimate break-up, which is coded passionately.

J. Barton Cunningham proposes a similar idea in his article "Feelings and interpretations during an organization's death", which is about layoffs in the case of "the organization's death". The marriage vows say, "till death do us part", and in Cunningham's article it is precisely the death of the company which separates employees. He writes: "An organization's death may have much in common with what an individual experiences when they discover that they or their loved ones have a terminal illness" (Cunningham 1997, p. 472). Often, there is unwillingness to accept the separation: "Like a loving relative who has lost a loved one, there are reactions of unwillingness to accept and adjust but to continue the fight to preserve what was" (Cunningham 1997, p. 483).

Thus, the semantics of layoffs provides a way to observe the conditions of possibility for the intimate strategies. Love communication and strategic planning are not each other's opposites. Nor were they opposites in the 1700s at the origins of the love semantics. Reading Don Juan is like reading strategy literature of an advanced kind. And the literature on layoffs is precisely strategic and recognizes passion as the communicative medium.

Finally, the semantics on firing provide a way to study changes in the memory function of membership as it moves towards self-enrollment. My thesis here is that there is a doubling of memory into formal and strategic memory.

THE SEMANTICS OF DIVORCE

Since my focus is not divorce as such but only the way in which its semantics plays a certain part in my argument concerning the semantics of layoffs, I have decided to settle on a rather limited archive. I have primarily focused on books and articles from the past decade and I have not followed the archive to its limit in the same way that I usually do in semantic analyses. Thus, my analysis does not claim to be a comprehensive analysis of the semantics of divorce. It has been written with an eye to the semantics of layoffs and I limit myself to observations of how a set of central questions are observed and conceived. I do not enter into specific questions such as where the child is going to live after divorce, and so on.

Taking a broad glance at the divorce literature, we observe certain characteristics: There are many conversation books (and conversation pieces on radio and television) in which a journalist leads a conversation among a group of people who have been through a divorce. Different books prioritize different perspectives: The child's perspective, the parents' perspective, the perspective of the new wife, the grandparents' perspective, and so on. The basic ethos is generally that conversation promotes understanding, which the participants can then make use of. There are also interview books that emphasize the description of personal experience in relation to divorce. Then, there are quite a few self-help books providing advice and counseling. These are often written by psychologists, but not always. Often, there are two professions involved: psychology and law, and in that way the question of divorce is continually split into the purely legal divorce on the one hand, and on the other hand the question of how to make it a "good" divorce.

The Good Divorce

A repeated theme is "the good divorce". Divorce is always defined as something fundamentally evil. And the question asked is whether this evil can be handled in a good way. In her conversation book *The Good Divorce (DK: Den gode skilsmisse)*, Irma Lauridsen writes: "But does divorce relegate you to chaos, guilt, sleepless nights, and thoughts about being a loser and that this is the end of the good life? (. . .) Is there a way to create a useful product from the many feelings and actions the divorce generates?" And she goes on: "Could it be that there are indeed good divorces, or at least decent ones? (. . .) Can a divorce ideally lead to new insights, greater self-awareness – and a better future life?" (Lauridsen 2009, pp. 7–8, own translations). The rest of the book is about the possibility of answering "yes" to these questions. Through many interviews and conversations, the book seeks out this "yes" and its particular manifestations in different divorce scenarios. The possibility of the "yes" relies on the distinction between choosing to cooperate as opposed to working against each other.

Another book by Dorthe Boss Kyhn is called *The Perfect Divorce* (DK: *Den perfekte skilsmisse*). In her introduction, Kyhn writes:

> I think that most people would reject the idea that there is such a thing as a perfect divorce! We can attempt it and we can suppress all our anger, bitterness, and pain when we are faced with the situation. But I believe that there is no such thing as the perfect divorce. How can something be perfect, which is about breaking up something as fundamental as a family? However, that does not change the fact that the book you hold in your hands has this provocative subtitle. Perhaps, if we say the word out loud, we can make it function as well and as perfectly as humanly possible when getting divorced. And if not for our own sake, then at least for the many children whose foundation is suddenly pulled from under them. (Kyhn 2007, p. 7)

Again, we see this insistence on the possibility of the good within the bad. This book does not only focus on cooperation but is about each of the parties playing a leadership role. If one does not take charge of the situation, the inner evil logic of divorce will set the agenda: "It might be difficult to handle separation and new routines, but we the parents are the adults – we are the ones who need to help the children make it through, and we don't do that by throwing mud at each other and fighting over the rights to the children" (Kyhn 2007, p. 8).

Children

The children are everywhere the most central point of reference in the construction of the good divorce. Obviously, there are numerous questions concerning children and divorce, for example: When to tell them that Mom and Dad are getting a divorce? Who tells them? How do the children react? Where will they live? What is the best way to share the children?

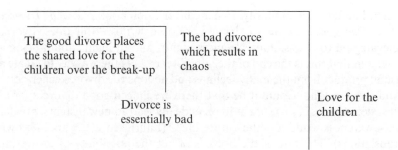

Figure 6.1   Children and the good divorce

How to share responsibility for the children? Ultimately, however, there is one element that dominates everything. Mom and Dad are getting a divorce. The parents have made the decision. The children undeservedly become victims of a divorce that causes their entire world to collapse. As Dorthe Kyhn writes: "The child might experience loneliness and become incapable of processing the emotions caused by the ongoing disagreements between the parents. So consider your child – speak nicely about and to the other parent in the presence of the child" (Kyhn 2007, p. 115, own translation). Likewise, psychologist Lotte Tvede writes:

> If the parents are always fighting and treat each other with a lack of respect it will greatly influence the child's ability to work through the crisis that a divorce will inevitably represent to her (. . .) If the parents are incapable of controlling their feelings – and perhaps even include the child in them – it can have very damaging effects, also long-term (. . .) If parents are exceedingly unhappy or angry, they need to try to find a different outlet for their emotions in order to protect the children. (Tvede 2007, p. 50, own translation)

The notion of the undeserving children who the parents love produces the imperative of having to effect a decent divorce for their sake. The concept of children becomes the constitutive other, which makes it possible for the good to be reintroduced into the bad. Because both of us love our children and because we can acknowledge each other's love for the children, we have to take joint responsibility for a loving divorce even if we no longer love each other. I have formalized this idea in Figure 6.1.

Figure 6.1 appears again and again in the literature both as good advice with examples of how it can be achieved, but also as a frightening example of how bad things can turn out if both parties do not acknowledge each other's love for the children and choose the good path in the land of evil. One example is the story of Jørgen and Jette in Irma Lauridsen's (2009) book. Here, Jørgen is interviewed about his relationship with Jette and about the divorce process. When Jørgen meets Jette, she already has a son. According to Jørgen, he chose both Jette and the boy. Jette and Jørgen get married and live together for eight years. Jette then meets someone else and Jørgen and Jette get divorced. Jørgen unambiguously considers himself the father of the boy, but when they get divorced Jette refuses to recognize Jørgen as the father or to consider his and the boy's emotional attachment to each other. She does not grant Jørgen visitation rights after the divorce and also does not see any reason why they would see each other despite her son's explicit wish to do so. The story works to show how the lack of recognition of the other's love for the child makes the good divorce impossible and renders it vehemently vicious. The book sums up the story like this: "Jørgen tells the story of his marriage to Jette who had a son when they met. Jørgen did not want to lose the boy after the divorce but Jette rejected his wishes with the reason that he did not have any legal rights to Kasper because he is not his father. Jørgen is now 54 years old. He loves Jette's boy as if he were his own son but has to fight to see the boy in secret" (Lauridsen 2009, p. 100, own translation).

The Heilberg/Wivel family appears in one of the books as an example of the good divorce. The heading of their story is "We worked at it." In the interview, the father says: "But I want to say that at no point did we have to discuss the fact that we wanted and had to behave properly. It was important for us that the children were doing as well as possible and sensed the divorced as little as possible" (Kyhn 2007, p. 120, own translation). The mother goes on:

> I think it was a matter of willpower on our part. It was important that everyone felt ok – even though we were getting divorced. I believed that if two people had at one point been so much in love that they decided to have three children together, then it makes no sense to not be able to be in the same room. I believe – and I thought a lot about it back then – that the most important thing for you had to be that Dad and I still cared about each other. We might not be able to live together and all that, but the fact that we care about each other so that you did not have to see your parents fight, that was important to me. (Kyhn 2007, p. 120, own translation)

There are two distinctions in play here, linked to "the good divorce for the sake of the children". Clearly, in the semantics articulated by the mother, the question is not whether or not she sincerely cares about her ex-husband but precisely that she commits to caring about her ex-husband because she loves her children. Her feelings for her ex-husband, in other words, are not contingent. They follow necessarily from her love for her children and sometimes require willpower. The other distinction, which is folded into itself, is the difference between dependence and independence.

Marriage implies choice of dependence. Divorce is about regaining independence. However, according to both parents' statements here, pure independence can only be gained at the children's expense. Continued dependence is entered into as a premise for regaining independence in the good divorce. In that sense, divorce does not represent a final termination of the relationship but simply the indication of new conditions for the relationship. Karl Moxnes writes in his book about "gentle divorce": "It is ironic, but while they have decided that they can no longer be married, they have to develop a shared effort around the children" (Moxnes 2004, p. 105, own translation).

The father from the above example is quoted as saying: "You have to tell yourself that the other party sees things differently than you and accept that that is the way it is." His ex-wife goes on: "I don't really believe that even though you force yourself to think rationally and consider the thoughts and feelings of the other, this is not only what drives you to rebuild a good life. It is primarily the awareness that it should not hurt the children" (Kyhn 2007, p. 124, own translation). Love communication defines the partner as the significant other and contains an expectation about the internalization of the other's perspective on the world. Divorce, in turn, can be described as a de-installment of one's partner as the significant other in one's life. Getting a divorce implies that one is no longer expected to internalize the other's perspective on the world. However, the above example indicates a semantics, which twists this logic so that the good divorce is seen as a loving termination of love. However, the loving termination of love is only possible through the installation of a strategic perspective on love, so that love is no longer necessarily something one surrenders to and exists within, but instead a game whose rules one chooses to follow to obtain a strategic gain. And the strategic gain is the children. Through love of the children, it becomes strategically possible to maintain the other as significant other while phasing out that very position. In other words, the articulated semantics constitutes the possibility of strategic relating in the language of love.

Grief Work and the Personal Crisis

A different set of texts take up divorce as personal crisis, where the good divorce is one in which one lives through a personal crisis and emerges on the other side equipped with new personal insight and possibilities. As an example, Lotte Tvede writes: "The divorce can become the grounds for re-discovering sides of yourself, which did not fit the relationship and were hidden away" (Tvede 2007, p. 19, own translation). This segment of the literature is dominated by psychologists. It focuses on personal feelings, learning processes and dreams, and the reader is often presented with a number of exercises. These might be reflection exercises aimed at describing and recognizing one's own feelings or exercises in which one has to put words to one's dreams, either present ones or, if one finds this difficult, past dreams from another period in one's life.

The concept of crisis as a description of a transformative period is central to this literature. Lotte Tvede defines crisis as "a situation in which previous experience is not sufficient to handle the present situation" (Tvede 2007, p. 30, own translation). Often, the writer divides the crisis into successive phases. Lotte Tvede describes how each phase creates preconditions for the progressing process of transformation: "If the emotions become 'encased', the crisis work does not progress and you never arrive at a new phase where you dare connect with others again" (Tvede 2007, p. 34, own translation). Psychotherapist Per Holm Knudsen makes a distinction between the phases of the divorce and the phase of the grief process. The phases of the divorce are: (1) Learning to live without my partner in practical terms, (2) Loss of illusions (I thought it was this way, but now I have to acknowledge...), (3) Acceptance of the past as it was (stand by one's feelings), (4) Acceptance of the present (It is what it is), and (5) Orientation towards the future (http://psyx.dk/skilsmisse/skilsmissefaser. htm). The grief process looks like this: (1) Acknowledgement of loss (what is lost IS lost), (2) Resolution of different emotions produced by loss, (3) Development of new skills, (4) Productive channeling of emotional energy (life is good again, and the loss is a part of my life story) (http://psyx.dk/tab.htm).

The Law

Finally, law is another theme. However, it is always defined as clearly separated from the above questions. The legal divorce is the shadow of the loving divorce, and it is considered a sign of failure if disagreements about the children result in a legal decision.

Therefore, the legal semantics is essentially about warning against taking conflicts to court. Moxnes puts it rather unambiguously: "I strongly advise parents against going to court over how to share their children; it may damage the children and most often makes it even more difficult to establish successful future cooperation" (Moxnes 2004, p. 157, own translation). The warning against legal action as the solution, thus, is based in part on the notion that it might damage the children but also on the view that legal action is a non-solution. She explains:

> The court's responsibility is to reach a verdict, that is, to make a decision. Most people and many judges consider the decision that is reached to be just and a

basis for cooperation between parents, which is designed to provide good conditions under which for the children to grow up. It does not always work that way. First, many parents do not respect the court's decision, precisely because they don't believe that it is fair or beneficial to the child. (Moxnes 2004, p. 157, own translation)

Thus, the line of argumentation is that in the case of divorce, legal action works differently than normally. It does not transform the conflict since the legal decision is often disregarded by the parties. The point is: there is no alternative to a loving divorce.

THE SEMANTICS OF FIRING

In this section my archival material consists of a rather heterogeneous mix of texts from professional legal explications of laws pertaining to hiring and firing via conversation books about losing one's job, guidelines from management organizations and unions, a wealth of articles from trade periodicals and consultancy books. A shared genre characteristic is the extensive use of "cut&paste" across different texts. Not only individual sentences but also often long passages or entire pages are repeated in much of the material.

Layoffs as Divorce

As will become apparent below, clear analogies are drawn today between the semantics of divorce and the semantics of firing. Most of these analogies consist of parallel questions and shared references concerning personal development, coaching, crises, phases, and so on. But there are also explicit connections, where layoffs are directly compared to divorces. One article, for example, is entitled "Being fired can be more difficult than divorce" (www.jobzonen.dk/for20%virksomheder/produkter/produktoverblik/genplacering). Gitte Schramm has even written a book about layoffs entitled *The Professional Divorce. How to Handle Being Fired*. She writes:

> Some employees find the process of being fired more difficult than a divorce. Remember that we often spend more of our waking hours at work than with our spouse. Plus a large part of our identity is located in our jobs. Firing, therefore, is a complicated process, which should be handled professionally by the management (. . .) Thus, you should consider firings from a broader perspective. And you will understand the kind of responsibility you carry on your shoulder in the context of firings. As a manger, it is your job to ensure that fired employees are given a dignified resignation. (Schramm 2008, p. 8, own translation)

And she concludes her book with these words: "Even though it is difficult and unpleasant, it is important that you as manager will consider it your responsibility to ensure that the divorce happens as professionally as possible in relation to all involved parties" (Schramm 2008, p. 26, own translation).

In the book *Bossa Nova – Management on the Ground* (DK: *Bossa Nova – Ledelse ude på gulvet*), Rumle Hammerich compares the work relationship to the love relationship and firing to a break-up:

> You have to remember that fired employees need to construct an image of the enemy. There is a certain level of drama in a relationship that is being determined, whether it is a love relationship or a professional relationship. It is ok to hate someone for a while and be really pissed off and kick a cardboard box and melt down. It is a human process, which there needs to be room for. This means that it should not necessarily be easy for the leader who delivers the message. As a leader, you have to be willing to accept the role of "bad guy" – and the burden it can be. (Jacoby and Bræstrup 2007, p. 226, own translation)

Finally, Rikke Høgsted compares being fired to going through a divorce. Her perspective is that of the fired employee: "When you lose a job that you liked, there will be feelings of grief for a while. In the same way that, right after the firing, you might think poorly of the workplace. You can both grieve the loss of your job and curse it at the same time, not unlike a divorce where you grieve the loss of your husband or wife while also being very angry at them" (Høgsted 2009a, p. 36, own translation). The comparison pertains to the loss of one's significant other and the grief that follows. The organization is the significant other, which one has lost and for whom one grieves. Thus, for Høgsted it is a question of how one handles one's grief. She speaks of the flow of grief and sees grief as an oscillating movement between three questions: "1. What have I lost?", "2. What do I have left?", and "3. How do I want to use it?" (Høgsted 2009a, p. 38, own translation).

The Sensitive Manager and the Dignified Layoff

When terms of employment are considered to shape identity and as having a wider reach than the relationship with one's spouse, and when being fired is framed along the same lines as breaking up with one's partner, the manager, in turn, is responsible for breaking off a highly intimate relationship and is assigned, in the words of Gitte Schramm, a special responsibility for the rejected employee.

Ultimately, this has certain implications for the codification of the dismissal notification. Giving notice to someone is no longer simply a formal resignation of an employee, and many leaders speak about their personal difficulties related to firing someone. Development director Frederik Bruun Rasmussen states:

> It is never pleasant to have to fire someone. I once had to fire a man who had a wife and two kids and a car. That was not easy. I could not fall asleep the night before. I lay in bed brooding for a long time. I had to write down what I was going to say to him. How do you formulate this kind of message? How do you say it in the best way? What are you going to do if he breaks down crying? How do you respond if he slams the door and flips you off? You have to have already thought about these scenarios. I was very relieved once I had said it. But of course I was left with a lump in my throat: what will happen with the employee in the future? (Jacoby and Bræstrup 2007, pp. 118–19, own translation)

The literature frames layoffs as heavy emotional tolls on the leader: "For many leaders, letting people go belongs to the most difficult part of the executive position. This is mainly a sign of health that bears witness to empathy and responsibility, but it can also become excessive. For some managers, layoffs also result in mood swings, sleep problems, and a lack of interest in social activities, food, sex, and perhaps even work" (Høgsted 2009b, p. 1, own translation). Gitte Schramm's advice to managers who have had to fire someone is to allow themselves to speak to others about the situation: "It is important that you acknowledge your response and make sure to talk about the way the experience affected you" (Schramm 2010, p. 37, own translation).

It has probably always been difficult to conduct layoffs and it is not ultimately sociologically relevant whether or not it pains managers to fire people. What is interesting, however, is the fact that these difficulties have become relevant to communication and become part of a particular self-description semantics pertaining to the firing manager. It has become relevant for leaders to ascribe emotional difficulties to themselves in relation to layoffs. This contributes to a particular construction of the question of layoffs as a highly intimate (and emotional) phenomenon.

In the same way that divorce is defined as an evil, layoffs are defined as awful, and in the same way that good is sought in the evil divorce, much of the semantics about layoffs today concerns the dignified layoff. The dignified layoff is not defined as one where the leader is sincerely upset about the situation. The dignified layoff is not simply defined in opposition to a cold layoff. Every emotional layoff is not loving. Chief executive officer (CEO) Brian Petersen reflects on the first time he had to fire someone:

> I remember when it was and who it was. I had a team of three people in which one of them did not work well. My emotions were conflicted. On one hand

I knew that firing the employee was the right decision. On the other hand I thought: "What am I doing to this man? What am I doing to his life?" What helped me was to put aside the conflicting emotions and put myself in his shoes: "What would be a good solution for him?" If you allow your emotions to take over, you are not helping the person. He left our company but felt that we had treated him well and has consulted me ever since whenever he has changed jobs. (Jelbo 2009, p. 27, own translation)

The question raised in this quote is about how to deliver an unloving message in a loving way while standing by the unloving message. Emotions are seen as simultaneously entirely relevant and yet also as an obstruction. Firing someone in a loving way is not possible if the leader did not think "What am I doing to this man? What am I doing to his life?" On the other hand, however, firing someone in a loving way would also not be possible if the leader was unable to (lovingly) disregard this feeling in his delivery of the message.

Standing by the unloving message means remaining loyal to the decision to fire someone. One must not create doubt about the decision that one is in the process of carrying out. That would be anything but loving:

Some employees might cry. This makes it more difficult for the leader because his feelings are affected by the situation as well. Still, he needs to remain in control of the conversation. If he does not stick to his role and begins to comfort the employee, he runs the risk of adding insult to injury. On the other hand, he must also be able to express his compassion. It will be remembered if he is noticeably affected by the situation. But his message has to remain clear. The leader cannot be disloyal to the decision to fire the employee or advance empty promises about future employment. (Chefgruppen HK/Kommunal 2009, p. 9, own translation)

Thus, the important thing is that the leader is expected to show compassion while maintaining the ability to break up without creating doubt about the firing. Generally, it becomes important to speak of emotional difficulties with respect to firing someone so that, in the specific situation, they can appear as someone who "puts aside" their emotions.

The unloving aspect of firing someone, today, is about the determination of a more or less intimate relationship. It is not only the determination of a legal relation and a financial transaction. It is also an intimate work relation between leader and employee. One article puts it this way: "Both employee and manager has had the experience of being equal partners, but this illusion is shattered with the introduction of the lay-off notice, which makes it a visible fact that employment is also a power relation in which the management acts on behalf of the owners, whether these are stockholders or the 'political owners' in the public sector" (Høgsted 2009b,

p. 2, own translation). The firing causes the existing relationship to be re-evaluated. Firing someone raises the question of whether there was ever another aspect to the relationship outside economic exchange.

Therefore, in this light there must also be limits to how many partners we can break with in one day: "A rule of thumb says that a Manager cannot dismiss more than five–six employees in one day. Then he gradually loses the ability to be sensitive to the employees' situation" (Chefgruppen HK/Kommunal 2009, p. 5). Although the dignified dismissal is not a simple negation of a cold layoff, the laying off situation makes "cold leadership" visible. It is expressed by Dion Sørensen in the following manner: "it may be difficult to understand, but there are actually leaders, for whom sackings are easy, yes maybe even attractive. And the reason is simply that business is full of men in suits who are emotionally blunt (. . .) A round of layoffs is a great opportunity to evaluate one's managerial colleagues. Do the managers show compassion and understanding for those being laid off, or do they show clearly that it does not mean anything to them?" (Sørensen 2009, pp. 85–6). Sørensen believes that when one has passed a layoff round one should layoff the managers who have exhibited psychopathic traits.

The Remaining Employees

Like divorce, there is a third party in an organization, who is a part of the family and who is affected by the break-up. The remaining employees are discussed in line with divorce-stricken children. They, too, are going through a divorce, although they have not made the decision, and they may begin to doubt how the management sees them. Firing someone is an attempt to end an organizational relationship with one specific employee, but the act also ends a whole range of collegial relationships and weakens the self-evidence of the remaining relationships. Medical Director Jørgen Lund puts it this way: "Those who 'survive' a round of layoffs often experience stress because of the many changes, the loss of colleagues, and fear of additional layoffs" (Løvbom 2008, own translation). Another article describes the situation in this way: "The layoff conversation is awful because almost all people who get laid off experience a sense of shock when they receive the notice; a shock that might cause a greater or smaller crisis for the person who has been laid off. In addition, it is awful because it sends the rest of the organization into a state of coma so that it takes time and an incredible amount of management energy to recreate culture, motivation, and work climate" (Otkjær 2009, p. 32, own translation). It is difficult to isolate the layoffs because the employee relation is not simply a formal relation but a nexus of partnerships.

This is why the semantics of layoffs addresses time and again the importance of caring for the remaining employees: "It is difficult to underestimate the situation and reaction of the remaining employees" (AS3 Outplacement 2009, p. 39, own translation). Vibeke Skytte from The Danish Association of Managers and Executives says: "It is as important to take care of those who remain. You have to focus on the future. Therefore, it is important to come up with a strategy for how to communicate this to the organization" (Skou 2008, p. 2, own translation). Chefgruppen HK/ Kommunal writes about those who remain: "It is a question of smoothing out emotions and creating closure so that the organization can move on. It can only move on if employees are motivated. The leadership must listen to criticism from employees and to their feelings and must articulate how they think about it (. . .) The conversation about criticism and emotions should last no longer than one hour. After that, managers and employees need to begin looking forward" (Chefgruppen HK/Kommunal 2009, p. 9, own translation).

If the organization is kept together by partnerships, layoffs will affect the entire organization: "The organization as a whole can be affected by decreasing efficiency. Motivation disappears, energy decreases, and passivity might spread across the organization" (Schramm 2008, p. 18, own translation). There is frequent mention of concepts such as energy loss, cold and cooling: "Like those who have been laidoff, those who remain go through a transitional process in order to regain their previous energy. The company's working climate has been put in the freezer" (Otkjær 2009, p. 33, own translation).

Dion Sørensen compares the organization affected by layoffs to a family in the middle of a break-up. His comparison does not employ the image of the divorce-stricken family but the family affected by forcible removal of children:

> The same problem occurs when authorities forcibly remove a child from its family due to neglect and places the child in foster care. Without a simultaneous effort to help not only the child but also the biological family, all the progress that might have been achieved during the child's stay in foster care would be lost as soon as the child is brought back into the biological family. In other words, the individual is part of the system that it partakes in, and the system has to continually integrate its individual members so they are in alignment with the general program. (Sørensen 2009, p. 103, own translation)

His point is that an organization affected by layoffs is like a scattered family in which the individual family member no longer knows her place and is doubtful as to what actually constitutes and defines the family. To Sørensen, it is a question of reuniting the family: "What meets the eye after this kind of process, however, is a group of employees who grieve the loss of a bunch of colleagues and also are concerned about what this means for them. The remaining employees need very clear information very quickly about what the plan is for the new organization and how they fit into the big picture" (Sørensen 2009, p. 97, own translation).

The challenge, according to Sørensen, is to recreate partnerships among the remaining employees. Thus, it is critical, in the aftermath of layoffs, to intensify teambuilding efforts and create events that bring people together and facilitate new relationships among employees: "Following structural changes, it is advisable, in addition to team activities, to create events for the whole organization. Not everything should be fun and games but it is a big advantage if employees can have fun together" (Sørensen 2009, p. 112, own translation). The family needs to be brought back together: "It is healthy to bring out laughter after a round of layoffs and it is also a good basis for creating new relations among people. In an organization, we often cooperate most productively with those we know best, which is why it is a good idea to organize events that provide employees with the chance to meet people from other teams and departments" (Sørensen 2009, p. 112, own translation). An example of such an event could be the game "A brand new day" (DK: *En helt ny dag*) designed by the Danish company Resonanz. The game focuses on the remaining employees and is designed to "mark a new beginning – a brand new day, and the development of focus and positive expectations about the desired future. A crisis also represents the possibility to rethink and create change" (Resonanz 2010, own translation). Management is defined as the supervision of collegial relations. The question is not whether or not layoffs in themselves are loving, or whether management care for the remaining employees, but whether management assumes responsibility for allowing employees to care for each other.

The notion of working climate among the remaining employees, who have not been laid off and whom the organization still loves, installs an imperative about having to ensure, for the sake of the remaining employees (and thus the organization), a dignified form of layoff. This is formalized in Figure 6.2.

Notions of climate and atmosphere become the constitutive other that makes it possible to reintroduce dignity into the undignified. However, in this case the re-entry takes on an asymmetrical form since it is uncertain whether the person who has been laid off wishes to assume responsibility for the climate among the remaining employees. It is a bit difficult to assign the same status of innocence to the working climate as to shared children in the context of a divorce.

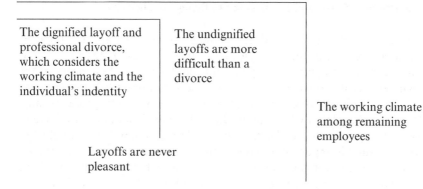

Figure 6.2   Working climate and dignified layoffs

The Uninterrupted Relationship

One of the issues in the literature on divorce is that the divorce does not fully terminate a relationship but changes it because mutual dependency, particularly when children are involved, can be experienced as stronger than before the divorce. Similarly, the literature on layoffs also emphasizes that the relationship is not entirely over after the layoff. Those who have been laid off represent both risks and possibilities for the organization. This pertains primarily to the organization's reputation both internally and in the environment: "The company has to make itself attractive in order to recruit the best employees and ensure its basis for recruitment. It has become critical for the company to have a good image, not only in relation to customers but also in relation to future and potential employees (. . .) And it quickly becomes known if a company has a tradition of kicking out old employees when they no longer have any use for them" (Schramm 2008, p. 7). Here, we see the articulation on the risk side of a dependence on laid-off employees in terms of reputation.

However, laid-off employees also represent the possibility of a positive continuation of the relationship on different terms: "It is important to pay attention to the fact that most laid-off employees often find employment within the same field and on a similar level in a new organization, and it does not require a great deal of imagination to think that you might one day run into one of your past employees in the role of customer, supplier, or competitor" (Schramm 2008, p. 7, own translation). In other words, layoffs have to happen in a way that considers the possibility that it does not represent a final termination of the relationship but merely a transformation of it.

The Personal Crisis and Its Phases: On Being Coached Out

The semantics on divorce addresses the personal crisis and the possibility of coming out of the other side as a "bigger" person. This question is framed in the semantics on layoffs in a similar way. The concept of the dignified layoff includes the organization's responsibility for ensuring that the employee assumes responsibility for moving on professionally. However, the person who communicates the layoff does not also have to assume responsibility for helping the employee to move on. As Fellinger writes: "But it is important to understand that since you are the messenger, you become the hangman in this context. And a hangman does not have the right to comfort the victim" (Fellinger 2005, p. 83, own translation).

But the organization as such can take responsibility, for example, in the property of "outplacement": "the fundamental principle in outplacement advice is that the terminated employee is attached to an external consultant, who works as a sparring partner in the job search process. Outplacement advice is a very central part of lay-off policies, giving the company by choosing this service signals a wish to help the employee further in other employment" (AS3 Outplacement 2008, p. 43, own translation).

The layoff itself is sometimes referred to as loving in the sense that if the reason for it is a dysfunctional, unloving or lukewarm relationship between organization and employee, then it is the manager's duty to fire, and being fired is then conceived as helpful since it liberates the employee in question by allowing her to find a better partner. Dion Sørensen formulates the loving layoff in this way:

> Typically, when someone is fired, it is due to the employee's relationships, mediocre performance, lack of competences, questionable attitude, etc. Most managers find it difficult to deliver this kind of message. Nonetheless, you are probably doing the employee a favor by setting them free if the relationship is not working. Nobody feels good about being in a job where things are not working out, where one's performance is unsatisfactory, and where one's colleagues think that one does not match expectations. This does not mean that the person in question is a bad person. Rather, it is a sign that the employee has not been matched with the right company and the right job. I have still to meet the person who cannot be successful in the right work context. It is about finding the right match and in order to do that, one might have to change companies a few times or lose one's job a few times. Unfortunately, that is often what happens. Indeed, because of our fundamental need for stability, it is often difficult for employees to do what it takes to move on from an employment situation that is not working. A push from a manager can prove to be rather useful. And although it is difficult for managers to fire employees who do not perform well, they can comfort themselves with the thought that they are probably doing both their employee and company a favor in the long run, and that

the employee more than likely will look back upon the decision and think of it as the right one. (Sørensen 2009, pp. 71–1, own translation)

Here, the manager is defined as someone who breaks up with the employee and at the same time sets the employee free. It would basically be wrong for the manager to retain the employee in a workplace if there is no true love, that is, the match is wrong. It might be difficult for the employee, but ultimately, it is considered a loving act to fire the employee and allow her to move on with her life. As Dion Sørensen writes: "Life is a roller coaster – it goes up and down and we actually learn a lot when it goes down" (Sørensen 2009, p. 120, own translation). He proposes five pieces of good advice to the laid-off employee: "1. Acknowledge your situation, 2. Accept the help people offer you, 3. Think positively, 4. Build new skills, 5. Work hard and be creative" (Sørensen 2009, p. 121, own translation). He writes a fictitious letter to a laid-off employee: "You did not choose to be fired. The decision was made for you by others. However, it is entirely your decision how you deal with being fired and with your plans for the future. You can choose to take a pessimistic view of the future and confirm for yourself that nothing is going to work out right. Or you can choose to approach the situation in a positive way and tell yourself: 'It might take some time but there is a job out there for me and I will do anything in my power to get it'" (Sørensen 2009, p. 122, own translation). The manager has set the fired person free, and now that person must assume responsibility for her freedom.

The notion that the fired person may ultimately gain something from being fired is a repeated figure in the semantics. Being fired is fundamentally seen as an awful event: "When you lose your job, you lose a meaning component in your story about yourself. This constitutes a loss of something immaterial, a loss of a part of yourself. Many people have a good deal of personal identity tied up in their work, and the result is the loss of your work identity" (Schramm 2008, p. 17, own translation). However, there is a solution. Similar to the divorce semantics, being fired is perceived as transformational: something is over and something new has to begin. And any such crisis has its phases. Chefgruppen HK/Kommunal distinguishes between four phases in the reaction of the laid-off person: (1) The immediate reaction, (2) The delayed reaction, (3) Processing and (4) Re-orientation. These phases are virtually identical to the phases of divorce, and there is also an obvious overlap in the bibliographies to books and articles about personal crises. And there is ultimately hope for the laid-off employee, even though many describe the crisis as extensive (one to one and a half years). About the final phase of the crisis, "reorientation", we read: "Reorientation represents the fourth and final stage of the crisis. The employee has managed to create some distance to the firing and can speak about it without being emotionally affected. He is able to focus on new possibilities, and if the crisis is overcome he usually comes out of it stronger than before" (Chefgruppen HK/Kommunal 2009, p.7, own translation).

The Law

Like the literature on divorce, the semantics about the loving layoff has a shadow-semantics about the legal layoff (Personalestyrelsen/State Employer's Authority 2004). Today, there is extensive legal articulation of layoffs from legal justification of layoffs, legal procedures for the decision to layoff, legal procedures for delivering the message to someone, options for the laid-off employee, and so on. Thus, layoff law has undergone a major development in the construction of the specific layoff. Here, it is only important to point out that despite its scope, organizations do not consider layoff laws functionally equivalent with the dignified layoff. While the dignified layoff has to obviously also be legally correct, the fact that a layoff is legally correct does not make it dignified or loving in the layoff semantics, which is why we see a doubling of the layoff operation into a legal layoff and a loving break-up.

CONCLUSION: WHEN STRATEGY IS LOVE AND LOVE IS STRATEGIC

What we see is that passion as a medium not only establishes a particular language for self-enrollment, but also for the determination of membership, both self-resignation as well as the organization's termination of the relationship. We see the emergence of personalized membership termination, emphasizing the importance of layoffs being not only legally correct but also loving.

The double membership gives us the double layoff. The formal layoff is about the termination of a membership contract, and although people involved in a formal layoff might obviously experience a range of different feelings, these feelings are not considered relevant to the communication. The central aspect is the compliance with formal layoff procedures designed to prevent the development of conflicts in the context of layoffs. The formal layoff has a number of built-in tensions because the code of law precisely excludes the question of justice. Thus, layoffs can be legally correct and still perceived as unjust, and this question cannot be addressed within the organization. The question of just layoffs is only present precisely as the excluded question – a question that cannot be addressed.

In the loving layoff and the termination of the membership of self-enrollment, a layoff is the suspension of a highly intimate relationship between the laid-off employee on the one hand and manager, colleagues, citizens (external partners) on the other. In a love relationship, passion is transformed over time to become shared history, and the shared history is what makes the relationship "steady". In this kind of relationship, one recognizes oneself in the other's expectations of oneself. In this context, a layoff constitutes a much more wide-reaching break-up that includes the self-relation of the involved parties because it is already folded into the expectations about the other's expectations. Loss, and not least loss of oneself, is part of the break-up, which includes a necessary reinterpretation of one's own history (Luhmann 2010, p. 54). One can no longer recognize oneself in the other's expectations, and the worldview that relied on the significant other breaks down. Contrary to the formal layoff, the loving layoff is precisely highly personal.

In conclusion, there are a number of points I want to touch upon regarding "the loving layoff". The first one pertains to organizational memory. Luhmann stresses the fact that formal membership performs a memory function in the organization. This memory function concerns the specific kind of structural coupling between organization and psychic system. Through membership, the organization is able to always compare the role and the generalized motives an employee was originally hired to fulfill with the actual development of the employee's contribution. This allows the organization to adjust its expectations about the employee in question and her interaction. The termination of membership abolishes the structural coupling with the employee and the organization is free to focus on something else. With the loving layoff, however, the problem looks different. First, memory functions differently in the membership of self-enrollment. When the generalized motive is established as personal motivation *as if* someone's motivation is the organization's, then the organization can only remember and adjust second-order expectations; that is, expectations about the employee's production of expectations about her own activities. Moreover, a loving layoff entails a transformation of memory rather than its abolishment. In a loving layoff, the employee is forgotten in the formal communication but continues to be remembered in the strategic communication in which the employee still represents both possibilities and threats to the organization and therefore is perceived as part of a reduced and changed but still existing reliance.

My second point is that love-codified communication does not exclude a strategic communicative perspective, almost quite the reverse. In the construction of the figure of "the loving layoff", a strategic perspective on the layoff and a strategic choice of a dignified layoff do not equal "false love". It is considered to be loving to show a certain distance from one's own emotions. And obviously, the decision to lovingly lay someone off is a strategic choice. This does not only pertain to the specific conditions of the highly personal codifications of layoffs but also to the management of highly personal relations in general. Love-codified communication does not preclude a strategic perspective, actually quite the reverse, since it opens up for an entire pallet of strategic relating to the highly personal and the intimately relational, whereas other strategic perspectives (for example, economic, political) would eradicate precisely these elements in their construction of the strategic actor as a rational actor with given preferences.

Clearly, the modern semantics on layoffs has framed a number of themes and concepts which run parallel to the semantics on divorce: (1) the re-entry of love into the disastrous divorce and layoff with the expectation of a loving un-installment of the significant other, (2) the doubling of emotions in the person initiating the break-up/layoff into "disregarded" emotions and strategic compassion, which remains loyal to the break-up, (3) the introduction of a third party (the children and remaining employees respectively), who also goes through a divorce while remaining outside the situation and who has not partaken in or been a part of the decision; an introduction which insists that the break has to be done in a loving way because other loved ones are watching and reflect themselves in the treatment of the rejected one, (4) the fact that the one who breaks up is responsible for caring for both parties and gives the other the freedom to find a new significant other who might be a better match, and (5) finally, the notion of the break-up as a new beginning, a process of transformation, which is both the work of grief but which may also provide strength and open up new possibilities and dreams. These parallels bear witness to the set of different questions that come into the picture when the organization or person is codified in the medium of passion. The organization is not free to choose to address certain aspects of love communication and disregard others. There is an entire package of expectation resulting from the observation of "the whole employee" who is "entrepreneurial", "responsible", and so on. The modern semantics about layoff represents a good example of this. It is not easy to combine a highly personal management style with an impersonal layoff. The layoff becomes highly personal as well – even in the case of mass layoffs. And as we have seen, this creates a specific set of challenges.

The question is whether we can draw further conclusions? Despite the fact that a more comprehensive study could have been done, it is clear that we are witnessing the creation of a form of divorce culture with a particular semantics of self-description concerning "the good divorce". And just as apparent is the formation of a particular culture of layoffs, a particular semantics of self-description pertaining to "the dignified layoff". Might these two cultures be reinforcing each other? Might the culture of divorce make it easier to develop a culture of layoffs and vice versa? I am aware of the fact that the present study is far from substantial enough to unambiguously claim this kind of connection. However, there are sufficient grounds to ask the question. We might ponder whether the thing that links the semantics about divorce to the semantics about layoffs is a particular experience of seriality; an experience of consecutive relationships, which follow each other serially.

Baumann makes the following statement about the experience of seriality with respect to intimate relationships:

> One may even (and one all too often does) believe that love-making skills are bound to grow as the experience accumulates; that the next love will be an experience yet more exhilarating than the one currently enjoyed, though not as thrilling or exciting as the one after next. This is, though, another illusion . . . The kind of knowledge that rises in volume as the string of love episodes grows longer is that of "love" as sharp, short and shocking episodes, shot through by the *a priori* awareness of brittleness and brevity. The kinds of skills that are acquired are those of "finishing quickly and starting from the beginning". (Bauman 2003, p. 5)

This experience of seriality appears to be parallel to the existing expectations in the semantics of layoffs (and more generally in the passion-mediated semantics about the responsibility-taking employee, cf. Chapter 3). These are expectations about enrollment through engagement that defines the organization as the significant other. One remains as long as both parties maintain the ability to reproduce this engagement. If the relation begins to assume the characteristics of a practical arrangement, it needs to be broken up. It was not a match after all. Perhaps the employee needs a little nudging in the form of a layoff in order move on and find a better match with a new engagement, at least for a little while. Transient love, in intimate relationships as well as at work, requires an intensive connection in the present, and once the intensity lessens, both parties must move on. And for the purposes of "finishing quickly and starting from the beginning" we have the semantics about the loving layoff and the loving divorce with a built-in professionalized grief work promising new and better relations "on the other side" of the transformation.

Perhaps we may trace a connection in Denmark between high divorce rates and the flexicurity model on the labor market. If nothing else, we can observe the development of semantics that support personal and organizational management of divorce in the workplace and thus the possibility of serial relationships and job shifts, which provide continual self-enrollment and total engagement.

7. Unbound binding: from employee contracts to partnerships

As we have said, organizations today exist within a regime of transience. Everything changes – or is imagined to be changing. The present moment is at all times the essential moment. And yet nothing can be decided since one needs to maintain the ability in the next similarly essential moment to make a different decision, to change direction and throw oneself at other possibilities.

This creates a particular challenge for the organization on the membership dimension about *how to take responsibility for ensuring that the individual takes responsibility for her own inclusion into the organization, which is continually in the process of becoming something else.* So far I have discussed the ways in which organizations seek to manage this challenge through the form of self-enrollment and its codification in pedagogy, love and play. Moreover, I have shown how organizations develop semantics for their reliance on the emotions of individuals, including the way that the attribution of emotions in organizations to individuals depends on the systemic perspective. Finally, I have addressed certain aspects of the question of the termination of membership within the membership form of self-enrollment.

What I am interested in here is the individual's self-commitment, or rather self-commitment as form, and the management of this self-commitment. As I have discussed, membership is about the way in which organizations make decisions about inclusion and exclusion of individuals. Membership is about the way that the organization addresses psychic systems and structurally links up with them and defines this linking as the decision premise for subsequent decisions within the organization. Organizational membership thus functions at the same time as an employee contract. Employee contracts are viewed by the organization as a specific decision, a membership decision; that is, as a decision about accepting the reliance on a particular person in the environment. However, for the employee the contract does not represent membership but only the commitment to the sale of one's services at a certain price, which makes sense both as a stage in a particular career development and as the possibility to live a particular private life with family, hobbies, and so on. This gives the contract an entirely different meaning and afterlife. In other words, the question of whether or not it is perceived as an employee contract or a membership depends upon the observer. When the contract is observed as contract, it is seen as the external binding of one's freedom. When it is observed as membership, it is seen as an internally decided premise for further decisions.

Therefore, a shift in the form of membership in the direction of self-enrollment has to also effect a shift in the form of the employee contract. This is the shift I am going to address next.

My basic assertion is that the contract becomes challenged in the regime of transience in a way that is equivalent to the challenge of membership. The challenge of the employee contract becomes a question of *how to establish mutually binding expectations between independent units with the expectation that expectations are constantly changing?* This challenge forces the contract in the direction of partnership in which the flexibility pressure is managed by having the contract assume a "meta" function. Instead of making an agreement, it is agreed to make subsequent agreements. It is the creation of a form of agreement, which is simultaneously an agreement and not an agreement; a form of withheld agreement according to which premises are still fluid but assume the character of second-order premises, that is, premises for subsequent premises. This creates a permanent management challenge about the continual recreation of partnerships. Whereas formal first-order contracts could be negotiated and agreed to, and then be functional for a while before being either broken or renegotiated, partnership are never fully agreed upon. They are always under-created and hence require permanent management effort.

I will begin with examples of the way in which the contractual relation becomes rearticulated as a partnership. I then go on to analyze the general contractual form. This analysis will subsequently allow me to analyze partnership as a specific dislocated form of contract.

TOWARD PARTNERSHIP

I have already addressed in Chapter 3 the formation of expectations pertaining to the organization-employee relation as a shared space in which management and employee *share responsibility*. The ministry of Finance, in the mid 1990s, emphasized that "Managers and employees need to assume a shared responsibility" (Ministry of Finance 1998b, p. 5, own translation) and that "public employees and managers have to take on shared responsibility for the development of the institution and its employees" (Ministry of Finance 1995, p. 179, own translation). Stress is placed on the need to create oneself in the other's image: "Institutions and employees need to mutually develop each other" (Ministry of Finance 1995, p. 179, own translation). What is expressed here is an ambition to ensure that the discrete contractual relation between organization and employee becomes much more than that; that it becomes a relational shared space.

We saw a similar semantic figure in Daniel Goleman (Chapter 4), who framed the organization as "the organizational marriage" and the relationship between manager and employee as "the vertical couple". A contract, thus understood, is not simply the linking of different interests. Rather, the ideal situation is for employees to commit to "making our goals and those of our organization one and the same" (Goleman 1998, p. 119). It is the notion that the contractual relationship between organization and employee is transgressed through the creation of shared space.

This sense of shared space manifests itself today in concrete agreements between manager and employee about the responsibility that they share and ways in which to help each other contribute to the organization as a community. Such agreements are often developed in or follow so-called staff development reviews. The staff development review is directed at the coordination of expectations based on the premise that a shared space needs to be generated. Promises are given about subsequent agreements aimed at addressing shared goals, and the written agreement that the review leads to symbolizes precisely that it is not simply a conversation but the formation or renewal of a partnership. Similarly, many organizations hold performance reviews with subsequent performance agreements.

I will give a few brief examples of what we may refer to as partnership agreements between employee and organization before attempting to present a diagnosis of the shift in the contract form.

Performance Agreement

My first example is the performance agreement. The performance agreement is part of a performance review concept from a nursing home in the Municipality of Copenhagen, Denmark. The standard agreement looks like that shown in Figure 7.1.

The competence review was introduced at the nursing home in 2000. The agreement page is part of the concept. The page is divided into left and right columns. The left column is designed to list promises about action. The right column gives the employee a space to justify her promised actions. In other words, it is not enough to act. One has to act for reasons that ideally define the employee's competence development within the context of the nursing home. Thus, the employee is expected to reflect on herself as competence but has to also reflect on this reflection in relation

Contract agreement for competence development for **Name:**	
I will particularly strive to improve: (list three things)	Comments (e.g. how these relate to the base values and competencies, is a helper required, time frame, etc.)
Suggestions for collective courses/instruction, etc. for the entire department staff	Comments (e.g. how these relate to the base values and competencies, is a helper required, time frame, etc.)
I will work to obtain more knowledge/ better qualifications within the following areas.	Comments (e.g. how these relate to the base values and competencies, is a helper required, time frame, etc.)

Date:

Signature: _____

Figure 7.1   Agreement page from Sølund Nursing Home

to the whole. It is the employee's responsibility to guarantee the agreement between competence development and the whole. The agreement asks the employee to make improvements in three areas. Why precisely three? In order for the promise to demonstrate self-reflection, it cannot be too easy. One promise is too little. That would be like writing down the first thing that came to mind. However, too many promises are also too easy. It would be a long unprioritized list, which, in its abundance, would neither demonstrate reflection nor promise. The employee then signs the form. But what does a signature mean in this case? It means a contractualization of the employee's self-relation. The employee enters into a contract with herself about herself, with the manager as the sanctioning and supervising authority (for more on personal contractualizations, see Andersen 2003a).

We might say that by entering into an agreement with oneself about one's self-development in response to one's perception of the needs of the nursing home, one simultaneously signs a partnership agreement with the nursing home in which the nursing home becomes a shared responsibility for both management and the individual employee. The self-contract is not a promise to carry out specific responsibilities for the nursing home. It is a promise to create oneself in the image of the nursing home in order to subsequently agree to specific promises about fulfilling the nursing home's future responsibilities.

In this case, we are dealing with a partnership that is primarily coded through pedagogy. The agreement is an agreement about the employee observing herself pedagogically within the code better/worse in terms of learning and allowing herself to be a formable medium open to competence development with the goal of fitting the competence needs of future nursing homes. There is also a secondary coding because the very agreement of acceptance or rejection can be read from the perspective of the code loved/not loved: The employee either installs the nursing home as her significant other to the extent that she has engaged in self-development for the benefit of the home, or she does not take the agreement seriously, which testifies to a lack of engagement and a distanced relationship from the home.

Contract Yourself

The next example is taken from a book of recipes of games and activities in organizations. One of the concepts in the book is called "Contracting with yourself". The example builds on the notion of so-called "psychological contracts". The idea is that there are always implicit psychological contracts between organizations and employees that extend beyond the formal legal contracts. Psychological contracts include unspoken mutual expectations about motivation, loyalty, support, and so on, and generate anger if they are perceived to be broken. The idea is for these psychological contracts to be made explicit in the form of written contracts about how to relate to one another. Management may promise possibilities for development and advancement, and the employees, in turn, promise to assume greater responsibility for their own hireability (Jørgensen and Jørgensen 1999; Rousseau 1995). "Contracting with yourself" advances the notion that the organization supports employees in the effort to establish a psychological contract with themselves. The support offered takes the form of an organizationally provided context (for example, an employee seminar), a concept and helping the employee formulate the contract, including the *identification* of the difficult self-relation that the employee wants to address and focus on by means of the contract, the *rationale* for wanting to change this relation, the definition of *goals* for the change, outlining a *plan* for the pursuit of the goal, and deciding on a *reward* for fulfillment of the contract. Finally, organizational support also entails helping the employee *externalize* the contract by putting it in writing, signing it and

---

Psychological Contract:

A commitment to yourself or others to make a change.

Requirements:

      1.   Awareness of a problem

      2.   Desire to change

      3.   Statement of objective

      4.   Plan for review of progress

      5.   Meaningful reward

Directions:

Write yourself a letter, committing to a change in behavior as a product of this seminar. Sign it, insert it in the envelope, address it to yourself, and we will mail it back for your review in one month.

Dear_____ :

_____

_____

_____

Sincerely,

_____

Figure 7.2   The psychological contract

subsequently sending it to the employee as a reminder of the contract as an external imperative. The standard contract is shown in Figure 7.2.

    The essence of the concept is that commitment to oneself means commitment to the group, and that the group, in turn, supports and aids one's self-commitment. In other words, one's self-contract becomes a part of one's partnership agreement about creating oneself as a partner to the partnership.

    It is not easy to answer the question of what code guides the writing of the contract. Is it a formal contract? If nothing else, the concept stresses the importance of putting the contract into writing so that the employee knows whether or not she has fulfilled the contract. The contract even has a built-in sanction in the form of a self-reward. At the same time, however, it is obviously not possible for an outside authority to independently thematize the employee's self-relation in terms of right and wrong. The contract can also be communicated about in terms of pedagogy. From a pedagogical perspective, the contract is an exercise in describing and relating to oneself in terms of problem, willingness, possibility, plan, self-care and self-commitment. It is an exercise for employees in observing themselves from a pedagogical point of view, and the organization functions, then, as the supervisor of employees' self-pedagogization. Finally, the contract can be seen as codified as play. One plays a game in which one enters into a contract with oneself, and the organization helps to make sure the game functions well. The fact that the contract is structured as a contract with goals, sanction and signature makes the game a serious one. It is a game that plays with the notion of relating to oneself contractually. Similar to the partnership's ambiguous stance on promises (one promises subsequent promises), the game effects the same ambiguity with the oscillation between contract and contract game; a form of contract that suspends itself through play but that can also suspend the game and become a contract with self-reward. Either way, the psychological contract produces expectations of employees. What is kept open is the question of what to expect of the produced expectations. Can we expect, for instance, that they turn into binding obligations or into norms that can be disappointed, or are they purely cognitive expectations, which, like the weather report, are forgotten or adjusted if they do not materialize?

A number of similar contract types exist; one example is the coaching contract given in Figure 7.3 (Greenwich 2000).

Employee Development Interview: Putting the Cards on the Table

My next example is a concept for employee development interviews designed by the Danish municipality of Græsted-Gilleleje (Lind 2001). The municipality's stated purposes behind employee development interviews are: (1) Ensuring a shared perception and acceptance of the work situation, including a clear understanding of the background, qualifications and future of the individual employee, (2) Generating a greater sense of engagement by aligning demands and expectations, giving and receiving feedback about performance, and (3) Increasing adaptability.

The concept, which was developed in 2001, involves a number of stages. First, a collective agreement is put in place with employees about guidelines for employee development interviews. Next, the interviews take place. The method "putting the cards on the table" is one of the interview tools

Coaching Record

Name: Coach:

Position: Coaching period:

Coaching goal:

_____

Benefits

To team member:

To customer:

To organization:

_____

What actions will help me accomplish my goal?

_____

How can we measure my success over the period?

_____

Evaluation of progress

My evaluation:

Coach's evaluation:

_____

Team member's signature_____ Date _____

Coach's signature _____ Date _____

Source: Greenwich 2000, p. 74.

Figure 7.3   The coaching contract

used. Finally, the idea is that the development interviews are followed up by a personal development plan, which has the character of a contract.

In the conversation *about* the employee development interview, a contract about the interview is negotiated and agreed upon by management and employees. The contract is about conditions for the conversation. These conditions are divided into seven points:

(1) The premise under which employee and manager meet each other. Here, the contract is about a commitment from both parties to the present rather than past issues or events.
(2) Prejudices one brings to the table. The contract asks for a commitment to being open without prejudgment.
(3) Respect. The contract defines limits for the use of private information.
(4) Delimitation of issues that can be brought up during the interview. This is both about showing courage and articulating how personal

and private the interview can be. The employee development interview provides a space for talking about personal issues that are not usually discussed, but there has to be a clear definition of boundaries prior to the interview.

(5)   An agreement about the issues, which need to be excluded from the interview, for example, agreement about speaking about personal issues but not about individual colleagues.

(6)   An agreement about shared responsibility for the agreement.

(7)   An agreement about the terms of renegotiation.

The municipality hopes to use such contracts to establish conditions for the employee development interview to meet its objectives. Contracts are meant to generate a sense of security, discipline and motivation in relation to the employee development interview, and the interviews themselves are not conducted until a collective agreement about the condition for the interviews is in place.

As part of the development interviews, the concept employs a method referred to as "putting the cards on the table". The objective is to incorporate questions of personal talents and skills into the conversation. The exercise works like this: In advance of the employee development interviews, the manager hands out two sets of ten blank cards to employees. Each employee is asked to carefully reflect on her skills and personal resources. On one set of cards the employee writes down ten skills that she believes to be the most fitting. These are then copied onto the second set of cards. The employee then prioritizes the cards using number one as the highest priority and ten as the lowest. The numbers are written on the cards. They may look like those in Figure 7.4.

The employee gives the manager the unnumbered set of cards. The manager then evaluates the employee in accordance with the skill categories she has been given by the employee. The cards represent the manager's preparation for the interview. At the interview, the employee begins by placing her prioritized cards on the table and the interview starts with the manager inquiring about the keywords on the cards. The manager is expected to provide the service of "not understanding" as the concept puts it. The manager inquires about the meaning of the different skills, and the employee has to explain them so that the manager understands. Having had the terms clarified, the manager then places her prioritized cards on the table and explains her prioritization. With the employee's and manager's cards side by side, the manager explains to the employee how she perceives her. Differences of perception will be obvious, and these become the focus of the conversation. The central question is: "What calls for learning?" The manager then removes her cards and leaves the

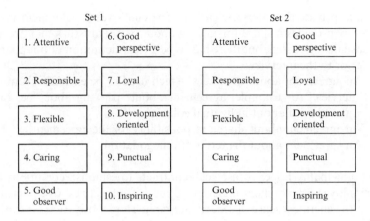

Figure 7.4   Putting the cards on the table

employee's on the table. The employee is asked to pick her two highest priorities. These are written down. According to the concept, these are skills that the employee can be proud of. The employee then selects two skill cards that need further development. They come to represent two goals for development, which need to be turned into operative goals. As part of the operationalization, the manager is expected to ask question such as: What will you do? How will this manifest itself? How will others know? How can you measure whether you have reached your learning objectives? The questions are asked in a way so that the employee can make the goals clear to herself.

How is an employee development interview using "putting the cards on the table" coded? It is probably a double coding. First, it is a conversation in the love code with the question "am I loved/not loved?" The manager explores the employee's engagement and conducts a form of authenticity check: "If you see yourself as engaged, what do you mean by that?" It suggests a form of meta-communication in the love code in which the relation and its nature is spoken about rather than performed. The manager can look into the depth of the engagement and the employee can get a sense of whether she is loved for who she is.

Second, the conversation becomes re-codified in terms of pedagogy, and the love indicators such as "responsibility", "attentiveness", and "engagement" are now observed as personal skills, which can be developed. The manager becomes supervisor and coach for the employee's self-pedagogization. By employing the "putting the cards on the table" method, the employee is invited to objectify herself as a competence resource. Moreover, the employee is invited to reflect on whether her self-perception seems reasonable, whether she may be perceived differently by others than how she perceives herself. The employee is made aware of her strong resources and is recognized for these when they are written down. This subsequently makes it easier for the employee to handle her weaker areas, which are never referred to as weak. The method is designed in a way so that the dialogue allows the employee to point to the skills that need development. The manager simply creates the procedures for the conversation. The important thing is not at all what the manager has to say. The important thing is that the employee is invited to turn herself and her skills into a self-project by defining learning objectives for personal skill development. The result is a pedagogical agreement about the employee's self-development.

As a result of the employee development interview and "putting the cards on the table", the manager and employee develop a "personal development plan". The plan is described like this: "The development plan is a mutual agreement between the closest manager and employee about how to implement the employee's requests for development – personal and work-related" (Lind 2001, p.10, own translation). The objective is the coordination of the employee's self-development with the group: "The aim is to ensure that the individual employee is offered qualified professional and personal development, which means: – that the individual continually evaluates her work situation, both in the short and long term, and is aware of strengths and weaknesses as they relate to her objectives, – that the development matches the goals and visions of the institution" (Lind 2001, p.14, own translation). The development plan consists of a personal and a professional part. It points four years into the future but has to be continually adjusted. Both manager and employee sign the plan. A standard plan with made-up content looks like that given in Figure 7.5.

Having outlined the plan, both the employee's and manager's responsibilities for the plan have been defined in concrete terms before both parties have signed the plan.

The development plan also suggests a double codification in the codes of power and pedagogy. Through the code of power, the contract can be read as a way for the power-superior to unload loosely formulated tasks onto the power-inferior, who has to independently define and manage these tasks by interpreting organizational intent. Moreover, in the code of power, the contract represents an empowerment technology, which asks the subordinate to increase her capacity for self-management. In addition, it is also a pedagogical contract, which asks employees to assume a pedagogical perspective on themselves with a view to self-development.

Professional	Personal
First year The institution's minibus. Actively participate in the development of the pedagogical initiative to make sure it is more than "a Sunday drive"	Participate in the "bus program" – actively work to ensure cooperation on the bus – be assertive Develop my skills to master the new functions and be responsible towards the management function. Accept coaching/supervision from my manager
Second year Coordinate the institution's project days (2 × 14 weeks)	Practice keeping a good perspective. This is achieved by overseeing an increasing number of management functions. Ask for help when I need it
Third year	
Fourth year	

Figure 7.5   Personal development plan

THE FORM OF THE FORMAL CONTRACT

The question is to what extent the above examples can even be viewed as contracts? In order to answer this question I will have to first analyze what we perceive as a contract more generally. In other words, how do we define the general form of contract? As a point of departure we might say that a specific form of contract corresponds with formal membership – a specific way for mutual reliance to be produced among independent units.

A contract can be seen as the unity of obligation and freedom (Luhmann 1981, p. 249). A contract communicates about mutual obligations. One gives a promise about the exchange of obligations. However, communication of obligation always presupposes the freedom of the parties as the contract's outside. A contract negotiation may not address the parties' status as free subjects, but this status is always presupposed because without this freedom the subjects are not in a position to agree to obligations. Being forced to do something is not a contract. Force does not produce obligation. Therefore, obligation has no meaning without freedom. Obligations both limit and presuppose freedom. Or as Durkheim puts it: "The only undertakings worthy of the name [contracts] are those that are desired by individuals, whose sole origin is this free act of the will. Conversely, any obligation that has not been agreed by both sides is not in any way contractual" (Durkheim1997, p. 158). Thus, a contract represents

| Obligation | Freedom |

Contract

Figure 7.6   Form of contract

the voluntary binding of one's own freedom. The form of contract can be formalized as shown in Figure 7.6.

However, a contract is always a multiplicity because mutual obligations are always perceived differently by different contract partners. Derrida writes:

> You can only enter into a contract (. . .) if you do so in your own tongue. You're only responsible, in other words, for what you say in your own mother tongue. If, however, you say it only in your own tongue, then you're still not committed, because you must also say it in the other's language. An agreement or obligation of whatever sort – a promise, a marriage, a sacred alliance – can only take place, I would say, in translation, that is, only if it is simultaneously uttered in both my tongue and the other's (. . .) There is no contract possible – no social contract possible – without a translation contract, bringing with it the paradox I have just mentioned. (Derrida 1988, p. 125)

In other words, a contract can only maintain its unity by being a multiplicity. Obligation has to always be read from the perspective of the free subject. Otherwise, contract would not be the "voluntary binding of one's own freedom". That means that obligation has to be read in a language that belongs to the contract subject. And since there are several contract subjects, the contract becomes a meeting place for these languages. If one language tries to forcefully and unambiguously interpret obligation, it is no longer a contract. The contract becomes a meeting place between languages, whose meeting doubles the mutual obligation.

In terms of systems theory we could say that the contract represents a coupling between communication systems and/or psychic systems, which otherwise remain closed to one another. As operative closed systems, they must assign meaning to the contract in each their own way. However, at the same time, the way in which one system defines the contract as meaningful has to also make sense to the other systems. One system's

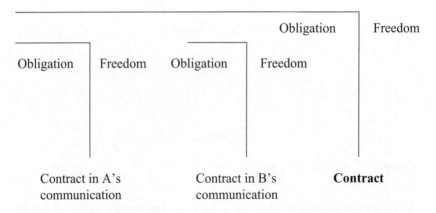

Figure 7.7 The multiplicity of contract

interpretation has to be recognizable as obligation to the other system. The paradox, in other words, is that a contract necessarily has to be both one and many at the same time. The contract between communication systems has to both be a shared contract and an individual contract. Contracts can only maintain their unity by remaining a multiplicity. I have tried to formalize this in Figure 7.7.

The fact that contract is both one and many means that it is a shore upon which languages meet *without fusing*. A contract precisely does not constitute a collective. A contract cannot be a collective with common language and horizon because that would cause the very distinction between obligation and freedom to collapse. The contract's form and multiplicity presuppose that the collective is defined as the form's constitutive outside; that is, that which a contract can never be, and up against which a contractual relation is always defined.

For a formal employee contract this means that the organizational system observes the contract as a premise for decision, that is, membership, and as such it proposes a contractual afterlife in the form of new management decisions. To the employee (the psychic system), however, the contract does not represent membership but only an obligation about the sale of one's services at a certain price, which is meaningful both as a stage in a particular career development and as the possibility to live a particular private life with family, hobbies, and so on. This gives the contract an entirely different meaning and afterlife. Moreover, the employee contract can be observed, within the career and educational system, as the possibility of acquiring new skills and subsequently as the documentation of a certain level of experience, which means that the employee can be ascribed further skills and qualifications.

THE FORM OF PARTNERSHIP

The employee contract comes under pressure at the same time as the formal membership. How does one commit to others under shifting conditions where one is unsure of what kind of commitment one even wants from someone? My argument is that in the contract forms I have discussed, the employee contract has been displaced to and doubled in partnerships, and that this displacement is equivalent to the displacement and doubling of membership to self-enrollment. The agreements that result from the employee development interviews, the competence reviews, and in the so-called psychological contracts and self-contracts, challenge the formal contract form. They constitute partnership agreements rather than formal contracts in a traditional sense, but they are still agreements. They are contracts that incorporate the logic of transience. A partnership, therefore, is not something entirely different from a contract. A partnership is a second-order contract. Partnerships are about committing to future commitment (for a more comprehensive analysis of partnerships, see Andersen 2006, 2008b). I have illustrated the relation in Figure 7.8.

Partnerships represent contracts about wanting to have contracts with each other in the future. Whereas first-order contracts pertain to promises, second-order contracts represent promises about promises. But a promise about a promise has a radically different social quality than a promise. A first-order contract presupposes a social order, legally and otherwise. A promise in a first-order contract refers beyond the contract to the law as the installation of order. Like self-enrollment, where the criterion for the assignment of membership basically is that one works continually on enrollment – never a member, always in enrollment – a promise about a promise does not presuppose an order but creates its own order. That is what a second-order promise is about: Creating conditions and premises for future promises. And this changes the temporality, factuality and sociality of commitment.

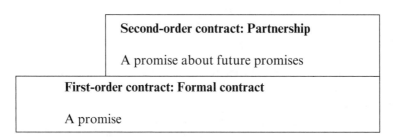

Figure 7.8   Partnerships as second-order contracts

Temporality

The act of formulating future horizons becomes essential in partnerships. In first-order contracts, a contract represents a presentification of the future. A first-order contract is meant to give a promise in the present about future obligations. A first-order contract works to create the future of the present, so to speak. A second-order contract on the other hand has to indicate a horizon in the present for future work with new possible obligations. In second-order contracts, thus, it is a question of making present future presentifications of future. That is, not only the future of the present but the future of the future. Future horizons do not represent a promise about concrete action at some point in the future. Future horizons are also not prognoses of specific developments of needs in order to better plan tasks. Future horizons represent images of what the collaboration might look like in the future, including entirely new tasks and visions. Future horizons are expectations about future expectations of the collaboration. A promise about future horizons and visions is a promise about a premise for subsequent promises. Second-order contracts thus concern the stabilization of expectations with the expectation of shifting expectations.

Factuality

On the factual dimension, first-order employee contracts are about specifying work tasks and fields; that is, specifying what kind of work to expect in return for what pay. Second-order contracts assign primacy to the temporal dimension because the object of exchange is development possibilities. In an employee partnership, there are no given work fields and therefore no given responsibilities because the organization's future area is open and remains open to a certain extent. Therefore, a partnership is not about issues (problems, tasks, areas) but about the commitment to a particular perspective on issues that do not yet exist. Factuality appears in partnerships as deferred. The factual perspective and the maintenance of this perspective is the central concern.

Sociality

Finally, partnerships are radically different from first-order contracts on the social dimension. First-order contracts presuppose, as I have already mentioned, contract parties as independent actors. This means that focus in contract communication is on mutual obligation but always with the presupposition of the parties' freedom to limit their own freedom. In partnerships, however, this is not quite as clear. What the employee promises

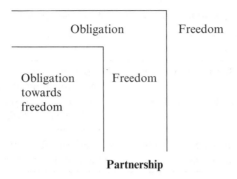

Figure 7.9   The form of partnership

is to create herself in the image of the partnership in order to remain a relevant partner in the future. The organization, in turn, promises to create
challenges and possibilities for development for the employees. On the
social dimension, thus, partnership becomes a promise about a collective
space in which the parties develop together and for each other. It is a question of the obligation to create oneself as a free and independent partner
for the partnership; a commitment to freedom in the image of the partnership. Like the membership of self-enrollment and its doubling and re-entry
of the distinction "general motive/person", we have here a doubling and
re-entry of the distinction "obligation/freedom" within the distinction
itself. In partnerships, freedom is re-entered as obligation, but has to at
the same time presuppose freedom since otherwise no freedom is possible.
This can be summed up as in Figure 7.9.

On the factual, temporal and social dimensions we see the erosion of
the conditions for establishing first-order contracts. The factual quality
of complexity changes: It is no longer a given what the object of exchange
is. The social quality of complexity changes: The definition of a relevant
partner has become fluid and multiple and something that is continually
being created (see Table 7.1).

Thus, partnerships can be seen as functionally equivalent to contracts
under conditions where the basis for first-order contracts disintegrates.
Partnerships represent a functionally equivalent response to shifting conditions. Partnerships stabilize expectations with the expectation of shifting
expectations. First-order contracts refer to conditions outside themselves,
which precede the contracts and are considered stable. Partnerships
refer to conditions defined by the partnership which are never perceived
as stable because a partnership only exists in its actual manifestation.
Therefore, partnerships are not only second-order contracts. They also

Table 7.1   Dimensional shifts on first and second order

Dimension	Contract	Partnership
Temporal	Presentification of future	Presentification of future presentifications of future
Factual	Specification of tasks	Indications of perspectives on the development of tasks that are yet unknown
Social	Contract partners are presupposed	Commitment to creating oneself in the image of the partnership

represent a second-order social order designed to always only exist in its emergence. As Maas and Bakker put it: "partnerships ask for 'unfrozen circumstances', in which dynamic, social spaces, and fluid forms can be examined as long as possible" (Maas and Bakker 2000, p. 198).

CONCLUSION: PARTNERSHIP AS SELF-SUSPENDING CONTRACT

Competence reviews, contractualized employee development interviews, and self-contracts transfer the contractual relationship between organization and employee from first to second order, from formal contracts to partnerships.

Partnerships introduce new levels of paradoxy into these relations. The fundamental paradox is that the competence reviews, and so on, are at once an agreement and not an agreement, at once desire mutual commitment but also strive for the noncommittal and for unconditional freedom. And this paradox is managed through the displacement and deferral of the promise: a promised promise.

However, there is another side to the paradox as well. Partnership is a form of contractualization that wants to become community (see Figure 7.10).

This represents a paradox because a contract defined by means of the distinction obligation/freedom is precisely constituted in a way so that it cannot constitute a community. As I mentioned earlier, freedom also consists in the freedom to give obligation an afterlife within the "own language" of the individual contract partner. The ambition to form a community is an ambition about shared language. That would dissolve the very form of contract and cancel the difference between obligation and freedom. The employee development interviews and the competence

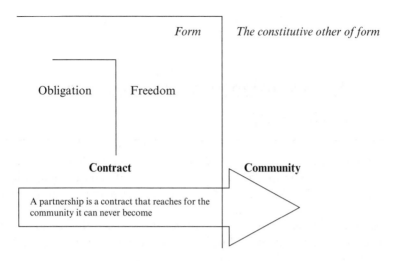

Figure 7.10   The contract that wants to be a community

reviews contain ambitions about the definition of a community made up of organization and employee. The new agreements strive to constitute that which is the contract's constitutive outside. They aim at the creation of contractual commitments to the one thing a contract cannot create commitment to. And they also pose the obvious question of who is authorized to define a shared language. A contractualized employee development interview in which the organization defines the language of community is unilateral force and not a mutual agreement. "Putting the cards on the table" is an example of how the language for employees' self-description becomes an object of management. The employee's language of self-description becomes contractualized. Freedom is desired and yet annihilated at the same time.

8. The organization as a nexus of partnerships

The Nobel Prize winner Oliver Williamson suggests that we observe market and hierarchy as different forms of contractualizations (Williamson 1983, p. 253). From this perspective, an organization is seen as a nexus of contracts. What if we similarly see the organization as a nexus of partnerships? And what do organizational possibilities look like if the organization is perceived to be in the process of becoming a nexus of partnerships?

What I want to address in this chapter is the fact that it is not only the contract relation between organization and employee that shifts in the direction of partnerships, it is also the relations between organization/ citizen, organization/student, organization/patient, organization/client, and so on, which develop in the direction of partnerships. (And again I want to stress that my primary point of reference is the public sector, although I believe that we might observe a similar development in the relationship organization/consumer. My knowledge in that field is rather limited.)

I begin with a few examples of contracts and partnerships between administration and citizen, which have evolved over the past 10–15 years. I aim to point to some of their peculiar traits of contract and partnership and will explore what kinds of media they form, including management questions they produce.

Second, I turn to function systems as my point of observation. From that point of observation, partnership becomes a symptom of a particular folding in the function system's way of producing roles. My point of departure is that function systems traditionally operate with a distinction between performance roles and audience roles (for example, teacher/student) when they produce roles and distribute communication relevance. Today, this distinction seems folded into programs for the creation of a performing public (for example, the student with responsibility for her own learning).

Finally, I will discuss what the organization ends up looking like if employees not only enter into partnerships with managers and colleagues but also into partnerships on behalf of the organization with a multiplicity of individuals from the organization's environment. Does this result in an organization that must be represented and created from its periphery, that is, an organization created on its boundary? If management is to represent the whole, what does management become in an organization, which at best is a nexus of partnerships? Management becomes management of partnerships.

WHEN THE CITIZEN IS EXPECTED TO CREATE HERSELF AS A PARTNER TO THE PUBLIC ADMINISTRATION

As I mentioned in Chapter 3, it is not only the manager who is responsible for representing the organization. The anticipation of the organization's needs points in many different directions for the individual employee. It involves the manager, but also colleagues, teams (internal and cross-organizational), citizens, users, customers, and so on. Therefore, I spoke about the fact that the love relationship with the organization takes on the properties of a harem. If this is accurate, the employee's partnership with the organization has to express itself not only by the employee entering into a partnership with the manager but with many other organizational representatives. And this is precisely the case. Employee teams can clearly be seen as a form of partnership among employees on behalf of the organization. But the employee also enters into partnership agreements with the organization's citizens and customers. The social services department works to make clients partners in their own cases through citizens' contracts. Similarly, programs for health promotion are developing strategies for making the patient a partner, and in the public schools system students are invited to see themselves as partners through the introduction of so-called student agreements.

Hanne Knudsen has addressed the creation of partnerships between schools and parents. She particularly emphasizes the creation of open-ended expectations about parent involvement in the classroom and in the school in general. She shows that the school–parent relation today precisely assumes the form of a partnership because the responsibilities of parents are not articulated as a simple obligation but as an expectation about a generally responsible attitude in relation to the school and in relation to establishing the best premises for learning both at home and in the classroom (Knudsen 2010). However, the partnership analyzed by Hanne Knudsen could also be described with an emphasis on the creation of expectations with respect to the individual teacher. The teacher's partnership with the parents is simultaneously a partnership with the school. The teacher represents the school in the partnership with parents at the same time as the building of a community with parents expresses the teacher's partnership with the school. We might say that the teacher lets down the school if she does not succeed in her efforts to build partnerships with the parents. Similar examples of partnerships between employees and citizens can be found in nearly all welfare areas and relate to the emergence of the concept of the "active fellow citizen". The active fellow citizen is a citizen who is invited to enter into a community with the public sector. The active fellow citizen thus comes in a peculiar way to represent a doubling of the concept of citizen. In its initial form, the citizen represents a case-based environment for the public organization. The citizen is an administrative category about whose cases the organization has to make decisions; that is, the citizen represents an external case-based relation with the organization. In its secondary and doubled form, "the active fellow citizen" is a citizen who has been given the option of limited membership if she enrolls and takes on the case-based relation as a collective responsibility. Under the heading "The citizen as employee", weekly magazine *Monday Morning* (*Mandag Morgen*) writes: "The citizen cannot simply expect an increasing level of services but has to also take on a new role as fellow citizen and active co-producer of services" (*Mandag Morgen* 2011, own translation).

Below I am going to provide a few examples of partnerships, which employees enter into with citizens on behalf of the organization. They in no way represent a comprehensive or sufficient typology for the organization-citizen partnerships. They only serve to make my argument more concrete and to show how varied and complex the phenomenon is. These examples have been selected precisely because they do not fit a simple type, which would allow it to be configured seamlessly within the distinction between first-order contracts and second-order contracts.

The Family Contract

The municipality of Vojens, Denmark, has developed a tool called "family contracts" (for a more comprehensive analysis see Andersen 2003a, 2004a, 2007a, 2008c, 2012a). Family contracts are agreements offered by the social services department to certain families, which give the families the possibility of influencing the decisions of the department and show their willingness to change, cooperate and commit.

In 2001, psychologist and administrative services director in the municipality Leif Petersen provided the following rationale for the family contracts:

> We are faced with a group of people who often has problems with alcohol, unemployment, little or no education, and shifting partners. There is often

domestic violence and the children experience a lot of moving in and out of the house. The result is single mothers. Now, we can tell these mothers that it is their responsibility to change (. . .) Parents sign a written psychological contract, which may entail requirements about alcohol treatment, about finding a job, job activation, or agreeing to not getting involved in a new relationship until the children are under control. (*Jydske Vestkysten* 2/11-01, own translation)

The municipality's vice-mayor and then rank-and-file member of parliament Hans Christian Schmidt stated in *Socialrådgiveren* (*The Social Worker*):

These are voluntary contracts, and when something is voluntary, it can be terminated immediately and without consequences (. . .) The objective of the contracts is to take control of one's life (. . .) Parents need to feel a greater sense of responsibility toward their children. And we get up close and personal when the contract articulates a requirement about limiting the number of different partners. But it is because we focus on the children. Constant changes are not good for the children. Everyone who works in the social field knows this or they walk through life blindfolded. (Paulsen 2001, p. 3, own translation)

Director of administrative services Leif Petersen elaborates: "A contract gets closer to the person and it is more elaborate. In a contract, the terms are concrete and rigid, and we hope we can make parents reflect and take their role as parents more seriously (. . .) But if the contract is broken, you are on the path to disqualifying yourself" (Paulsen 2001, p. 21, own translation). Thus, the willingness to enter into a contract is perceived as willingness to become an active partner with the municipality about changing things together. If the client breaks the contract or lacks the willingness to effect change, the client reclaims the status of object and becomes a mere observer of administrative decisions.

The contract clearly addresses the obligation towards freedom. The clients commit to the effort to create themselves as free so that they may take responsibility for themselves and their families. And by creating themselves as free, they make themselves qualified to become partners in a partnership with the administration, and this partnership temporarily suspends the legal relationship and unambiguous decisions about the family as case.

Thus, the family contract represents a unilateral invitation to mutuality. The citizen as subject is invited to become a fellow citizen on the condition that she enters into a partnership with the administration, and part of this partnership agreement is a self-contract in which the citizen commits to create herself as a good employee and hence partner in the partnership with the municipality. I have tried to illustrate this in Figure 8.1.

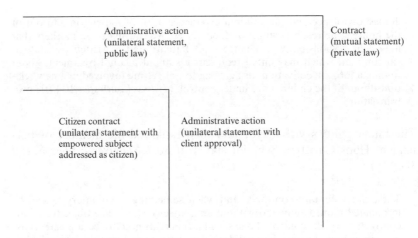

Figure 8.1   Citizen contract as unilateral invitation to mutuality

However, the unilateral nature of the exchange is not abolished with the partnership and citizen role since it remains a unilateral invitation to mutuality. As a contract, the citizen contract is voluntary, but if the clients refuse to partake in the creation of a contract, the administration has to respond with administrative action. Only if the citizen is found capable of committing to her own freedom is the citizen really considered a fellow citizen with individual communication relevance and the ability to form a partnership. Otherwise, the client is seen as someone who has no willingness towards self-development, who is passive, weak and dependent, and therefore as someone without a position of sovereignty from which to negotiate. Or in other words: the citizen's individuality is denied and she is (again) seen as part of the masses (cf. the concept of the masses in Stäheli 2003).

But is a family contract legal in the same sense as administrative action? In administrative action, the right to make unilateral statements is located outside the administrative action in the delegation of authority. Similarly, the right to mutual statement in the context of private contracts is secured outside the contract, not through delegation but through freedom rights of different kinds. What happens when the difference is re-entered in the form of family contract is that both the power of the authorities as negotiator and the power of the client as negotiator become defined as something which is produced internally in the interaction between social worker and client as part of the creation of the citizen contract itself, which is then confirmed by the signature of the partners. Thus, unlike the legal order, the family contract does not precede the interaction. The family contract represents a partnership which is meant to create its own order. Not only the family contract but also its conditions in the form of empowered negotiation partners are established through the formulation of the contract. The contract process transforms client and social worker into empowered partners.

The peculiar thing is that the administration has to suspend administrative law in order to make itself a partner to the client. The partnership is presented as an obligation but is not in a legal sense. The family contract as partnership is precisely only binding to the extent that it simultaneously suspends administrative law!

What does the administration gain from this suspension of its own legal basis for making unilateral decisions? The administration sees that it is unable to help or intervene unless the citizens want it too. The administration is put in a situation in which its ability to act depends on the other's willingness to act on the administration's action. The precondition for the administration's power to act becomes the citizen's power to act. This is what the contractualization of the citizen is about: bilateral empowerment (Andersen 2003a, p. 184, 2004a, 2012a). The family contract allows the administration to become a partner in the client's creation of her own life and obligation-freedom relation. The administration renounces its legal authority in order to achieve the status of conversation and negotiation partner in areas that otherwise reside outside the scope of legal authority. It is an administration that seeks its own self-empowerment in relation to citizens. Finally, this suspension of the law means that, as partner, the individual citizen can function as the shared focal point for an administrative network among different institutions and individual employees. So family contracts are not only partnerships between administration and citizen, but also partnerships among a number of primarily public welfare institutions, though at times also private ones. And in this way they also become partnerships for the individual employee and organization, represented here through the concern for the citizen and other cross-organizational administrations.

However, this self-suspension of the law can of course itself be suspended. And the possibility of the suspension of the suspension establishes the legal shadow of a deferred order that constitutes the possibility of the partnership.

Yum-Yum: A Partnership about a Partnership

My next example of a partnership between administration and citizen is from the campaign "healthy through play", designed by the Danish Veterinary and Food Administration in collaboration with the National

Board of Health (for a more comprehensive analysis of this campaign see Andersen 2009). The campaign "healthy through play" is a third-order campaign; it is a ministerial campaign directed at health professionals that encourages them to organize a campaign directed at vulnerable families who are encouraged to organize campaigns in relation to themselves and their habits concerning health, food and exercise. My focus is on a single element from the campaign: the so-called agreement forms designed for the families for purposes of contractualization.

The basic idea is that parents and children in the individual family enter into an agreement with one another about food and exercise. The role of the health professionals is to sell the idea and supervise the agreement conversation. The campaign has eight preprinted agreement forms, each of which covers a different issue that the agreement may include. The issues are based on the campaign's eight pieces of diet advice. The idea is for the agreements to be in effect for a limited time so that a new agreement about another dietary piece of advice can be made once the first agreement expires, and so forth.

The campaign addresses health professionals: "As a health professional you can use the agreement forms to find out, via dialogue with the family, which dietary guidelines are of particular interest to the family. The family then writes down the agreement as a specific goal, e.g. 'take a thirty minute walk twice a week'" (www.legdigsund.dk/Services/forfagfolk/forfagfolk. htm, own translation). It is not only that health professionals intervene in the eating habits of the individual family; it is the fact that they intervene in family members' internal social relations by giving the social space a particular form to exist within, namely, the form of contract, but without a dialogue about contract as a particularly value-laden form. It affects the social space. Sharing family norms about, for example, not putting sugar on breakfast cereal, means something very different from making an agreement about the same issue. It is a question of trying to contractualize internal family relations (see also Andersen 2003a, 2007a, 2008c). It contributes to the creation of the family as a negotiating family, where unilateral management intentions are made to look like voluntary action. The point is to make it appear as if the incorporation of particular health precepts is the family's own initiative. The campaign does not like the use of force and raised fingers. It is important to make it seem as if the family has independently formulated the contract, that it has been created from the ground up and is the expression of a horizontal relation of mutuality among family members.

I have included an example of this kind of agreement in Figure 8.2. On the right side of the form the campaign's diet advice is listed, together with nutritional information. The right side is where the health professional

Source: http://www.legdigsund.dk/NR/rdonlyres/6FCE7BF1-AE69-492D-A07F57CCA10B90D4/0/1Aftaleark_samlet_LOW.pdf.

Figure 8.2   Yum-Yum agreement chart

begins her dialogue with the family by advising and informing about health issues. The right side unilaterally defines the framework for understanding within which a mutual agreement in the family can subsequently be reached. On the form's left side is a space called "our agreement", where the family's agreement is written down. At the top of the form is written, "tear here". The idea is that once the agreement is made, the right side of the form is torn off and the left side with the agreement is posted on the refrigerator. Why not the entire form? Because in order to make the agreement look as if it has been generated from within the family, the right side of the form has to be removed. The unilaterally defined framework for the agreement, which is the form's right side, has fulfilled its function and can be removed. This allows the family to forget the unilateral origins of the agreement.

Below the agreement is a monthly chart. This is a place to write down a family member's contribution to the agreement. As the campaign material states: "The children can put stickers on the agreement form every time they do something to honor the agreement" (www.legdigsund.dk/Services/forfagfolk/forfagfolk.htm, own translation). We might say that filling out the agreement form constitutes the actual signature on the agreement (Derrida 1988, pp. 124–6). It is by proving one's commitment to the agreement that the agreement is given an afterlife and becomes an actual agreement (Derrida 2007, p. 213). At the same time, this method of gradually filling in the chart makes it possible for the family to check themselves and keep track of their eating and exercise habits, that is, to see if they have become better at eating six different vegetables a day, if this happens to be part of the agreement.

It is not only the form of the agreement that is peculiar, however. The campaign also expresses a certain sense of embarrassment about the agreement form. The agreement pages have been designed to not look like actual agreements, and colors and drawings create a fun, childish and inviting appearance. Despite the fact that these agreements are about the promotion of health in at-risk families, whose health is often threatened by poor nutrition and lack of physical exercise, this seriousness is lacking from the agreement pages. Emphasis is on "health promotion" not "health risks". It focuses on positive attitude and motivation, not on the "un-fun" obligation that comes with any contract. Addressing the families, the campaign writes: "Make agreements with your child. Your child watches you and reflects herself in your habits – also when it comes to food and exercise (. . .) It is a good idea to create little rituals in your daily routine, e.g. cross out a space on the chart every day after you pick up the children. Many children take agreements very seriously; make it fun and a game to keep the agreements" (www.legdigsund.dk/Lav_aftaler_med_dit _barn/aftaler.htm).

Here, the embarrassment associated with contracts is transformed into the notion that contracts are in fact fun. They are a game. And keeping a promise is like playing a game. This creates a strange form of double communication according to which the contract is on the one hand a contract with mutual responsibilities and on the other hand a contractual game, where it is fun to fill out the table. There is, in fact, a difference between breaking a promise made as part of an agreement and losing a game by not scoring a certain number of vegetables for the week. The health professional and the family enter into a partnership about the creation of the family as a health partnership.

The Dialogue Circle

My final example is what, in the municipality of Herlev Denmark, is referred to as "the dialogue circle", which is an agreement between parents and a childcare center about how to describe the child. The dialogue circle is part of a greater concept called the "Framework for pedagogical work with children ages 0–10". The program basically addresses the coordination of the municipality's differentiated pedagogical efforts in relation to the individual child. The program is designed to ensure coherence between the municipality's child policies and the concrete efforts in the municipality's pedagogical institutions, including daycare centers, schools and after-school programs. The program is meant to ensure synchronous cohesion among institutions so that they are coordinated in their pedagogical effort in relation to the individual child's development. Moreover, the program is to ensure cohesion diachronically by establishing continuity in the pedagogical effort, for example, in the transition from preschool to kindergarten. The program does not represent a hierarchical program in a narrow sense. Instead, it is a program for the creation of partnerships across institutions and across the institution/family/student relationships. The point of departure is:

> Collaboration means making a shared effort to address an issue, which can only be solved collectively. This is characteristic of the responsibilities and effort that is needed in professional child services. It is not possible to qualitatively take on the task alone – it requires significant cooperation to generate a qualified comprehensive effort for children. Therefore, we need everyone who works professionally with children to commit to collaboration. And similarly, parents have a responsibility to partake in the effort concerning their children. (Herlev Kommune 2005, p. 22, own translation)

There are no specific guidelines for who to collaborate with or how. The childcare professionals are expected to independently establish the necessary partnerships:

> One of the collaborative efforts that all childcare professionals must partake in is the collaboration around transitions in the child's life. We expect that all childcare professionals gather knowledge and work together in the districts and with parents about the program content. Children and parents must be able to feel the effects of this effort as a recognizable pedagogical praxis in all programs and schools that the child participates in. (Herlev Kommune 2005, p. 24, own translation)

The program develops a concept called "children's traces". Traces are defined as different signs and expressions of who the child is and what motivates it. Traces could be the child's drawings and notes about something she has said or done. It is considered a pedagogical task to collect, sort and interpret traces. The municipality places great emphasis on such traces. In the present context, it suffices to note that the traces become a form of medium for cross-institutional partnership creation because the traces can be transported from one institution to the next and from one conversation to the next. In addition to the concept of traces, there is the concept of a "suitcase", which travels with the child and in which the child's traces can be stored. The suitcase is designed to help "preserve the child's life story" and "create respect around the child, its interests and products" (Herlev Kommune 2005, p. 33, own translation). Thus, the gathering of traces becomes the precondition for the creation and development of a partnership around the child across the boundary institution/parents and

institution/institution: "Children's traces are gathered through observations, log books – children's and adults' –, the suitcase, visible trace charts
and dialogue. When working with children's traces it is important: to work
systematically with the collection and interpretation of children's traces,
to plan on the basis of traces, that the process is not just an adult-guided
learning process but also a process of collaboration" (Herlev Kommune
2005, p. 28, own translation).

It is in this context that Herlev Municipality in 2010 developed the so-
called dialogue circle, which is meant to guide the transition from daycare
to school. The dialogue circle is shown in Figure 8.3.

The dialogue circle is provided in advance of the conference to parents
and the daycare centers. The partners prepare for the conference by each
filling in the dialogue circle. Thus, the parents and the childcare professional are asked to describe the child in the language and concepts of the
circle. This means that there is a predefined language that the partners
use to describe the child and to make an agreement. The concept material
emphasizes that the language it provides is inclusive and multifarious:
"With a few words, the dialogue circle encourages multiple interpretations
of and approaches to the child's resources and development potential"
(Herlev Kommune 2010, p. 9, own translation). However, it is obvious
that only a pedagogical approach to the child as medium is considered
relevant to the communication. Parents and childcare professionals are
invited to describe the child in the language of pedagogy and not in the
language of love, for example. The parents are invited to look at their
child as it appears to the pedagogical institutions. Yet, the concept is seen
as allowing for "a nuanced image" of the child. At the parent–teacher
conference, parents and childcare professionals present their description
of the child, and the objective is then to combine the two dialogue circles
into one circle, which both parents and institution sign. The agreement is
about how the child is when described through its skills. It is an agreement
about a factual perspective on the child, which establishes the premise for
future agreements. That is, an agreement about which factual premises
regarding the child's skills will form the basis of a continued collaboration
between parents and institution. However, the parents simultaneously
agree to let the daycare share the dialogue circle with the school as the
premise for their partnership. As Hanne Knudsen from the Danish School
of Education writes in her analysis of the partnership: "The signature thus
both represents a 'yes, you can share the information' and a 'yes, this is
what my child is like'" (Knudsen 2011, own translation). The municipality's idea is that the daycare institution and school engage in a dialogue
across the dialogue circle about what kind of child the school is taking
over, what expectations the school can reasonably have in relation to the

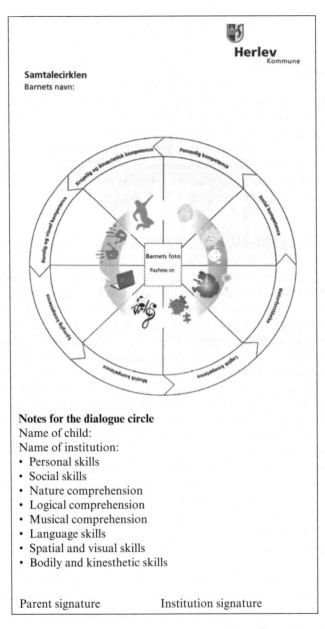

Notes for the dialogue circle
Name of child:
Name of institution:
• Personal skills
• Social skills
• Nature comprehension
• Logical comprehension
• Musical comprehension
• Language skills
• Spatial and visual skills
• Bodily and kinesthetic skills

Parent signature   Institution signature

Source: Herlev Kommune 2010.

Figure 8.3   The dialogue circle

child, what action plans the school can develop, and so on: "Which skills do the circle show that the school can then focus on in the child. Is there something from the circle that may lend itself to an action plan?" (Herlev Kommune 2010, p. 13, own translation). Furthermore, the idea is that the first parent–teacher conference in kindergarten is based on the dialogue circle. Thus, the circle comes to represent a form of partnership handover. The parent–teacher partnership does not have to be built from scratch but is based on agreed premises from the previous partnership between parents and daycare center. The dialogue circle is further developed in the school–parent partnership and is gradually supplemented/replaced by equivalent concepts such as "the student plan" and "the child's skills portrait" (Herlev Kommune 2010, p. 14, own translation).

PARTNERSHIPS WITH THE PERFORMING AUDIENCE

Now, the question is the extent to which these examples of attempts to create partnerships between administration and citizen even concern the question of membership (which ultimately is the central concern of this book). There are at least two questions in play: When an employee (a professional) establishes a partnership with a citizen, can this partnership simultaneously be said to also be a partnership between the employee and the organization? In other words, when an employee enters into partnership relations with a third party, does she simultaneously enter into a partnership agreement with her organization about the goals of the partnership? The second question is about whether the citizen similarly becomes part of the organization through the partnership? When the citizen/student/patient/client accepts an offer of becoming a partner for the administration, are they also assigned membership? And if so, what kind of membership? Formal membership? Self-enrolled membership? A third form of membership? My thesis is that they are assigned a form of *monstrous membership of self-enrollment* where they are invited to join on the condition that they remain outside.

In order to begin to answer these questions, I will have to shift my point of observation from organizational systems to function systems. This is needed in order to arrive at a reasonable description of the production of categories such as citizen, client, student. Without such clarification, the discussion of how these categories become challenged in citizens' contracts and partnerships makes no sense.

Let me begin with a few very general premises. I mentioned previously that, as decision systems, organizations are linked to function systems such as the legal system, the financial system, and so on, when decision

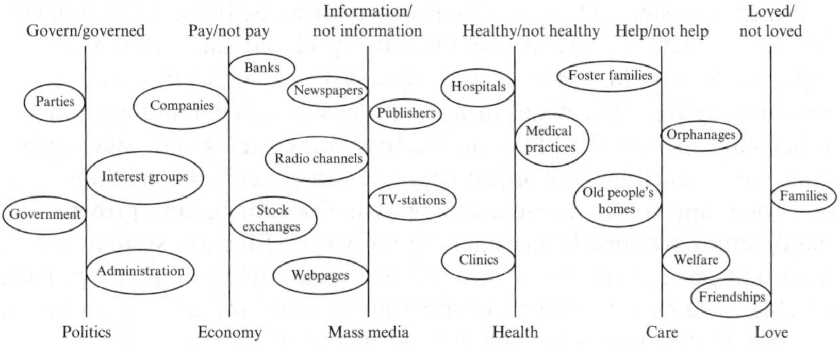

Figure 8.4 Functionally specialized organizations

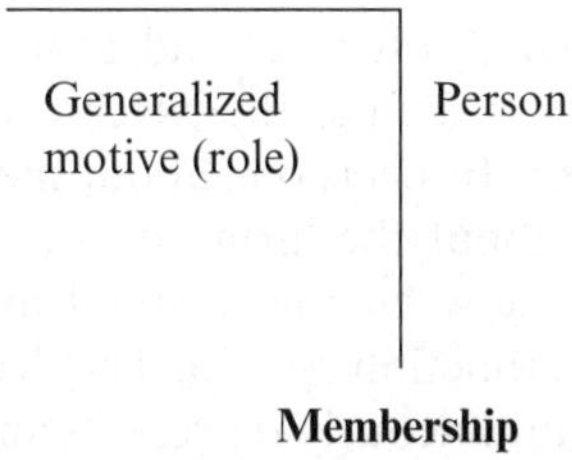

Figure 8.5 The form of the formal membership

operations form communication media from the function systems. If a decision forms the medium of money, we get an economic decision, which "colors" the decision system in a particular way. The environment is then construed as a market. Society's differentiation into different function systems happens concomitant with the development of organizational systems, which specialize in the formation of particular media of communication that belong to the individual function systems. I have written elsewhere about *homophonous organizations* whose specialty is their coupling to particular function systems (Andersen 2003c). This can be roughly illustrated in the model in Figure 8.4.

The coupling between organization and function system is a result of membership decisions and the definition of roles, among other things. This is because the definition of roles is both a communicative operation in an organizational system and in a function system.

For the organizational system, the definition of roles is about making decisions about generalized motives in relation to the association of a specific person with the organization. I summed this up in Chapter 3 with the form of membership (see Figure 8.5).

Function systems also communicate about roles, but not about membership. Function systems are operatively closed and employ binary codes such as right/wrong in the legal system and pay/not pay in the economic system. The codes mean that the system's communication can either link up with the plus side (motivation) or the minus side (reflection). One can either pay or not pay, one can either call something right or wrong, and so on. These are the possibilities for linking provided by the function systems. Over time, the individual function systems create roles that serve purposes of both inclusion and exclusion. Roles provide psychic systems with communicative possibilities for linking up in the function system that allow someone to be recognized as a person within the function system in a way that simultaneously disregards other roles. One is addressed as a physician in the medical function system, and the role of physician disregards the other roles one fulfills in other contexts, for example, mother, wife, volunteer and athlete. Thus, in relation to function systems, role both defines the psychic system's communication relevance and irrelevance. In decisions about membership in a hospital, for example a decision about the hiring of a surgeon, it is obviously a question of a coupling between the hospital as organizational system and the health system as function system. The decision about the general motive for a surgeon simultaneously represents an operation in the organizational system and in the medical health system and its development of role-related expectations.

Function systems historically operate with distinctions between *performance roles* and *audience roles*. We all know these distinctions: actor/ audience, doctor/patient, social worker/ client. Rudolph Stichweh writes about the relationship between role and audience: "The concept of inclusion means that all those members of society who are not involved in the operations of a function system via performance roles are nonetheless important as an audience of this function system. That is, there are specific roles for members of the respective *audience*: roles for voters, consumers, sports spectators, and religious laypersons" (Stichweh 1997, p. 97). Niklas Luhmann reflects on the role of the *audience* as a specific form of parasite on the function system. Speaking of the political system in which the code is government/opposition, he writes:

> In our case the example is the political parties that are forced by the code to locate themselves either within the government or opposition and then the audience (as the parasite). Understood formally, this is a question of the re-inclusion of the excluded third value. Whoever is excluded assumes a position through the exclusion from which one surreptitiously, secretly, unnoticed (!) sneaks oneself back in (. . .) But the unity of the excluded third possibility exists only through exclusion, thus only in the illusion of politics. The omni-

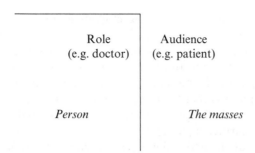

Role (e.g. doctor)	Audience (e.g. patient)
Person	*The masses*

Figure 8.6   The function systems' distinction between role and audience

presence of the audience is actualized through the schema of government/ opposition just as much as the secret power of this parasite. (Luhmann 1990a, pp. 178–9)

For Luhmann, the audience is "the excluded third value" (next to the binary code). The audience is primarily an internal fantasy within the function system about a "third" role one can enter with a very limited role script. A third role, which is parasitic in the sense that one does not perform in relation to the operations of the function system but primarily acts as an observer. And as observer, the audience contributes by being observed by the function system, for example, when political parties reference "the audience opinion" and make themselves representatives of this opinion. Thus, we have a distinction between, on the one hand, performance roles, which gives the one who takes on the role the possibility of being assigned the characteristics of a person, and, on the other hand, audience roles where the observer is merely assigned the characteristics of "the masses" without being recognized in the communication as individually performing. I have illustrated that in Figure 8.6.

Each function system produces both its own performance roles and its own fictitious audience. And each fictitious audience defines its own horizon of expectations of the citizen. The health system sees a patient, the educational system sees a student, the care systems sees a client, and so on. Going to school one knows what the expectations are and which rules of acceptance apply in the communication, for example, the fact that the teacher asks questions and the student answers them. When going to see a doctor, a different set of expectations applies. The doctor also asks questions, but one knows that the questions do not represent a way to test one's knowledge but an attempt by the doctor to gather information for the purpose of reaching a diagnosis. The different fictitious audiences serve the function systems so that they address citizens in a functionally relevant way, including encouraging individual citizens to contribute to their communication and practice. Fictitious audiences stabilize citizens' expectations concerning the meeting with the doctor, the teacher, the social worker, and so on. In other words, we end up with an explosion of different citizens figures linked to the individual function systems. However, my point is that the distinction between performance role and audience has been challenged over the past 20 years – and that this is what causes the new partnership efforts.

The concept of the active fellow citizen effects a strange doubling of the fictitious audiences that the function systems employ. The active fellow citizen is, as mentioned, one who creates herself as free and takes responsibility for herself and her destiny by taking on the collective. This self-relation, however, looks different from the perspective of different function systems. It means something very different to be an active fellow citizen in the care system, educational system, and so on. What the perspectives share in common, however, is that the individual citizen is expected to relate to herself in a proactive way through the codes and languages of the systems. This means an expectation about not only relating to the doctor, teacher or social worker on the systems' conditions but also about creating oneself in the image of the individual system. In addition to previous audience fictions about student, patient, and so on, we get what I call second-order audience fictions (Andersen and Born 2005). With second-order audience fictions, the citizen is encouraged to see herself from the perspective and code of the function system. One is not only expected to create oneself as free and responsibility-seeking, but as free and responsibility-seeking from within the perspective of the individual function system. Therefore, the individual function system develops fictions for the citizen's self-relation. What takes place is a re-entry of the distinction performance role/audience on the side of the role. The excluded massified audience is included as performing but has to be individualized in order to do so. The student is expected to contribute to her own learning. The patient is expected to partake in her own diagnosing and treatment. The client is expected to help herself. The consumer is expected to contribute to the production of the product and become a co-producer. It is an individualization of the audience, which allows the client, student and patient to be assigned a certain status of personhood within the function system. However, the masses as parasite do not disappear. The idea of the masses is maintained as the shadow of the individualized audience. As a self-helped client, one is addressed as a person at the mercy of the function system. The citizen is expected to be able to observe herself from the perspective of the system but is not recognized for general systemic observation skills. One is expected to contribute

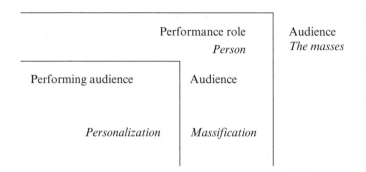

Figure 8.7   Second-order audience fiction

to one's own learning, to see oneself pedagogically, but if one tries as a citizen to direct the pedagogical perspective outward at other students or at the teacher one is perceived as acting aggressively. One is interfering in something that does not concern one. On the one hand, the individual member of the masses is given the chance to gain personhood. On the other hand, the citizen is constantly in danger of losing her personhood and disappearing back into the masses if the function system does not recognize her self-reflection as that of the system's. The active citizen is, not unlike Alice in Wonderland, both inside and outside. The active fellow citizen becomes a *monster*, symbolically connecting what cannot be connected: system and environment. The active fellow citizen is invited inside on the condition that she remains outside (see also Knudsen 2010). I have tried to illustrate that in Figure 8.7.

The student is expected to take responsibility for her own learning. Project work, student plans, personal logbooks, social games and student contracts are examples of this new practice. Each student has to define goals for their own learning but also for their own improved capability to learn. It is called developing one's social and personal skills, for example, social skills for how to inhabit the classroom as a space for learning with learning teams, and so on (Hermann 2003; Andersen 2003a).

The unemployed is expected to be active and to make action plans for the development of her work life (Jensen and Born 2001), and *the social client* is expected to be an active fellow citizen (Järvinen et al. 2002; Andersen 2007a, 2008c). Today, social policy is not about solving clients' problems. Acting on the client's problem is to make the client dependent on the system. It is no longer the social administration that looks and the client who is looked at. The ideal is no longer a comprehensive view of the client. Rather, it is about having a shared view, of seeing together with

Table 8.1   First and second-order audience roles

Function system	Code (plus/ minus)	The code's folding	Performance role	First-order audience role	Second-order audience role
The pedagogical system	Better/worse in terms of learning	Learning is to learn to learn	Teacher	Student	Responsible for own learning
The political system	Power superiority/ power inferiority	Power to empower	Politician	Citizen	Active fellow citizen
Care system	Help/no help	Help through self-help	Social worker	Client	Self-helped client
Health system	Healthy/sick	Preventive lifestyle	Doctor	Patient	The healthy citizen
The economic system	Pay/not pay	Pay for others' payments	Producer	Consumer	Political consumer and the consumer as co-producer

the client. The purpose of support is no longer solving problems caused by the client's particular circumstances, but to create a self, which is capable of creating herself and her own circumstance.

The consumer is expected to be a political consumer. Today, the consumer is not to be victimized by having the public authorities and semi-public institutions such as The Consumer Council speak for them and secure them in every way. Today, The Consumer Council is expected to turn consumers into active political consumers who relate to themselves as a particular consumer type and know the kind of market power they hold when they make a purchase. New types of trademarks and new kinds of information and focus group studies of consumers are elements in this development (Halkier 1999; Sørensen 2004).

As the Norwegian health minister has said, *the patient* today is expected to be her own health minister (Hydle 2003). It is not only a question of treatment but also prevention. The body is no longer the only object of treatment, but also lifestyle. Physical ailments have become symptoms of lifestyle ailments. We are all potential patients and are expected to pre-empt ourselves as such through preventive risk management (Christensen and Andersen 1999; Dahlager 2001; Svendsen 2004). This shift from first-order public fictions to second-order public fictions can be summed up as shown in Table 8.1 (Andersen and Born 2005):

THE ORGANIZATION AS A NEXUS OF PARTNERSHIPS AND THE CITIZEN'S MONSTROUS MEMBERSHIP

Let us return to partnerships. The emergence of these individualized public fictions makes it possible for an organization to multiply into a large number of individualized partnerships. Not just partnerships between manager and employee and among employees (for example, teams), but also partnerships between employee and citizen (for example, client contracts, family contracts, school–parent agreements, student contracts, weight-loss contracts, job application contracts and rehabilitation contracts). Such individualized contracts serve two simultaneous functions: one function is that such contracts represent the preferred self-technology for responding to the challenge of shifting citizens from being responsible to being responsibility-seeking, from recognizing *their public roles* in the first-order fictions to recognizing *themselves* in the second-order fictions. Here, partnerships represent strangely unilateral invitations to limited mutuality. They pretend to be concerned with the empowerment of citizens, but their basic function is to empower the administration to gain access to the individual citizen's private self-relation, which otherwise remains inaccessible to it. By unilaterally inviting mutuality, public administrations expect that the individual citizen receives the invitation positively and reciprocates it by inviting the administration to talk about the citizen's self-relation (Andersen 2004a). We may say that the citizen (the student, parents, client, patient, and so on) is offered a monstrous organizational membership. This form of membership is monstrous because one is never recognized as a person with independent motives. One is invited on the condition that one does not take the invitation literally by pretending to be a full member of the organization. One is only included as a token of one's self-relation. Acting as an actual member results in one's exclusion and returns one to an administrative category.

The other function is about the selection of public. From the perspective of the function systems, the public is no longer a given. As an example, the political function system experiences increasing expectational pressure from its public and voters. Moreover, voters seem segmented into different masses, each with their own perspective and set of expectations. Which public should one choose? The concept of "voter contracts" can be seen as an attempt to select among competing public opinions and reduce external expectations. Similarly, the health system also experiences growing expectational pressure with more and more people asking for a diagnosis. There are competing associations of publics (for example, patient associations). Again, partnerships appear to function as a way to select and control the public. In the public school, for example, the theory of the 12 types of intelligence implies that the public is not simply a mass of students. Students are segmented into types with different expectations of the school. They may expect special education, or they see themselves as tactile children who need a particular form of pedagogy. We could run through the list of function systems. The point is that each function system has competing publics. And partnership seems to offer itself up as a form through which function systems can relate to competing publics and seek to define conditions for the observational horizon of these publics.

The third function concerns the binding of employees in partnerships with organizations in a way that is equivalent to the organization's complexity, and it means that the employee has not only one but many relationships with the organization. These partnerships are a way for the organization to short-circuit and deconstruct its own hierarchical machine of complexity-reduction. The re-entry of "public" on the "performance role" side has the curious effect that it allows for the folding into the organization of the public as a systemic phantasm, where it is given a voice and a body so that agreements can be made about it. The public as the system's internal phantasm is brought to life as some kind of slumbering monster. And the organization allows itself to be strangely represented from outside itself if the member of the public accepts the invitation to become a member of the organization. In the individualized partnership that the employee enters into, the organization allows itself to be represented by means of the personalized parasites of the function systems. Instead of a hierarchically based organizational self-description, the unity of organizations can now be described from its interfaces through multiple partnership descriptions. Observing the organization from this perspective raises a couple of interesting questions about current organizational conditions for asserting influence. Each time a partnership is formed, the organization is given a specific set of visions and future images, but the effect is also the dissolution of the organization into numerous partnerships. The organization becomes a network or a nexus of partnerships.

MANAGEMENT AS SUPERVISION OF PARTNERSHIPS

My final point in this chapter is about what happens to the organizing role of an organization when it assumes the form of a nexus of partnerships. To the extent that the organization lets itself be described as a nexus of partnerships, the function of the organization becomes to create conditions and a framework for its employee's countless partnerships, internally with colleagues and managers in teams and projects and externally with active fellow citizens. As a result, the organization emerges primarily as the supervision of partnerships and partnership formation. Managing the organization means to create possibilities for the relations within the organization as well as with the environment in the form of performing publics.

Anders la Cour and Holger Højlund address this question in a context where the municipality is seen as the supervision of partnerships among welfare institutions – public, voluntary and private. They speak of the *polyphonic supervision of partnerships* when a number of alternative communication media are available for a third party seeking to assume the role of supervisor of collaborations. Their point is that "the selected code defines very different conditions for the individual collaboration forms by showing the collaborating actors how to construct images of each another within the collaboration" (La Cour and Højlund 2008, p. 221). The actors in the La Cour and Højlund study are primarily public and voluntary organizations. I believe that this thesis can be extended to partnerships in relation to individual partnerships among employees, between employees and the organization and between employees and citizens. Moreover, La Cour and Højlund stress that, "inconsistency and internal contradictions continually threaten any supervision, which is sought coded in several different codes. At the same time, however, polyphony also proposes flexible possibilities for making oneself relevant as supervisor in variant work relations" (La Cour and Højlund 2008, p. 222).

Table 8.2 expands upon a similar table by La Cour and Højlund (2008, p. 221)

To the extent that we can perceive an organization as a nexus of partnership, management is transformed into the supervision of partnerships, which, depending on its perspective on differently coded partnerships, is given a range of possible ways of supervising. To view an organization as relations, therefore, is not an unambiguous perspective. Relations represent a polycontextual phenomenon, which depends on the observer's perspective. Relations and partnership are not something in themselves, they are only something to an observer. Thus, the question of what the organization is as a nexus of partnerships oscillates according to the communicative choice of code.

If an organization can be said to be a nexus of partnership and a partnership represents a transient form of agreement, which both seeks to bind and remain unbound, then management becomes the management of transience. This is a form of management, which is relegated to being a parasite on fragile partnerships that never *are* but that are always in their becoming. It is also a form of management which itself is exceedingly

Table 8.2 The polycontextual partnership

Code	The construction of partnership	The construction of the partner	Supervision of partnership formation
Power superiority/power inferiority	Constitution: decision of decision	Partners are construed as independent decision-making actors	Delegation of authority and autonomy
Pay/not pay	Economic alliance with exchange of possibilities for exchange	Partners are construed as *homo economicus*, having entered a long-term economic alliance	Communication of vision and strategy. Investment in the partnership
Better/worse in terms of learning	Mutual learning process, exchange of experience and knowledge sharing	Partners are construed as oscillating between the position of teacher and student	Facilitation of framework for partnership formation. Guiding and coaching
Right/wrong	Promise about future promises	Partners are construed as legal subjects with converging interests	Conflict mediation and conciliation. Procedural regulation and forced reflection
Loved/not loved	A vertical or horizontal "marriage" in which partners develop together	Partners are construed as lovers, blind to each others flaws and deficiencies	Family therapy Creating a space for partners to allow each other to give to each other
Help/no help	A collective of mutual compassion	Partners are construed as codependent on each other's help and care	Caring for the partners' care for each other
Play/reality	A collective of serious playmates	Partners are construed as playmates	Organization of partnership-promoting games such as teambuilding and speed-dating

238

fragile, because even though management facilitates speed-dating, delegates skills, coaches, mediates, and so on, it cannot create and maintain, not to mention control, these partnerships. The organization can organize speed-dating among employees, it can develop agreement forms for citizens, but it can never create a partnership. Partnerships can only be created from within. And it is always up to the partnerships to decide whether the organization supports them or just functions as noise in the environment. The organization becomes a fragile nexus of fragility, a nexus of transient relations, which continually become displaced into the future through promises about subsequent promises, endless suspensions of bonds and expectational fixations.

Conclusion: transient relationships – towards the intensity machine

I began this book with a set of general observations about a non-normative diagnostics of the present. I posed the question of how to perform a diagnosis of the present without a fixed "outside" from which to describe and diagnose. I tried to outline a gradual strategy for the development of an "outside" from within, and I have sought to pursue this strategy in my work. What are the results? How does my specific diagnosis relate to other similar diagnoses? Below I address two different diagnoses of the present:

The most renowned present diagnosis of the development of work relations in recent years is probably Richard Sennett's book, *The Corrosion of Character* (1998). Sennet explores the effects of flexible capitalism on work's possibility to create a coherent personality and character. Sennett's "outside", that is, the place from which he diagnoses the present, is *character formation*. Character, he says,

> particularly focuses upon the long-term aspect of our emotional experience. Character is expressed by loyalty and mutual commitment, or through the pursuit of long-term goals, or by the practice of delayed gratification for the sake of a future end. Out of the confusion of sentiments in which we all dwell at any particular moment, we seek to save and sustain some; these sustainable sentiments will serve our character. Character concerns the personal traits which we value in ourselves and for which we seek to be valued by others. (Sennett 1998, p. 10)

To Sennett, character has no independent history. He chooses character formation as a point of fixation, which makes changes to work and capitalism observable and an object of evaluation. The question for Sennett, accordingly, is: "How can mutual loyalties and commitments be sustained in institutions that are constantly breaking apart or continually being redesigned?" (Sennett 1998, p. 10). Throughout the book he shows how loyalty and mutual commitment cannot be maintained under such conditions. When long-term employee contracts are replaced by short-term ones, when the workforce becomes increasingly mobile, when routines break down and work becomes flexible, when security is replaced by risk-taking, it becomes increasingly difficult for the individual worker to form a character in Sennett's sense. The effect is a psyche that "dwells in a state of endless becoming – a self-hood which is never finished. There can be under these conditions no coherent life narrative, no clarifying moment of change illuminating the whole" (Sennett 1998, p. 133). This, according to Sennett, is eroded character: "A pliant self, a collage of fragments unceasing in its becoming, ever open to new experience – these are just the psychological conditions suited to short-term work experience, flexible institutions, and constant risk-taking" (Sennett 1998, p. 133). In Sennett's book, the only bright spot, which is not really a bright spot, is a group of computer programmers who, having failed in life, their careers destroyed, gradually create a new life narrative in the attempt to heal themselves. However, for Sennett this ultimately remains a tragic development: "In the flexible, fragmented present it may seem possible only to create coherent narratives about what has been, and no longer possible to create predictive narratives about what will be" (Sennett 1998, p. 135).

"Flexibility" and "transience" seem to connote similar directions, but they ultimately represent rather different observations. In Sennett's analysis, the logic of flexibility negates the possibility of a long-term perspective with fixed-term contracts and broken down routines. In my diagnosis, transience does not equal a negation of a directedness towards the future. Transience is not constituted by the fact that employee contracts are short term but by the fact that they continually defer membership. What is transient about self-enrollment is that one never really becomes a member, and that, in turn, is a long-term phenomenon. Becoming a member includes requirements about directedness towards the future whether as future needs for skills, anticipation of the organization's future, or play with possible organizational and personal futures. Focus is on the future, but the future of the present is transient. It becomes engulfed in the same undecidability as the rest of the organization. It is a present future without any notion that it will some day become a present present. Decisions are organized in a way that images of the future never unambiguously come to function as a premise for new decisions. That does not mean that stability has been negated. There can be plenty of stability in the sense that the constant shifting of images of the future is stable. Similarly, we can also imagine "stability" in the autopoiesis of the psychic system, albeit in the second order; a narrative of coherence and lack of coherence in different self-narratives.

Peter Fleming, who wrote the 2009 book *Authenticity and the Cultural Politics of Work*, provides a different diagnosis of the present. The book focuses not only on flexibility in the form of short-term contracts, but in the form of new expectations about freedom in work, which is often accompanied by the ideology of "just being yourself". What is the

"outside" from which Fleming observes? In Fleming's text, this is articulated as an explicit problem. He cannot place "character" outside because
it has become a management object when managers tell employees to "be
yourselves". Peter Fleming's project becomes to salvage authenticity as a
critical figure, even though he is highly aware that this is not an easy task.
One chapter is dedicated to a critique of critical management theory. The
main point here is that critical management theory has been discovered
as a reservoir that companies can parasitize on. Critique can no longer
simply take place from the perspective of an ideal about how employees
must find authenticity in the workplace. This ideal has been appropriated
as a management discourse. Peter Fleming conducts a discourse analysis
of the distinction work/non-work. One becomes authentic, according to
Fleming, through non-work. Work defines non-work as play, sex, leisure
time, counterculture and fun. As soon as authenticity becomes a management ideology, non-work becomes an "exploitable reservoir" for the companies, for example, through play and games in the workplace (Fleming
2009, p. 8). Companies copy non-work and fold it into the company where
it becomes the fabric of (in)authenticity. This results in a peculiar double
perspective on the distinction work/non-work because non-work simultaneously appears as tied to the discursive figure of work, and hence is
a discursive element, while also representing the "real" outside of work.
This double standard allows Fleming to argue that the "be yourself" ideology only *mimes* the outside of work, including anti-capitalist movements.
His discourse analysis turns into ideology critique based on a distinction
that comes exceedingly close to the distinction true/false consciousness.
The "be yourself" ideology is described in normative terms as *parasit-
izing* on non-work: "it parasitically draws upon the world of non-work,
both outside the organization (in terms of leisure, lifestyle, and popular
counterculture) and inside the formal organization (in terms of informal
interactions, discretion, subcultures, and organizational 'slack'" (Fleming
2009, p. 137). And he continues: "What is being arrogated in the sphere
of non-work (fun, sexuality, lifestyle, domestic rituals, etc.) are signs of
an 'elemental communism' whereby gestures of cooperation, non-market
forms of life, and interaction (both inside and outside the firm) are reified
into a productive resource" (Fleming 2009, p. 138). Fleming's point is that
the articulation of "just be yourself" means precisely that the employee
cannot be herself. However, what then does "being oneself" mean in the
true, authentic way? Fleming suggests that we link authenticity to an ideal
about freedom *from* work. Only thus can the concept of authenticity be
salvaged as a critical concept. He provides the following normative definition: "I define freedom here simply as *having a life*, reclaiming it from
work so that self-identity (or personal authenticity) might be achieved"

(Fleming 2009, p. 149). And he goes on: "Authenticity cannot be achieved in or around the corporation without its conceptualization and enactment being implicated in reproducing the production process" (Fleming 2009, p. 164). The ideal is "a life of full positivity" (Fleming 2009, p. 156).

Again, we can trace many parallels to the diagnosis of the present moment that this book proposes. Like Peter Fleming, I observe the way in which authenticity has become articulated as an organizational employee expectation. However, my point is not simply that authenticity comes to constitute an intensified organizational way to control employees. My point is also not that play, love, and pedagogy are simply exploited for purposes of capitalist productivity. I do not hold an ideal, which has to be upheld at all costs. Indeed, expectations about pedagogical, passionate and playful authenticity can become a psychological strain on the individual. However, it is interesting to observe that such expectations also become an incredibly heavy strain on the organizations themselves. Because Fleming is so focused on salvaging his critical project and appearing as an (authentic?) critical organizational researcher, he fails to see that new discourses also significantly and constitutively affect organizational conditions for being an organization – and hence the micro-political conditions for the struggle for membership. Ultimately, his efforts fail to produce a precise description of the present moment.

Both Sennett and Fleming presuppose an outside, which is normative and functions as judging authority. Sennett argues that flexible capitalism erodes the possibility of personal character formation for the individual employee. Although I am very fond of Sennett's analysis, the problem is that the ideal on which his perspective is based relies so heavily on the notion of the formal membership and its distinction between role and person. To a great extent, his narrative becomes a history of decline, whose tragic tone indeed contains a great deal of beauty but which fails to comprehend the present moment. How can Sennett's critique be put to productive use rather than simply mourn what has been lost?

Peter Fleming argues that the "just be yourself" ideology represents a further sophistication of corporate and capitalist control over the individual. The "be yourself" ideology provides companies with access to control over additional aspects of the individual employee's personality. The "be yourself" ideology creates new possibilities for companies to ascribe to individuals responsibility for organizational flaws and dysfunctions. The "be yourself" ideology produces fun, sex and counterculture as a reservoir of exploitation for purposes of production (which is anything but good). The problem with Fleming's critique is that, despite many important insights, it ends up being rather too purist. There is no responsibility towards the present, in this case not because a previous form of identity becomes idealized resulting in a history of decline, but because the ideal identifies any form of organization, any form of work, any form of instrumentality as exploitative and destructive. We need not mourn what is lost but wait for the revolution and until then work in the autonomous pockets of society. According to Fleming, one is only authentic and autonomous in non-work, outside the codependence of capitalism.

What is the objective of this form of critique? I am inspired to quote Reinhart Koselleck's famous study of the history of the concept of critique in his book *Critique and Crises*. He shows that the concept of criticism emerged in the seventeenth century in opposition to the absolutist state. Criticism becomes the art of judgment: "Its function calls for testing a given circumstance for its validity, its rightness or beauty" (Koselleck 1988, p. 103). However, gradually criticism leads to hypocrisy and the critics "became the victims of their own mystification (. . .) Criticism goes far beyond that which has occasioned it and it transformed into the motor of self-righteousness. It produces its own delusion" (Koselleck 1988, pp. 117, 119). And he continues: "Reaching towards infinity, the sovereignty of critics seemed to continue its upward climb. Pushing criticism to its utmost limits, the critic saw himself as the King of Kings, the true sovereign" (Koselleck 1988, 119). Peter Fleming seems to position himself in the King's seat. I am not sure what to make of his position.

I do not subscribe to an explicit normative ideal that might have provided me with a platform from which to critique. And yet I do not refrain entirely from criticism. I also do not provide a set of comprehensive answers to the challenges that clearly accompany the regime of transience. Perhaps less will do – for now?

Contingency

I have pointed out different forms of contingency in the relationship between organization and employee. I have described the shift in the form of membership from formal membership to the membership of self-enrollment. But I have also shown the contingency of the medium and language formed by self-enrollment. I have tried to show the formation of at least three languages involved in the membership of self-enrollment (pedagogy, love, play), each of which defines its own conditions of possibility for self-enrollment. Thus, I have illuminated the way that managers, unions and employees respectively can play with the established contingency. The relationship between membership and self-enrollment is not given, the language of self-enrollment is not given, but represents a terrain for the unfolding of different strategies.

This has opened up a horizon of impractical questions: How does it work in your organization – formal membership or self-enrollment? Do you communicate in the code of pedagogy, love or play? Are you aware of the rules of the game that apply to the different media? Are you aware of the strategic possibilities provided by each of these languages? But there are also problems, challenges, risks, and so on. For example, loving self-enrollment can result in quite uncaring upward spirals of stress and experience of never having done enough to deserve others' love and recognition, and that the playful self-enrollment can lead to a further denial of realities, which can be quite difficult to handle both for the organization and for the individual.

Additionally, I have shown how organizations, with the form of self-enrollment, make themselves dependent upon emotions in the psychic systems. I have described the development of alternative semantics for the thematization of emotions, including love, pedagogy, care and play. The question, therefore, is not how to access the "real" emotions of employees or managers, but instead which language to use for the discussion of emotions. And how do we handle this talk when, on the one hand, we find it absolutely necessary because it seems essential to us to learn whether colleagues, managers or employees are getting serious with us and take the project as seriously as we do. And how do we handle this talk when we, on the other hand, are well able to see that the claim on an authenticity-proof regarding engagement and passion is absurd. The choice of language significantly changes both the communication and the possibilities for experience and action.

This opens another horizon of questions: If you discuss emotions in your organization, what language do you subscribe to? What communicative rules do you submit to when you choose particular forms of emotional communication? Is there a sense of competition in your organization around the desire to appear authentic? Do you have a competition on initiatives and engagement? Who is the most entrepreneurial? Or is it rather a competition on essential life pain? Who is under the most pressure? And what are the right forms of the pressure? Whose pain demonstrates total self-investment in work? And which strategies for the articulation of emotion do you support? Is someone primarily perceived as authentic when trying to communicate involvement, when being positive and disciplined emotionally, or when playing up the role as pain-struck employee (or manager)?

Of course, there are also questions for the manager: What games are permitted between employees? How far do you go in your intimacy with your employees? Is work and friendship mixed? Is there at all an alternative? How large a part in your total managerial work is emotional management? What happens when you try to withdraw yourself from the high intimacy zone? Is it accepted?

I have discussed the development of a rather extensive expectational structure in the organization's relationship with employees, with different "bundles" of expectations, which are heterogeneous and sometimes even contradictory, and a machine of expectation acceleration in the code of love, which continually poses the question of whether or not one has contributed enough to be loved. I do not have a satisfactory answer to the question of how to reduce expectations or the heterogeneity of expectations. Taking responsibility for employees is not, as I have shown, a possible answer. The impractical question, therefore, is how to actually manage the acceleration of expectations, heterogeneity and double binds, given their prevalence? The answer cannot be found in the effort to force back the logic of transience. That is one thing that does not seem contingent. Perhaps, instead, it is possible to force it forward by precisely observing these expectations as transient and develop a culture that allows for "minor failures" as a strategy for recovering from disappointment in each other and in ourselves. It would have to be about finding a way to devaluate the excess of expectations. As it is, new expectations continue to develop. So, why is focus on disappointments and fraud linked to long since dissolved expectations?

Paradoxes

Moreover, I have pointed out a series of paradoxes, which necessarily accompany the transience of self-enrollment.

First, I have shown how the logic of transience itself installs a paradox. It begins in the semantics of change with the question of how to effect change when the only perceived form of stability is change. This places the organization in a paradoxical situation in which it is at once responsible for creating itself through recursive decision and also has to desire undecidability. This leaves us with an organization that simultaneously makes decisions and suspends the very same decisions in order to be able to continually be something else.

The paradox of transience is then multiplied. We get the paradox of membership, which consists in the fact that the shift from formal membership to the membership of self-enrollment is not a from-to movement, but a both-and shift. The membership of self-enrollment is also a formal membership, self-enrollment is a fold on the formal membership: It is a decision about formal membership, which simultaneously suspends itself. And this produces the fundamental management of self-management paradox with its double communication: "Do as I say – be independent", and which similarly puts the power superior in the paradoxical situation of only having power through the suspension of power and only as the subordinate's voluntary attribution of it. And in the termination of membership, the paradox translates into: "We are firing you – but only out of love because we still love you, and wish you a new and better partner."

Second, there is the paradox of incommunication. When, in the form of self-enrollment, the organization makes itself radically more dependent on the emotions of the psychic systems and on the authenticity in their communication, organizational communication about employee emotion increases without necessarily resulting in improved communication of these emotions. The increase in emotional communication causes an increase in the incommunicability of emotions. And this once again directs communicative attention away from information in the communication towards communicative noise.

Third, there is the paradox of contract, which consists in the fact that the shift from contract to partnership is a both-and shift. A partnership is also a contract. It is a contract about a contract, a promise about future promises. As such, a partnership is also a contract that suspends itself: We have an agreement but not quite yet. And this produces two fundamental personnel management paradoxes with the double communication: "We want to commit to an agreement – the agreement must be unbound" and "Let us create a community – let us respect each other's independence."

Finally, there is the paradox of inclusion, which similarly is about the fact that the shift from citizen as category to fellow citizen as member is a both-and shift. It is a folding of the difference performance role/public role, resulting in the performing public, which is simultaneously included and excluded. This produces a monstrous membership, forced to unfold a paradox with the double communication: "You are invited to participate – (if you) stay outside."

Management is often forced to unfold such conditions of impossibility. And employees and managers often find themselves in double binds, which can be experienced as rather uncomfortable. My impractical message is: What is attempted is impossible but at the same time necessary. It is important for a manager or employee to face impossibility. Ultimately, this does not prevent becoming a victim of it, but it does increase one's space of action and experience. It is important to recognize the fact that where there are paradoxes, there are sure to be politics and negotiation. The paradoxes each reflect a fundamental undecidability, which has to be decided, but with no given model for how to decide. This creates tension, which calls for management but also resistance.

In relation to such paradoxes, the semantics (pedagogy, love, play) function as strategies for deparadoxification. They are ways in which paradoxes can be handled, deferred, hidden and made productive without ever being resolved. And whereas the paradoxes are not contingent, to the extent that there is transience and self-enrollment, the semantics for deparadoxification, in turn, are contingent.

Diagnostics of the Present

Together, these paradoxes and semantics constitute a regime of transience, which has significant effects for organizations' possibilities for being organizations. The very notion of organizing is challenged with the forms of self-enrollment and partnership.

I have shown that the logic of transience creates an organization which does not only create itself but also deconstructs itself by suspending the very decisions that it makes, thus deconstructing not only the individual operation but also the possibility of recursively linking operations to operations and forming the network we usually refer to as an organization.

I have also shown that the differentiation into a number of heterogeneous languages that each seeks to solve the problems of authenticity caused by self-enrollment multiplies the problems of authenticity rather than solving them. The result of this is what I have referred to as the "trembling organization". The trembling organization is one that places greater emphasis on incommunicable noise than on communication itself. The many different emotional languages increase the level of noise in the organization's structural couplings to the psychic systems. It is not only a question of how management of self-management intensifies how much the organization irritates the psychic system. It is significant that there is also an escalation in the organization's irritability in relation to psychic systems. The organization becomes hypersensitive.

Finally, I have shown that the organization seems to move in the direction of becoming a nexus of partnerships among employees, between employee and manager, and between employee and citizen. This organization is one that in a peculiar way allows itself to be represented from the outside as long as the public accepts membership of the organization. In the individualized partnerships that employees partake in, the organization allows itself to be represented through the personalized parasites of the function systems. Instead of a hierarchically oriented organizational self-description, the organizational whole can now be described from the perspective of its interfaces through multiple partnership descriptions. The organization becomes a network or a nexus of partnerships.

Is this a positive or negative development? Do partnerships and self-enrollment deliver what they are intended to for the organization? What is the overall significance of the form of partnership and self-enrollment in their multiple manifestations for the relationship between organization and psychic system? Sennett argues that it causes personal character to decline. Fleming argues that it leads to increased control over the individual and to the exploitation of the "outside" of work for capitalist ends. Both of these perspectives see the employee as a victim of her circumstance. I prefer not to propose an alternative perspective – because I do not know where such a perspective would come from. However, I might be able to suggest a few points from the inside based on the distinctions I have observed. I have already pointed to the development of new double binds, to the employee being subjected to expectations that are difficult to live up to. But these points can also be formulated differently, and in a way that makes it easier to understand why the revolution Fleming is waiting for has yet to become a reality.

The logic of transience causes two formal shifts: from contract to partnership and from formal membership to self-enrollment. I have addressed this in different ways throughout the book. Perhaps the most significant shift is a qualitative change in the coupling between organization and psychic system from fixed point to universe; whereas both contract and formal membership simply implied a *punctual coupling* of organization and psychic system with fixed obligations and descriptions of roles, partnership and self-enrollment entail that the coupling between organization and psychic system develops *its own universe of fluid conditions*. It is almost a question of independent system formation in the forms of both self-enrollment and partnership. Precisely because both forms are transient, they have to be continually recreated and exist only in their becoming. This kind of system formation oscillates between being an organizational subsystem and an organizational parasite respectively. In any case, the result is a shift in the direction of ongoing communication about the partnership as partnership, and similarly ongoing communication about self-enrollment that never happens. In the punctual coupling of the contract and the formal membership, one could speak of a *zone of indifference* between the psychic system and the organizational system which allowed for a great deal of freedom with respect to the factual development of the relationship without having to speak about the relationship as such. Partnership and self-enrollment turn this logic on its head: here, the relationship between organization and psychic system is *always* in question. Instead of a zone of indifference we have a *zone of intensity*. Or rather, an *intensity machine*, since it is not simply "an intense space" but a continual production and exploration of intensity and possibilities for intensity in the form of highly intimate couplings between organization and psychic systems. The intensity machine accelerates the psychic system's possibility for linking to the organization. The psychic system can perceive itself as relevant in many different ways. The intensity machine increases the inter-penetration between the organizational system and the psychic systems. Fundamentally speaking, a social system is always a parasite on psychic systems. The social presupposes the psychic and lives off the autopoiesis of psychic systems. But social systems are also guests, who contribute to the table with semantic cultivation, which can enrich the inner complexity and autopoiesis of the psychic systems. With the shift from an organizational zone of indifference to a dynamic intensity machine, the psychic systems are given new possibilities for pursuing affect in the organizations – with all its possibilities and risks.

Including the body and biological systems as system references we might talk about a management of potentiality aiming at creating a zone of intense interpenetration between the organization and psychic systems, inter-human interpenetration and the interpenetration between psyche and body. In *management of potentiality* the creation of possibilities is put far above the realization of possibilities, and interpenetration becomes the *medium* for potentialization. This is a regime of intensity suspending present future in favor of the future of future.

Bibliography

Administrationsdepartementet (1987), *Årsberetning 1987*, København.

Amhøj, Christa Breum (2004), "Medarbejderens synliggørelse i den transparente organisation: Om styring af frihed og usynliggørelse af ledelse", in Dorthe Pedersen (ed.), *Offentlig ledelse i managementstaten*, København: Samfundslitteratur, 268–86.

Amhøj, Christa Breum (2007), "Det selvskabte medlemskab: Om managementstaten, dens styringsteknologier og indbyggere", Samfundslitteratur, PhD Series, 23, Frederiksberg.

Andersen, Niels Åkerstrøm (1995), *Selvskabt forvaltning. Forvaltningspolitikkens og centralforvaltningens udvikling i Danmark 1990–1994*, København: Nyt fra Samfundsvidenskaberne.

Andersen, Niels Åkerstrøm (2003a), *Borgerens kontraktliggørelse*, København: Hans Reitzels Forlag.

Andersen, Niels Åkerstrøm (2003b), *Discursive Analytical Strategies – Understanding Foucault, Koselleck, Laclau, Luhmann*, Bristol: Policy Press.

Andersen, Niels Åkerstrøm (2003c), "Polyphonic organisations", in Tor Hernes and Tore Bakken (ed.), *Autopoietic Organization Theory, Abstakt, Liber*, Oslo: Copenhagen Business School Press, 151–82.

Andersen, Niels Åkerstrøm (2004a), "The contractualisation of the citizen – on the transformation of obligation into freedom", *Social Systems*, JG. 10, Heft 2, 273–91.

Andersen, Niels Åkerstrøm (2004b), "Ledelse af personlighed – om medarbejderens pædagogisering", in Dorthe Pedersen (ed.), *Offentlig ledelse i Managementstaten*, København: Samfundslitteratur, pp. 241–67.

Andersen, Niels Åkerstrøm (2006), *Partnerskabelse*, København: Hans Reitzels Forlag.

Andersen, Niels Åkerstrøm (2007a), "Creating the client who can create himself and his own fate – the tragedy of the citizens' contract", *Qualitative Sociology Review*, 3 (2), 119–43.

Andersen, Niels Åkerstrøm (2007b), "The self-infantilised adult and the management of personality", *Critical Discourse Studies*, 4 (3), 331–52.

Andersen, Niels Åkerstrøm (2008a), *Legende magt*, København: Hans Reitzels Forlag.

Andersen, Niels Åkerstrøm (2008b), *Partnerships: Machines of Possibility*, Bristol: Policy Press.

Andersen, Niels Åkerstrøm (2008c), "The world as will and adaptation: the inter-discursive coupling of citizens' contracts", *Critical Discourse Studies*, **5** (1), 75–89.

Andersen, Niels Åkerstrøm (2009), *Power at Play. The Relationships between Play, Work and Governance*, London: Palgrave Macmillan.

Andersen, Niels Åkerstrøm (2010), "Luhmann as analytical strategist", in John René, Anna Henkel and Jana Rückert-John (eds), *Die Methodologien des System. Wie kommt man zum Fall und wie dahinter?*, Wiesbaden: VS Verlag, 97–117.

Andersen, Niels Åkerstrøm (2011), "Conceptual history and the diagnostics of the present", *Management & Organizational History*, **3**, 248–67.

Andersen, Niels Åkerstrøm (2012a), "Citizen's contract as a tricky steering medium", in Niels Thyge Thygesen (ed.), *The Illusion of Management Control – A Systems Theoretical Approach to Managerial Technologies*, London: Palgrave Macmillan, pp. 108–32.

Andersen, Niels Åkerstrøm (2012b), "Organization and decision", in Olivar Hahraus, Armin Nassehi, Maroi Grizelj, Irmhild Saake, Christian Kirchmeier and Julian Müller (ed.), *Luhmann-Handbuch. Leben – Werk – Wirkung*, Stuttgart/Weimar: Verlag J. N. Metzler, 202–209.

Andersen, Niels Åkerstrøm (2012c), "To promise a promise – when contractors desire a life long partnership", in Niels Åkerstrøm Andersen and Inger Johanne Sand (eds), *Hybrid Forms of Governance – Self-Suspension of Power*, London: Palgrave Macmillan, 202–209.

Andersen, Niels Åkerstrøm and Asmund Born (2000), "Complexity and change: two 'semantic tricks' in the triumphant oscillating organization", *System Practice and Action Research*, **13** (3) 297–308.

Andersen, Niels Åkerstrøm and Asmund Born (2001), *Kærlighed og omstilling. Italesættelsen af den offentligt ansatte*, København: Nyt fra samfundsvidenskaberne.

Andersen, Niels Åkerstrøm and Asmund Born (2005), "Selvet mellem undersøgelse og bekendelse – En inklusions- og eksklusionsmaskine", *Grus*, **74**, 94–114.

Andersen, Niels Åkerstrøm and Asmund Born (2007), "Emotional identity feelings as communicative artefacts in organisations", *International Journal of Work Organisation and Emotion*, **2** (1), 35–48.

Andersen, Niels Åkerstrøm and Asmund Born (2008), "The employee in the sign of love", *Culture and Organization*, **14** (4), 225–343.

Andersen, Niels Åkerstrøm and Inger-Johanne Sand (eds) (2012), *Hybrid Forms of Governance – Self-Suspension of Power*, London: Palgrave Macmillan.

Antonacopoulou, Elena and Yiannis Gabriel (2001), "Emotion, learning and organizational change", *Journal of Organizational Change*, **14** (5), 435–51.

Argyris, Chris (1960), "Organizational effectiveness under stress", *Harvard Business Review*, **38** (3), 137–46.

Ariès, Philippe (1973), *Centuries of Childhood*, Harmondsworth: Penguin Books.

AS3 Outplacement (2008), *En værdig opsigelse*, København.

Baecker, Dirk (1999), "The form game", in Dirk Baecker (ed.), *Problems of Form*, Stanford, CA: Stanford University Press, 99–107.

Barnard, Chester I. (1968), *The Functions of the Executive*, Cambridge, MA: Harvard University Press.

Bateson, Gregory (1955), "The message 'This is play'", in Bertram Schaffner (ed.), *Group Processes, Transactions of the Second Conference October 9, 10, 12, 1955, Princeton, N.J.*, New York: Josiah Macy JR. Foundation, 145–242.

Bateson, Gregory (2000), *Steps to an Ecology of Mind – Collected Essays in Anthropology, Psychiatry, Evolution, and Epistemology*, Chicago, IL: University of Chicago Press.

Bauman, Zygmunt (2002), *Society under Siege*, Cambridge: Polity Press.

Bauman, Zygmunt (2003), *Liquid Love: On the Frailty of Human Bonds*, Oxford: Polity Press.

Bauman, Zygmunt (2004), *Flydende kærlighed*, København: Hans Reitzels Forlag.

Bauman, Zygmunt (2008), *The Art of Life*, Cambridge: Polity Press.

Bjerg, Helle and Dorthe Staunæs (2011), "Self-management through shame – uniting governmentality studies and the 'affective turn'", *Ephemera*, **11** (2), 138–56.

Blum, Fred H. (1958), "Social audit of the enterprise", *Harvard Business Review*, **36** (2), 77–86.

Bojesen, Anders and Sara Louise Muhr (2008), "In the name of love: let's remember desire", *Ephemera*, **8** (1), 79–93.

Borch, Christian (2009), "Organizational atmosphere: foam, affect and architecture", *Organization*, **17** (2), 223–41.

Burke, Richard (1971), "'Work' and 'play'", *Ethics*, **82** (1), 33–47.

Caputo, John D. (1997), *Deconstruction in a Nutshell. A Conversation with Jacques Derrida*, New York: Fordham University Press.

Caroselli, Marlene (1996), *Quality Games for Trainers*, New York: The McGraw-Hill Companies.

Chang, Richard (2001), *The Passion Plan at Work*, San Francisco, CA: Jossey-Bass.

Chefgruppen HK/Kommunal (2009), *En værdig afskedigelse?*, København, 23–27.

Christensen, Gudrun and Niels Åkerstrøm Andersen (1999), "Spisningens sygeliggørelse", *Grus*, **59**.

Christensen, S. (1987), "Fremtidens personalepolitik i staten", *Samfundsøkonomen*, **3**, 19–21.

Clam, Jean (2000), "System's sole constituent: the operation', *Acta Sociologica*, **43** (1), 63–80.

Clarke, John and Janet Newman (1997), *The Managerial State*, London: Sage Publication.

Clough, Patricia Ticinito and Jean Halley (2007), *The Affective Turn. Theorizing the Social*, Durham, NC and London: Duke University Press.

Costea, Bogdan, Norman Crump and Kostas Amiridis (2007), "Managerialism and 'infinite human resources': a commentary on the 'therapeutic habitus', 'derecognition of finitude' and the modern sense of self", *Journal for Cultural Research*, **11** (3), 245–64.

Costea, Bogdan, Norman Crump and John Holm (2005), "Dionysus at work? The ethos of play and the ethos of management", *Culture & Organization*, **11** (2), 139–51.

Costea, Bogdan, Norman Crump and John Holm (2006), "Conceptual history and the interpretation of managerial ideologies", *Management & Organizational History*, **1** (2), 159–75.

Cour, Anders la (2002), "Frivillighedens pris", ph.d.-afhandling 21. København: Sociologisk Institut, KU.

Cunningham, J. Barton (1997), "Feelings and interpretations during an organization's death", *Journal of Organizational Change Management*, **10** (6), 471–90.

Dahlager, Lisa (2001), "I forebyggelsens navn", *Distinktion*, 91–102.

Dalton, Melville (1959), *Men Who Manage. Fusions of Feeling and Theory in Administration*, New York: John Wiley & Sons, Inc.

De Man, Henry (1927), *The Psychology of Socialism*, New York: Henry Holt and Company.

Derrida, Jacques (1988), *The Ear of the Other*, London: University of Nebraska Press.

Derrida, Jacques (1992a), "Force of law: the 'mystical foundation of authority'", in Drucilla Conell, Michel Rosenfeld and David Gray Carlson (eds), *Deconstruction and the Possibility of Justice*, New York: Routledge, 3–67.

Derrida, Jacques (1992b), *The Gift of Death*, London: The University of Chicago Press.

Derrida, Jacques (1996), "Remarks on deconstruction and pragmatism", in Chantal Mouffe (eds), *Deconstruction and Pragmatism*, London: Routledge, 77–88.

Derrida, Jacques (2007), "Des tours de Babel", in Jacques Derrida (ed.), *Psyche. Inventions of the Other, Volume 1*. Stanford, CA: Stanford University Press, 191–225.

Dilts, Gordon (1966), "Developing desirable employee attitudes", *Industrial Management*, **8** (7), 5–8.

Dodgson, Mark, David Gann and Ammon Salter (2005), *Think, Play, Do*, Oxford: Oxford University Press.

Durkheim, Émile (1997), *The Division of Labor in Society*, New York: Simon and Schuster.

Ekman, Susanne (2012), *Authority and Autonomy. Paradoxes of Modern Knowledge Work*, Hampshire: Palgrave Macmillan.

Epstein, Robert (2000), *The Big Book of Stress-Relief Games. Quick, Fun Activities for Feeling Better*, New York: The McGraw-Hill Companies.

Ewing, David W. (1964), "Tension can be an asset", *Harvard Business Review*, **42** (5), 71–8.

Fellinger, Åsa-Mia (2005), *Svære medarbejdersamtaler – bliv en bedre chef*, København: Jyllandspostens forlag.

Fineman, Stephen (ed.) (1993), *Emotions in Organizations*, London: Sage Publications.

Fineman, Stephen (1997), "Emotion and management learning", *Management Learning*, **28** (1), 13–25.

Fineman, Stephen (2006), "Emotion and organizing", in Stewart R. Clegg, C. Hardy, T. Lawrence and W. Nord (eds), *The SAGE Handbook of Organization Studies*, London: Sage Publications, pp. 675–700.

Fineman, Stephen (2010), "Emotion in organizations – a critical turn", in Barbara Sieben and Åsa Wettergren (eds), *Emotionalizing Organizations and Organizing Emotions*, London: Palgrave Macmillan, pp. 23–41.

Flaubert, Gustave (2010 [1857]), *Følelsernes opdragelse*, København: Rosinante.

Fleming, Peter (2009), *Authenticity and the Cultural Politics of Work. New Form of Informational Control*, Oxford: Oxford University Press.

Foerster, Heinz von (1989), "Wahrnehmung", in J. Baudrillard, H. Börhringer, V. Flusser, H. Foerster, K. Friedrich and P. Weibel (eds), *Philosophien der neuen Technologie*, Berlin: Merve Verlag, pp. 27–41.

Foerster, Heinz von (1992), "Ethics and second-order cybernetics", *Cybernetics & Human Knowing*, **1** (1), 9–19.

Foerster, Heinz von (2003), *Understanding Understanding: Essays on Cybernetics and Cognition*, New York: Springer-Verlag.

Forbess-Greene, Sue (1983), *The Encyclopedia of Icebreakers*, San Diego, CA: Applied Skills Press.

Foucault, Michel (1988), "The ethic of care for the self as a practice of freedom", in James Bernauer and David Rasmussen (eds), *The Final Foucault*, Cambridge, Massachusetts: The MIT Press, 3–20.

Fox, Shaul and Yair Amichai-Hamburger (2001), "The power of emotional appeals in promoting organizational change programs", *Academy of Management Executive*, **15** (4), 84–95.

Frankel, Christian and Niels Thyge Thygesen (2012), "Management as a temporal hybrid", in Niels Åkerstrøm Andersen and Inger-Johanne Sand (eds), *Hybrid Forms of Governance. Self-Suspension of Power*, Hampshire: Palgrave Macmillan, 102–123.

Frost, Peter J. (2003), *Toxic Emotion at Work. How Compassionate Managers Handle Pain and Conflict*, Boston, MA: Harvard Business School Press.

Frost, Peter J., Jane E. Dutton, Sally Maitlis, Jacoba Lilius and Monica C. Worline (2006), "Seeing organizations differently: three lenses on compassion", in Stewart Clegg, Cynthia Hardy, Thomas Lawrence and Walter Nord (eds), *The SAGE Handbook of Organization Studies*, London: Sage Publications, 843–866.

Fuchs, Peter J. (2004), "Wer hat wozu und wieso überhaupt Gefühle?", *Soziale Systeme*, **10** (1), 89–110.

Gadamer, Hans-Georg (1985), *Truth and Method*, New York: Crossroad.

Glennon, J.R., W.A. Owens, W.J. Smith and L.E. Albright (1960), "New dimension in measuring morale", *Harvard Business Review*, **38** (1), 106–107.

Goethe, Johann Wolfgang von (2008 [1774]), *Den unge Werthers lidelser*, København: Søren Gyldendals Klassikere.

Goleman, Daniel (1998), *Working with Emotional Intelligence*, New York: Bantam Dell.

Goleman, Daniel (2008), *Følelsernes intelligens på arbejdspladsen*, København: Borgens Forlag.

Greenwich, Carolyn (2000), *Fun and Gains. Motivate and Energize Staff with Workplace Games, Contest and Activities*, Sydney: McGraw Hill.

Habermas, Jürgen (1987), *The Philosophical Discourse of Modernity*, Oxford: Polity Press.

Halkier, Bente (1999), "Politisering af forbrug i risikosamfundet", in Kurt Nielsen, Anni Greve, Finn Hanson and Klaus Rasborg (eds), *Risiko, politik og miljø i det moderne samfund*, Forlaget Sociologi, 337–367.

Herlev Kommune (2005), *Rammeplan for det pædagogiske arbejde med de 0-10-årige*, Herlev.

Herlev Kommune (2010), *Tillæg til Rammeplanens afsnit om det betydningsfulde samarbejde*, Herlev.

Hermann, Stefan (2003), "Fra folkeskole til kompetencemiljø – tendenser i videnssamfundets kapitallogik", in Christian Borch and Lars T. Larsen (eds), *Perspektiver, magt og styring. Luhmann & Foucault til diskussion*, København: Hans Reitzels Forlag, 231–266.

Herzberg, Frederick, Bernard Mausner and Barbara B. Snyderman (1967), *The Motivation to Work*, 2nd ed., New York: John Wiley & Sons.

Hochschild, Arlie Russell (2004), "Gennem sprækker i tidsfælden. Fra markedsmanagement til familiemanagement", in Michael Hviid Jacobsen and Jens Tonboe (eds), *Arbejdssamfundet*, København: Hans Reitzels Forlag, 109–30.

Høgsted, Rikke (2009a), *Kom på benene igen. Sådan klarer du en fyring*, Viborg: Dansk Psykologisk Forlag.

Høgsted, Rikke (2009b), *Sådan fyrer du med værdighed*, Væksthus for ledelse, lederweb.dk.

Hohmann, Luke (2007), *Innovation Games. Creating Breakthrough Products through Collaborative Play*, London: Addison-Wesley.

Huberman, John (1964), "Discipline without punishment", *Harvard Business Review*, **42** (14), 62–8.

Hughes, Jason (2010), "Emotional intelligence: Elias, Foucault and the reflexive emotional self", *Foucault Studies*, (8), 28–52.

Huizinga, Johan (1971), *Homo Ludens*, Boston, MA: Beacon Press.

Hydle, Ida (2003), "Fra pasient til risikant", in I. Neuman and O. Sending (eds), *Regjering i Norge*, Oslo: Pax Forlag A/S, 154–175.

Ibarra, Herminia and Jennifer L. Petriglieri (2010), "Identity work and play", *Journal of Organizational Change Management*, **23** (1), 10–25.

Jacoby, Nicoline and Lise Bræstrup (2007), *Bossa Nova. Ledelse ude på gulvet*, København: Børsens Forlag.

Järvinen, Margaretha, Jørgen E. Larsen and Niels Mortensen (2002), *Det magtfulde møde mellem system og klient*, Århus: Aarhus Universitetsforlag.

Järvinen, Margaretha and Nanna Mik-Meyer (eds) (2003), *At skabe en klient*, København: Hans Reitzels Forlag.

Jelbo, Michael J. (2009), "Den første gang", *Berlingske Nyhedsmagasin*, (5), 27.

Jennings, Elizabeth and Francis Jennings (1951), "Making human relations work", *Harvard Business Review*, **XXIX** (1), 29–55.

Jensen, Per H. and Asmund W. Born (2001), "Aktivering og handleplaner som integrationsinstrumenter – hvor ligger muligheden for kritik?", in Jørgen G. Andersen and Per H. Jensen (eds), *Marginalisering integration velfærd*, Aalborg: Aalborg Universitetsforlag, 199–214.

Jones, Alanna (1996), *The Wrecking Yard of Games and Activities*, Revensdale: Idyll Arbor Inc.

Jones, Alanna (1998), *104 Activities that Build*, Richland: Red Room Publishing.

Jones, Ken (1994), *Icebreakers – A Sourcebook of Games, Exercises and Simulations*, London: Kogan Page Limited.

Jones, Ken (2002), *Emotional Games for Training. 15 Games that Explore Feelings, Behavior and Values*, Aldershot: Gower.

Jørgensen, S. and J.K. Jørgensen (1999), "En ny psykologisk kontrakt?", *Ledelse i dag*, (35), 271–83.

Juelskjær, Malou, Hanne Knudsen, Justine G. Pors and Dorthe Staunæs (2011), *Ledelse af uddannelse. At lede det potentielle*, Frederiksberg: Samfundslitteratur.

Jydske Vestkysten, accessed 2 November 2001 at www.jv.dk.

Kaagan, Stephen S. (1999), *Leadership Games*, Thousand Oaks, CA: Sage Publication.

Kane, Pat (2000), "Play for today", *Observer*, **22** (10).

Kane, Pat (2004), *The Play Ethic: A Manifesto for a Different Way of Living*, London: Macmillan.

Katz, Robert (1955), "Skills of an effective administrator", *Harvard Business Review*, **33** (1), 33–42.

Katz, Robert (1960), "Toward a more effective enterprise", *Harvard Business Review*, **38** (5), 80–102.

Kelly, Joe (1970), "Make conflict work for you", *Harvard Business Review*, **48** (4), 103–13.

Kieser, Alfred (1989), "Organizational, institutional and societal evolution: medieval craft guilds and the genesis of formal organizations", *Administrative Science Quarterly*, **34**, 540–84.

Knudsen, Hanne (2010), *Har vi en aftale?*, Frederiksberg: Nyt fra Samfundsvidenskaberne.

Knudsen, Hanne (2011), "Lærerroller i skole-hjem-samarbejdet', in Claus Madsen (ed.), *Grundbog i pædagogik – til lærerfaget*, Århus: Forlaget Klim, serien PTT: Pædagogik Til Tiden, 243–263.

Kofoed, K.H. (1928), "Bør Tjenestemandstillingen være en egentlig livsstilling eller et tidsbegrænset kontraktsforhold?", *Nordisk Administrativt Tidsskrift*, 1–17.

Koselleck, Reinhart (1988), *Critique and Crisis. Enlightenment and the Pathogenesis of Modern Society*, Oxford: Berg Publishers Limited.

Koselleck, Reinhart (2004), *Futures Past*, New York: Columbia University Press.

Kotter, John P. (2002), *The Hearth of Change*, Boston, MA: Harvard Business School Press.

Kristensen, Anders R. (2011), *Det grænseløse arbejdsliv. At lede selvledende medarbejdere*, Copenhagen: Gyldendal Business.

Kyhn, Dorthe Boss (2007), *Den perfekte skilsmisse*, København: Forlaget DR.

La Cour, Anders and Holger Højlund (2008), "Velfærd gennem det superviserende samarbejde", in Camilla Sløk and Kaspar Villadsen (eds), *Velfærdsledelse*, København: Hans Reitzels Forlag, 197–226.

Landgraf, Edgar (2002), "Self-forming selves: autonomy and artistic creativity in Goethe and Moritz", *Goethe Yearbook*, **11**, 159–76.

Landgraf, Edgar (2004), "Romantic love and the enlightenment: from gallantry and seduction to authenticity and self-validation", *The German Quarterly*, **77** (1), 29–46.

Landgraf, Edgar (2006), "Comprehending romantic incomprehensibility. A systems theoretical perspective on early German romanticism", *MLN*, **121** (3), 592–616.

Lauridsen, Irma (2009), *Den gode skilsmisse, Elleve interviews om skilsmisse*, Bjerringbro: Forlaget Cadeau.

Levinson, Harry (1967), "What you can do when the problem is personal", *Management Review*, **56** (4), 66–9.

Levinson, Harry (1972), "Easing the pain of personal loss", *Harvard business ness Review*, **50** (5), 80–88.

Lind, J. (2001), "MUS og PUP samtaler", *Notat*, Græsted-Gilleleje Kommune.

Linder, Marc-Olivier, Johan Roos and Victor Bart (2001), "Play in organizations", Working Paper 2, Lausanne, Switzerland: Imagination Lab.

Løvbom, Tina (2008), "Det gør også ondt ikke at bliver fyret", www.arbejdsmiljøviden.dk, blad no. 3, Videncenter for Arbejdsmiljø.

Luhmann, Niklas (1979), *Trust and Power*, Chichester: John Wiley & Sons Ltd.

Luhmann, Niklas (1981), "Communication about law in interaction systems", in K. Knorr-Cetina and A.V. Cicourel (eds), *Advances in Social Theory and Methodology. Toward an Integration of* Micro- and *Macro-Sociologies*, London: Routledge & Kegan Paul, 234–256.

Luhmann, Niklas (1982a), *The Differentiation of Society*, New York: Columbia University Press.

Luhmann, Niklas (1982b), "The world society as a social system", *International Journal of General Systems*, **8**, 131–8.

Luhmann, Niklas (1986), "The individuality of the individual: historical meanings and contemporary problems", in Thomas Heller, Morton Sosna and David Wellbery (eds), *Reconstructing individualism*, Stanford, CA: Stanford University Press, 313–325.

Luhmann, Niklas (1988a), *Erkenntnis als Konstruktion*, Bern: Benteli Verlag.

Luhmann, Niklas (1988b), "Frauen, Männer und George Spencer Brown", *Zeitschrift für Soziologie*, **17** (1), 47–71.

Luhmann, Niklas (1989), *Ecological Communication*, Chicago, IL: University of Chicago Press.

Luhmann, Niklas (1990a), "The autopoiesis of social systems", in *Essays on Self-Reference*, New York: Columbia University Press, 1–20.

Luhmann, Niklas (1990b), "The cognitive program of constructivism and a reality that remains unknown", in Wolfgang Krohn, Günter Küppers and Helga Nowotny (eds), *Selforganization. Portrait of a Scientific Revolution*, Boston: Klüwer Academic Publishers, 64–85.

Luhmann, Niklas (1990c), *Political Theory in the Welfare State*, Berlin: Walter de Gruyter.

Luhmann, Niklas (1992), "Operational closure and structural coupling", *Cardozo Law Review*, **13** (5), 1419–41.

Luhmann, Niklas (1993a), "Deconstruction as second-order observing", *New Literary History*, **24**, 763–82.

Luhmann, Niklas (1993b), "Die Paradoxie des Entscheidens", *Verwaltungs-Archiv. Zeitschrift für Verwaltungslehre, Verwaltungsrecht und Verwaltungspolitik*, 84. Band, heft 3, pp. 287–99.

Luhmann, Niklas (1993c), *Gesellschaftsstruktur und Semantik*, Bd. 1, Frankfurt am Main: Suhrkamp, 9–72.

Luhmann, Niklas (1993d), "'Was ist der Fall' und 'Was steckt dahinter?' Die Zwei Soziologien und die Gesellschaftstheorie", *Zeitschrift für Soziologie*, jg. 22, heft 4, 245–260.

Luhmann, Niklas (1994a), "Speaking and silence", *New German Critique*, (61), 25–37.

Luhmann, Niklas (1994b), "'What is the case' and 'what lies behind it': the two sociologies and the theory of society", *Sociological Theory*, **12** (2), 126–39.

Luhmann, Niklas (1995a), "Kærligheden som symbolsk generaliseret kommunikationsmedie", in Jens Christian Jacobsen (ed.), *Autopoiesis II*, København: Politisk Revy, pp. 58–78.

Luhmann, Niklas (1995b), "Lykke og ulykke i kommunikationen inden for familien: om patologiernes genese", in Jens Christian Jacobsen (ed.), *Autopoiesis II*, København: Politisk Revy, 79–91.

Luhmann, Niklas (1995c), *Social Systems*, Stanford, CA: Stanford University Press.

Luhmann, Niklas (1995d), "Why 'system theory'?", *Cybertics & Human Knowing*, **3** (2), 3–10.

Luhmann, Niklas (1996a), "Membership and motives in social systems", *Systems Research*, **13** (3), 341–8.

Luhmann, Niklas (1996b), "On the scientific context of the concept of communication", *Social Science Information*, 257–67.

Luhmann, Niklas (1997a), "Globalization or world society: how to conceive modern society?", *Journal of Review of Sociology*, **7** (1), 67–79.

Luhmann, Niklas (1997b), "Kunstens medie", in *Iagttagelse og paradoks*, København: Gyldendal.

Luhmann, Niklas (1998), *Love as Passion. The Codification of Intimacy*, Stanford, CA: Stanford University Press.

Luhmann, Niklas (1999), "The paradox of form", in Dirk Baecker (ed.), *Problems of Form*, Stanford, CA: Stanford University Press, 15–26.

Luhmann, Niklas (2000a), *Organisation und Entscheidung*, Wiesbaden: Westdeutscher Verlag.

Luhmann, Niklas (2000b), *The Reality of the Mass Media*, Cambridge: Polity Press.

Luhmann, Niklas (2000c), *Sociale Systemer*, København: Hans Reitzels Forlag.

Luhmann, Niklas (2001), "Notes on the project 'poetry and social theory'", *Theory, Culture & Society*, **18** (1), 15–27.

Luhmann, Niklas (2010), *Love. A Sketch*, Cambridge: Polity Press.

Lynch, Rob (1982), "Play, creativity, and emotion", *Studies in Symbolic Interaction*, **4**, 45–62.

Maas, A. and D.-J. Bakker (2000), "Managing differences in a multi-paradigmatic partnership", in Tharsi Taillieu (ed.), *Collaborative Strategies and Multi-Organizational Partnership*, Leuven-Apeldoorn: Garant Publisher, 189–198.

Mainemelis, Charalampos and Sarah Ronson (2006), "Ideas are born in fields of play: towards a theory of play and creativity in organizational settings", *Research in Organisational Behaviour: An Annual Series of Analytical Essays and Critical Reviews Research in Organizational Behaviour*, **27**, 81–131.

Mandag Morgen (2011), "Den mentale frikommune", **9/5** (2011), 15–17.

Marcuse, Herbert (1970), "The end of Utopia", in *Five Lectures. Psychoanalysis, Politics, and Utopia*, London: Allen Lane, The Penguin Press (org. in German, 1967; Danish edition, "Utopiens død", in *Politiske Essays*, Gyldendal, 1970).

Massumi, Brian (2002), *Parables for the Virtual. Movement, Affect, Sensation*, Durham, NC and London: Duke University Press.

McMurry, Robert N. (1951), "The executive neurosis", *Harvard Business Review*, **30** (6), 33–47.

Ministry of Finance (Finansministeriet) (1994), *Medarbejder i Staten – Ansvar og udvikling*, København.
Ministry of Finance (Finansministeriet) (1995), *Værktøj til velfærd. Effektive institutioner*, København.
Ministry of Finance (Finansministeriet) (1998a), *Personalepolitik i staten. Fra ord til handling*, København.
Ministry of Finance (Finansministeriet) (1998b), *Personalepolitik i staten. Fra ord til handling, Sammenfatning*, København.
Moe, Sverre (1998), *Den modern hjelpens sosiologi. Velferd i systemteoretisk perspektiv*, Stavanger: Apeiros Forlag.
Moeller, Hans-George (2012), *The Radical Luhmann*, New York: Columbia University Press.
Montgomery, Kevin (1985), "The most mismanaged emotion", *Nonprofit World*, **3** (5), 22.
Moxnes, Kari (2004), *Skånsomme skilsmisser – med barnet i fokus*, København: Hans Reitzels Forlag.
Münch, Richard (1992), "Autopoiesis by definition", *Cardozo Law Review*, **13** (5), 1463–71.
Mumby, Dennis K. and Linda L. Putnam (1992), "The politics of emotion: a feminist reading of bounded rationality", *Academy of Management Review*, **17** (3), 465–86.
Nassehi, Armin (2005), "Organizations as decision machines: Niklas Luhmann's theory of organized", *The Sociological Review*, **53** (November), 178–91.
Nassehi, Armin (2007), "The person as an effect of communication", in Sabine Maasen and Barbara Sutter (eds), *On the Willing Selves*, London: Palgrave Macmillan, pp. 100–20.
The National Association of Municipalities and KTO (Kommunernes Landsforening & KTO) (1995), *SKUP i leder og medarbejdersamarbejdet*, København.
The National Association of Municipalities and The Municipal Folk School (Kommunernes Landsforening & Den Kommunale Højskole) (1997), *Rekruttering og uddannelse*, København.
Newstrom, John and Edward E. Scannell (1998), *The Big Book of Team Building Games*, New York: McGraw-Hill.
Otkjær, Tage (2009), "Den forfærdelige samtale", *Berlingske Nyhedsmagasin*, (5), 32–3.
Paulsen, Susan (2001), "Vojens: Om prævention og partnere", *Socialrådgiveren* (24/01: 3–21).
Pedersen, Michael (2008), "Tune in, break down, and reboot – new machines for coping with stress of commitment", *Culture & Organization*, **14** (2), 171–85.

Perlis, Leo (1959), "Workers have emotions", *Vital Speeches of the Day*, **21** (21), 1434–6.

Personalestyrelsen (2004), *Håndbog om afskedigelse*, København: Finansministeriet.

Plejecentret Sølund (2001), *Kompetenceudvikling med udgangspunkt i værdigrundlag*, København.

Pors, Justine Grønbæk (2012), "Avoiding unambiguity – tensions in school governing", in Niels Åkerstrøm Andersen and Inger Johanne Sand (eds), *Hybrid Forms of Governance – Self-Suspension of Power*, London: Palgrave Macmillan, 30–45.

Pors, Justine Grønbæk (2011b), "Evalueringssamtale mellem skole og kommune – Selvledelse og gæstfrihed", in Malou Juelskjær, Hanne Knudsen, Justine Grønbæk Pors and Dorthe Staunæs (eds), *Ledelse af uddannelse. At lede det potentielle*, Frederiksberg: Samfundslitteratur.

Pors, Justine Grønbæk (2011c), "Noisy management – a history of Danish school governing from 1970–2010", Ph.d.-afhandling, CBS.

Porter, Lyman and Edward Lawler (1968), "What job attitudes tell about motivation", *Harvard Business Review*, **46** (1), 118–26.

Putnam, Linda L. and Dennis K. Mumby (1993), "Organizations, emotion and the myth of rationality", in Stephen Fineman (ed.), *Emotion in Organizations*, London: Sage Publications, 36–57.

Randall, Frederic (1955), "Stimulate your executives to think creatively", *Harvard Business Review*, **33** (4), 121–8.

Reitman, Jason (2009), *Up in the Air*, Paramount Pictures.

Rennison, Betina Wolfgang (2007a), "Cash, codes and complexity – new adventures in the public management of pay scales", *Scandinavian Journal of Management*, **23** (2), 146–167.

Rennison, Betina Wolfgang (2007b), "Historical discourses of public management in Denmark", *Management & Organizational History*, **2** (1), 2–26.

Rennison, Betina Wolfgang (2007c), "Intimacy of management – codified constructions of personal selves", *Philosophy of Management*, **6** (2), 47–60.

Rennison, Betina Wolfgang (2011), *Ledelsens genealogi – offentlig ledelse fra tabu til trend*, Frederiksberg: Samfundslitteratur.

Resonanz (2010), "En helt ny dag", accessed at www.resonanz.dk/side12.html.

Robertson, Robin (1999), "Some-thing from no-thing: G. Spencer-Brown's *Laws of form*", *Cybernetics & Human Knowing*, **6** (4), 43–55.

Roerlich, Jay B. (1980), *Work and Love. The Crucial Balance*, New York: Summit Books.

Roethlisberger, F.J. (1951), "Training supervisors in human relations", *Harvard Business Review*, **29** (5), 47–57.

Roethlisberger, F.J. (1953), "The administrator's skill: communication", *Harvard Business Review*, **31** (5), 55–62.

Roos, Johan, Victor Bart and Matt Statler (2004), "Playing seriously with strategy", *Long Range Planning*, **37**, 549–68.

Rousseau, D.M. (1995), *Psychological Contracts in Organizations.* Thousand Oaks, CA: SAGE Publications.

Roy, Donald F. (1960), "'Banana time': job satisfaction and informal interaction", *Human Organization*, **18** (4), 158–68.

Salamon, Karen Lisa (2002), "Beåndet ledelse", Ph.d.-serien 11, CBS.

Salamon, Karen Lisa (2007), *Selvmål: Det evaluerede liv*, København: Gyldendal.

Sandelands, Lloyd (2010), "The play of change", *Journal of Organizational Change*, **23** (1), 71–86.

Saxenian, Hrand (1958), "Criterion for emotional maturity", *Harvard Business Review*, **36** (1), 56–68.

Scannell, Edward, John Newstrom and Carolyn Nilson (1998), *The Complete Games Trainers Play, II*, New York: The McGraw-Hill Companies.

Scannell, Mary (2010), *The Big Book of Conflict Resolution Games*, New York: The McGraw-Hill Companies.

Schrage, Michael (2000), *Serious Play*, Boston, MA: Harvard Business School Press.

Schramm, Gitte (2008), *Den professionelle skilsmisse – Sådan håndterer de en opsigelse*, København: BusinessSumup.

Schramm, Gitte (2010), *Den professionelle opsigelse*, København: Employment Care ApS.

Sciulli, David (1994), "Interview with Niklas Luhmann", *Theory, Culture & Society*, **11**, 37–68.

Seijts, Gerard and Grace O'Farrell (2003), "Engage the heart: appealing to the emotions facilities change", *Ivey Business Journal*, February, 1–5.

Sennett, Richard (1998), *The Corrosion of Character – The Personal Consequences of Work in the New Capitalism*, New York: W.W. Norton & Company.

Serres, Michel (2008), *The Five Senses. A Philosophy of Mingled Bodies*, London: Continuum.

Sieben, Barbara and Åsa Wettergren (eds) (2010), *Emotionalizing Organizations and Organizing Emotions*, London: Palgrave Macmillan.

Sirota, David (1959), "Some effects of promotional frustration on employees' understanding of, and attitudes towards, management", *Sociometry*, **22** (3), 273–8.

Skou, Marianne Troelsen (2008), "Fokus: Dårligt klædt på til fyring", Arbejdsmiljøviden.dk, blad no. 8, Videncenter for Arbejdsmiljø.

Sørensen, Dion (2009), *Kriseledelse*, København: Børsens forlag.

Sørensen, Mads (2004), *Den politiske forbruger*, København: Hans Reitzels Forlag.

Spencer-Brown, George (1969), *Laws of Form*, London: George Allen and Unwin.

Spicer, André and Carl Cederström (2010), "For love of the organization", in Carl Cederström and Casper Hoedemaeckers (eds), *Lacan and Organization*, London: MayFlyBooks, pp. 133–67.

Stäheli, Urs (2003), "The popular in the political system", *Cultural Studies*, **17** (2), 271–96.

Statler, Matt and Johan Roos (2002), "Preparing for the unexpected", *New Practice from Imagination Lab*, **1** (3), 1–2.

Statler, Matt and Johan Roos (2007), *Everyday Strategic Preparedness. The Role of Practical Wisdom in Organizations*, Basingstoke: Palgrave Macmillan.

Staunæs, Dorthe (2009), "A very sick (challenge) of leadership", in C. Åsberg et al. (eds), *Gender Delight*. Linköping: Linköping University Press, 85–98.

Staunæs, Dorthe (2012), "Governing the potentials of life itself? Interragating the promises in affective educational leadership", *Journal of Educational Administration and History*, **43** (3), 227–47.

Stenner, Paul (2004), "Is autopoietic systems theory alexithymic? Luhmann and the socio-psychology of emotions", *Soziale Systeme*, **10** (1), 159–85.

Stichweh, Rudolf (1997), "Professions in modern society", *International Review of Sociology*, **7** (1), 95–102.

Svendsen, Mette N. (2004), "The space in the gap. A study of the social implications of cancer genetic counselling and testing in Denmark", Ph.D.-afhandling, Institut for Antropologi, Københavns Universitet.

Teubner, Gunther (1991), "Autopoiesis and steering: how politics profit from the normative surplus of capital", in Roald Veld, Linze Schaap, Catrien Termeer and Mark Twist (eds), *Autopoiesis and Configuration Theory: New Approaches to Social Steering*, London: Kluwer Academic Publisher, 127–141.

Teubner, Gunther (1996), "Social order from legislative noise? Autopoietic closure as a problem for legal regulation", in Gunther Teubner and Alberto Febbajo (eds), *State, Law, and Economy as Autopoietic Systems*. Milan: Dott. A. Giuffré Editore, 609–649.

Thiagarajan, Sivasailam (2006), *Thiagi's 100 Favorite Games*, San Francisco, CA: John Wiley & Sons, Inc.

Thommen, Beat and Alexander Wettstein (2010), "Culture as the co-evolution of psychic and social systems: new perspectives on the person – environment relationship", *Culture & Psychology*, **16** (2), 213–41.

Thomson, Kevin (1998a), *Emotional Capital*, Oxford: Capstone.

Thomson, Kevin (1998b), *Passion at Work*, Oxford: Capstone.

Thygesen, Niels (ed.) (2012), *The Illusion of Management Control*, London: Palgrave Macmillan.

Townley, Barbara (2008), *Reason's Neglect. Rationality and Organizing*, Oxford: Oxford University Press.

Tvede, Lotte (2007), *Skilsmisse. Kom helskindet gennem krisen*, København: Libris.

Weber, Max (1978 [1922]) *Economy and Society*, London: University of California Press (org. *Wirtschaft und Gesellschaft*, 1922).

Weber, Max (2003), *Udvalgte tekster*, bd. 2, København: Hans Reitzels Forlag.

Weiss, Howard M. and Arthur P. Brief (2001), "Affect at work: a historical perspective", in Roy L. Payne and Cary L. Cooper (eds), *Emotions at Work*, Chichester: John Wiley & Sons, pp. 133–71.

Williamson, Oliver (1983), *Market and Hierarchies*, London: The Free Press.

Yerkes, Leslie (2007), *Fun Works. Creating Places Where People Love to Work*, San Francisco, CA: Berrett-Koelers.

Index

Svendsen, M. 234
systems theory
contingency limit 23–4
examples 12
inside and outside distinctions 22–3
interpenetration in systems theory,
understanding of 165–7
and order from noise principle 33

tension *see* stress
termination of membership *see*
membership termination and
break-up strategies
Teubner, G. 20, 33
Thiagarajan, S. 90, 92
Thommen, B. 114
Thomson, K. 136–7
Thygesen, N. 37
Townley, B. 22
transience
and adaptability *see* adaptability and
machine of transience
"be yourself" ideology 241–4
contingency factors in organization/
employee relationships 244–6
contract *see* contracts
employee expectation levels 246
freedom from work and authenticity
241–4
language choice when dealing with
emotions *see* semantics
managerial decisions on involvement
245–6, 247

and membership deferral 241, 243
nexus of partnerships 248
organizational change *see*
organizational change
management
paradoxes *see* paradoxes
semantics *see* semantics
work/non-work distinction 242
trembling organization *see* authentic
self-enrollment feelings,
management of
Tvede, L. 178, 180, 181

uncertainty
dealing with 160–61
employee management of
unexpected, play strategy 84–5

Von Foerster, H. 30, 33

Weber, M. 22, 109, 121
Weis, H. 110
Wettergren, Å. 107
Wettstein, A. 114
Williamson, O. 216
work–life balance
membership to self-enrollment in
organizational image, intimacy
strategy 71–4
and play 151–3
work/non-work distinction 242

Yerkes, L. 151–3, 170